The Captain Who
Burned His Ships

The Captain Who Burned His Ships

Captain Thomas Tingey, USN, 1750–1829

GORDON S. BROWN

Naval Institute Press
Annapolis, Maryland

Naval Institute Press
291 Wood Road
Annapolis, MD 21402

Library of Congress Cataloging-in-Publication Data

Brown, Gordon S.
  The captain who burned his ships : Captain Thomas Tingey, USN, 1750–1829 /
Gordon S. Brown.
    p. cm.
  Includes bibliographical references and index.
  ISBN 978-1-61251-044-6 (hbk. : alk. paper) 1. Tingey, Thomas, 1750–1829.
2. United States. Navy—Officers—Biography. 3. Ship captains—United States—
Biography. 4. Washington Navy Yard—History. 5. Washington (D.C.)—History—
19th century. 6. Washington (D.C.)—Biography. 7. United States—History,
Naval—To 1900. I. Title. II. Title: Captain Thomas Tingey, USN, 1750–1829.
  V63.T55 2011
  359.0092—dc23
  [B]
                                                2011018580

♾This paper meets the requirements of ANSI/NISO z39.48-1992 (Permanence of
Paper).

Printed in the United States of America.

19 18 17 16 15 14 13 12 11   9 8 7 6 5 4 3 2 1
First printing

Contents

Preface

When Captain Thomas Tingey came to Washington in 1800, the federal city was little more than a set of hamlets clustered around the building sites of the Capitol and the president's house. The federal government itself was only ten years old, while the U.S. Navy in which Tingey was a senior officer had been formed only two years previously. His task was to create yet another new institution. He was to build a shipyard from scratch, on a parcel of land that included hill, marsh, and mudflat, a job that was to be achieved for a Navy whose very existence was under political attack. A purposeful and organized man, he set aside any doubts he may have had about his role and went to work.

His achievement, in the end, made a difference. The navy yard he built became the principal facility of the nation's Navy, and in it the ships that soon won renown were prepared and supplied for war. Tingey himself was neither a heroic nor a flamboyant figure like some of his uniformed colleagues, yet it was his work and the work of his yard that, to a considerable degree, put the more renowned captains in a position to win their battles, and the Navy to win its place in the hearts of Americans.

A quarter century after taking charge, Tingey could look back with satisfaction. The establishment he had brought into service had become a vital part of a successful, proud, and respected Navy. The yard had become Washington's major industrial facility and employer outside the bureaucracy, and Tingey himself was a respected leader in a town that was slowly maturing into a decent place to live. The ships that gained the Navy its glory in the early days of the War of 1812 had been prepared for battle in the yard that he and his colleagues had built up. The fortunes of war had obliged him to put his creation to the torch, but he had then taken the opportunity afterward to rebuild and enlarge it, with a new industrial emphasis that would guarantee its future.

This book, while a biography of the captain, is also about those transitions—at the navy yard, and simultaneously in the Navy itself, as well as in the city of Washington. At a time when our new nation and its institutions were taking form through a process of invention and adaptation, Tingey's role in the process of growth and development was not one he chose deliberately. But, in doing his job and in being the man he was, he contributed meaningfully to the history of both the Navy and the city.

The contribution of the navy yard to the growth of the city is worthy of further study, and I hope that this work will serve as a point of departure. This volume leans, of course, on the work of my predecessors in research, notably Lewis D. Cook, who in the 1930s gathered and made available so much of Tingey's life story and letters. I am particularly grateful to two current colleagues in research—John G. Sharp, on whose extensive research into the work environment at the early navy yard I have greatly relied, and Eben W. Graves, whose genealogical work has brought Tingey's family history into clearer focus. I thank them for their unstinting support, their information, and particularly for their enthusiasm. Mr. Graves, a Tingey descendant, also has helped me get in touch with other family members who have offered advice and assistance. Among those, I am particularly thankful for the support offered by Joseph DeKay of Maine, Eckford DeKay of California, and Truxtun Craven and Richard Malm of Washington state. I have appreciated the encouragement and assistance given to me by staff at the Naval History and Heritage Command in Washington, situated in the navy yard that still hosts many memories of its first commandant.

The Captain Who
Burned His Ships

CHAPTER ONE

A New American

Close-hauled as she moved smartly north by northwest with the strong wind, His Majesty's sloop *Nautilus* came abreast of York Point. The air was clear, with none of the fog and rain of the past days, and the wide bay opened up before the ship and her crew. Holding the same heading, they soon were sailing in less-troubled waters. The dramatic basaltic cliffs of Castle Island, to seaward, had broken the force of the wind as if to welcome them. To the west, across the sun-bright waters of the outer bay, the mass of Whale Island protected the entrance to still another spacious bay. The ship moved quickly but evenly through the calm waters toward little Eskimo Island, when Commander James Jones ordered the mainsail down and a turn to port. Straight ahead, finally, was the opening to the cove called Pitt's Harbor. They were almost there.

Midshipman Tingey could see why the bay had been called one of the finest harbors in the world. Chateau Bay, the French had called it, after the magnificent castle-like islands guarding its entrance, and the old name had stuck in spite of an English effort to rename it York Bay. After the desolate and rugged coastline the *Nautilus* had been following on the trip up from St. John's, Newfoundland, the bay provided a spacious and safe anchorage, while its various coves sheltered groves of valuable trees, and offered some protection from the elements. In the bright light of the early August morning, the place looked almost idyllic.

As the *Nautilus* dropped anchor in fifteen fathoms of water at the mouth of Pitt's Harbor, the details of their destination became clearer. A clutter of boats, fishing gear, huts, and fish-drying racks lined the shores, testimony to the principal occupation of the residents. The fort stood at the north side of the entrance, overlooking both the inner harbor and the outer bay, and a sec-

CASTLE ISLAND, CHATEAU BAY, LABRADOR
*(By Rev. William Grey, 1857; courtesy of the Centre for Newfoundland Studies,
Memorial University Libraries, St. John)*

ond Royal Navy sloop, the *Otter*, lay at anchor nearby. The bulk of the fort
loomed impressively in comparison to the raggedness of its surroundings,
but a closer look showed that it was only a two-story log blockhouse with a
stone-built magazine attached. Mercifully, it was made a bit more homelike
by the Royal Navy's penchant for order: the surrounding earthworks, two
hundred feet on each side, were kept neat and tidy; even the brass cannon
looked clean and ready for a (scarcely foreseeable) battle. A British flag flut-
tered at the corner of the blockhouse, and the fort's inhabitants could be seen
gathering excitedly to welcome the newcomers, who were in many cases also
their relievers.

Fort York, it was called. It had been built only some five years earlier, in
1766, after the British had wrenched this stony coast of Labrador and the
rest of Canada from the French in the Seven Years' War. It had been built not
to protect the new British territory from encroachment by foreign powers—
the Royal Navy's strong presence made that an unlikely prospect—but
rather to protect the monopoly the British sought to enforce over the coast's
lucrative cod fishery, and whale- and seal-hunting grounds. The magnificent

harbor's location allowed its occupiers to control the mouth of the vital Belle Isle Strait between Labrador and Newfoundland, through which the fish and whales migrated, and provided a sheltered spot from which the summer fishing fleets from England could operate. The fort, its garrison, and the vessels had been placed where they could oversee all activity in the bay, the better to enforce the monopoly and protect the fishermen in summer. In winter, after the fishing fleet had left, the garrison was responsible for enforcing the peace and His Majesty's rules for the seal hunt. It also provided a year-round presence that would protect the fishing equipment left on shore against raids by parties of native Eskimos or Beothuks, who resented the loss of their traditional free use of the hunting grounds.

"Appointed to Command the Fort and Garrison in Chateau Bay," Tingey's orders read.[1] Land duty might seem like a strange assignment for a young man aspiring to become a naval officer, who might more profitably have been learning his seacraft on warships rather than on the motley collection of small craft—a shallop, a yawl, and two wooden boats—that were the garrison's naval equipment. But the Royal Navy was supreme at this new and remote corner of His Majesty's dominions. The navy's senior officer in the area was at one and the same time "Governor of Newfoundland and the Coast of Labrador, and Commander in Chief of the Squadron of His Majesty's Ships and Vessels Employed for the Protection of the Fisheries." In that latter role, he was responsible for all that happened along the Labrador coast and in the fisheries. A junior naval officer like Tingey, as well as the fort he was to command and the small craft attached to it, were all parts of the commander in chief's "squadron."

Thomas Tingey was twenty years old that summer of 1771. He had come to the American shore as part of the four hundred–man crew of the 60-gun warship HMS *Panther*, on which he had served since May. How long he had been a midshipman, or on what other ships he had sailed, is a story that was never passed down. Tingey apparently did come, however, from a seafaring tradition: his father, William Tingey, was from the North Sea fishing town of Lowestoft, and his elder brother was a ship's pilot.[2] Thomas was the sixth child of the marriage between William Tingey and Ann Pilot, and he was their only child not born in Lowestoft. The family had moved, sometime after 1746, to London, where Thomas was born in September of 1750. Before Thomas' ninth birthday, however, disaster struck. Both William and his eldest son, also called William, died within a month of each other in the spring of 1759—quite likely from one of the endemic diseases, typhus and smallpox, that together killed one in four Londoners even in that non-epidemic year.[3] Sometime in the next few years, the widow Tingey and her children moved back to Lowestoft.

Thomas, however, soon went to sea, leaving just before his fifteenth birthday.[4] Before then, he evidently had been given good basic schooling in London and Lowestoft, as attested by his easy writing skills, fine hand, and solid if pedestrian use of language. He may have fulfilled the navy's entry requirement for midshipman of three years' experience at sea by following the practice of signing on as an officer's servant, but we know none of the details. By the time he shipped on board the *Panther*, in any event, he had six years' experience in the navy and was somewhat older than the normal midshipman. He certainly had received a sound, practical, education, as well as (if his own story is accurate) some experience in the Royal Navy's shipyards.[5] He was, at least, considered competent enough to be given command of a sizeable detachment of men in an isolated and difficult outpost.

His orders were signed by Captain the Honorable John Byron, governor and commander in chief in Newfoundland since 1769. Also known as "Foul Weather Jack," Byron had fought in Newfoundland waters during the recent Seven Years' War, was already a renowned explorer, and would soon become an admiral, only to play an undistinguished role in the naval campaigns of the American war for independence. Given the scope of his duties at the beginning of July 1771, Byron probably had little idea as to who, exactly, young Midshipman Tingey was. But he needed to fill a minor job at Fort York, and Tingey had presumably been proposed by someone down the chain of command. Accordingly, Captain Byron appointed Tingey as commander of the fort and its garrison. A few days later, at the beginning of August, Tingey and his detachment of twenty sailors boarded the *Nautilus* to make the four days' sail to Chateau Bay.

Midshipman Tingey, as commander of the fort, would command a party of some twenty men: a dozen Marines with their sergeant and corporal, plus another midshipman and six sailors to man the boats. His duties, it can be assumed, were similar to those assigned to his predecessor: he was to be justice of the peace, with the primary task of maintaining order along the coast "by every means in your Power, to protect and defend His Majesty's Subjects resorting thither, with their Ships from Britain, and their Effects, Fishing Works, &c as above-mentioned, . . . and to be very careful to keep a proper Guard and make a proper disposition for being always secure against any Surprise or Attacks from the Savages." While enforcement of the fishing rules during the season would be the responsibility of navy ships sent for the purpose, the Fort York garrison was entrusted to keep a vigilant eye out for "lawless Crews from the Plantations [meaning the southern colonies, especially in New England, who] . . . have been guilty of all kinds of disorders."[6]

The detachment was small, but the job was not necessarily easy. Young Tingey would need to exercise command over an isolated group of men with mixed chains of command, to coordinate his work with navy ships like the *Nautilus* and *Otter* that controlled all the action at sea, and try to enforce royal regulations over the shore activities of a disorderly group of independent fishers and hunters. The job involved mediating regular squabbles with and among the fishermen about use of the land facilities, reporting on catches that they preferred to keep confidential, and keeping order among a notoriously independent and competitive group of men. There also was room for feud and fraud on a grander scale: Tingey's predecessor, Lieutenant Samuel Davys, had distinguished himself—for bad or good—by confiscating the seal oil harvest of a renowned local operator, Nicholas Darby, on what appeared to have been trumped-up charges that very probably fattened Davys' pocketbook.

The first week in harbor was full of routine affairs: transferring cargo from the *Nautilus* to the *Otter* and the fort, and sending parties ashore to cut wood and brew spruce beer for the crew's consumption. It was not until 13 August, a week after their arrival, that the contingent from the *Nautilus* formally relieved those sailors at Fort York who were finishing their tour of duty. According to the ship's records, however, only seventeen of the twenty men taken on in St. John's were put ashore, and it is not clear whether Tingey was one of the men who stayed with the ship, or if he was at the head of the party that relieved the garrison. The *Nautilus*, in any event, sailed from Chateau Bay five days later, and did not return that year. The *Otter*, on the other hand, stayed in the bay for another month enforcing the fisheries regulations (her crew even sank some French craft that were fishing outside their permitted areas). When the *Otter* sailed back to England in mid-September, the fort was isolated until the navy ships and the fishermen returned to Labrador the following summer.

Surprisingly, Midshipman Tingey was neither in charge of nor even among the garrison that winter. If he ever took command of the fort, it was only for a short time: by October he was already on his way back to England, either on the *Otter* or back on board the *Panther*.[7] Tingey would tell his family much later that his position at Fort York had become untenable because of personality clashes, and that he had asked to be relieved, and subsequently resigned from the Royal Navy.

Something, it seems, did occur at Chateau Bay that led to a setting aside of Tingey's orders. If there was an argument or confrontation between himself and another officer at the fort, it seems at least that it passed as routine since there is no record of such an event in the ship logs, nor of disciplinary action being taken. Throughout his career, Tingey showed himself to be quick to defend his honor. He was not, however, the type to seek a fight, and in the event of a confrontation he would have been likely to prefer an honorable withdrawal to a lingering confrontation—or the brutality of a duel. Other factors, too, were surely at play in forming his decision, among them the lure of new opportunities in the American colonies, and Tingey's middling prospects in the Royal Navy. At age twenty-one, he was already beyond the age at which most midshipmen were tested for appointment as lieutenants, and, moreover, he did not have the sort of important social connections that could ease his way through the career. An incident at Fort York, combined with what looks to have been relatively poor prospects for advancement, may well have given him adequate reason to resign—or for a superior officer to advise him to do so. We do know that Tingey, on 31 December 1771, or some six weeks after the *Panther*'s return to Spithead, was discharged from the Royal Navy.[8] He had decided to try his prospects in the colonies.

Tingey next appears in Philadelphia, sometime in 1772. Or, to be more accurate, he attested many years later (in May 1795, to be exact) that he had been a resident of the city for twenty-three years. Why he chose to go to Philadelphia is not known. Whatever his particular reason, Tingey was by no means alone in selecting life in the colonies over the homeland. Many British seamen were following a similar path. Maritime business in the American colonies was booming, and British sailors were easily tempted by the better pay and conditions available to them on American ships. This migration of skilled mariners from the home country and Newfoundland to the American colonies so concerned British officials, in fact, that they had already begun to limit the departure of skilled men from Newfoundland. The following year, Captain Byron's successor, Admiral Molyneux Shuldham, issued a directive forbidding "carrying of British subjects to the Continent of America" and requiring American captains to enter into obligations that they would not carry away passengers without his written permission. Also, all British captains were instructed to return to their home ports, under penalty of law, with as many sailors as they had left with (deaths, of course, excluded).[9] Tingey's move to the colonies came before the Americans' political problems with the mother country broke out into warfare, but it was simply one of many cases of attempted migration that, in due course, would cause a major dispute between British and Americans about the impressment of American sailors onto the admiralty's warships.

Philadelphia in the early 1770s was the biggest and most sophisticated city in the colonies and, more importantly to a newcomer like Tingey, a thriving seaport. With a population of about thirty thousand, it was exceeded in British territory only by London and Liverpool as a commercial center. Vital to the colonies' grain trade, the city had ridden a wave of increasing exports throughout the 1760s that had enriched both merchants and shipbuilders.

Most of the exports went to the West Indies, where the sugar plantations demanded great quantities of foodstuffs, lumber, and other mainland products to maintain their profitable exploitation. And even though the sugar business had begun to slow down, Philadelphia's exports to southern Europe had grown to compensate. In short, it was a good time and place for a young man with sea experience, and with professional training courtesy of the Royal Navy, to find work.

Five years passed. In what jobs, on which ships, or in what capacity Tingey found work during those years we can only speculate, in the absence of documentary proof. But it is clear that, at least for some of those years, he was engaged in the West Indies trade, and that he had good prospects. In late March of 1777, at the age of twenty-six, Thomas Tingey married a young lady of his own age, and of good family. The marriage took place on the island of St. Croix, where we must assume that the two lovers met.

St. Croix was at the time a Danish colony, neutral in the war that had broken out between the American colonies and the British Crown. As a result of its neutral status, it was a convenient and key point for the trade—both legal and contraband—that blossomed between the colonies and the European countries during the struggle. Exactly what Tingey's business interest in St. Croix was is unclear; it is also unclear if he was master of his own ship. But he was evidently in Christiansted harbor long enough, or often enough, to meet and woo his bride. A later family tradition held

CHRISTIANSTED, ST. CROIX, IN 1811
(Courtesy of Photographic Collection, Naval History and Heritage Command)

that Thomas played an active part in the revolutionary struggle, yet there is no evidence that he served in the continental or colonial navies, or even on any of the privateers that operated out of the Indies (many of which were owned by Philadelphians). But it is possible that he—like his friend Thomas Truxtun—was involved in the smuggling of arms, gunpowder, or other supplies between neutral trading centers like St. Croix and the American revolutionaries. In the absence of evidence, however, Tingey's supposed contribution to the war effort will necessarily remain family legend.

The bride was Margaret Murdoch, also of Philadelphia. Her parents, Protestants from northern Ireland, had emigrated to the city along with two infant children more than forty years earlier.[10] William, the father, had done well enough as a Philadelphia tailor to own a number of properties by the time of his death in 1760, and his wife Mary had survived him for ten years. Margaret, the eighth of nine surviving children, was ten years old at the time of her mother's death. Most of her siblings had homes in Philadelphia or nearby with whom she may have spent her childhood. At some point she moved to stay with her eldest sister, Mary, on St. Croix. Mary had married another Philadelphian, George Beale, but they had long resided on the island where Beale owned what the family considered to be "two of the finest plantations on the island."[11]

The marriage between Thomas Tingey and Margaret Murdoch was celebrated on Easter Sunday 1777 at the Beale home; the service was performed by the Reverend Cecil Wray Goodchild, minister of St. John's Church in the town of Christiansted. The newlywed couple settled down to life on the island. Whether or not they stayed in town or on a plantation during their time in St. Croix, the Tingeys had inescapably become part of the slave-owning plantation society of that place. For all its green hills and inviting coastline that draw today's tourists, its picturesque wind-driven sugar presses and quiet coves, the island at the time was one of the more brutal sugar colonies. Even the towns, with their merchants, sailors, taverns, and brothels, ultimately depended on the sugar business. Trade, in spite of its wartime increase, largely supported the plantation economy and the comfortable lifestyles of the planters. That lifestyle was enjoyed at some moral and emotional cost—conditions on the plantations were murderous. The black slaves outnumbered the white population by twelve to one, and the possibility of insurrection loomed perpetually. But the Tingeys, it appears, nonetheless found their life on the island to be quite agreeable. They stayed for several years, and would subsequently return. Like many of their fellow Anglicans from Philadelphia, they did not share the revulsion of their Quaker friends toward the institution of slavery, and would own and employ slaves most of their lives.

The Tingeys' stay on St. Croix was marked by both joy and sorrow: their first child, Anne, was born early in 1778 but buried only nine months later. Thomas himself was absent at the time of baby Anne's funeral: he was commander of a brig called the *Lady Clausen*, on a seven-month voyage from the island to Scandinavia, and return. But their two years or so on the island allowed them to avoid another unpleasantness—the British occupation of Philadelphia, which ended in June of 1778.

By the summer of 1779, the couple had moved to Philadelphia. Family records give us a clue as to the reason. Mary Beale had returned to her native city. We can only suppose that Mary, whose husband George had died, was accompanied on the voyage home by her younger sister Margaret and Margaret's husband Thomas. But we do know that Margaret, at least, was in Philadelphia by October, because she gave birth to a son, called Thomas, at that time. In any event, we find that the two sisters acted in concert with their Murdoch siblings and their spouses when, in the spring of 1780, they finally settled the estates of their father and mother. In the various deeds that document the disposition of William Murdoch's real estate, Thomas Tingey is noted as a mariner, and a resident of Philadelphia.

But the Tingeys did not stay long in the city; they were still tied to St. Croix. Mary Beale, in the legal documents conveying her father's property, had listed herself as a continuing resident of the island. She apparently returned there to settle her affairs, and it is probable that the Tingeys accompanied her. We do know that they returned to the island, and the records give us a date by which they were back in residence. In early summer of 1781, Margaret gave birth to a third child, Mary, on the island. But in what must have seemed a tragic and discouraging pattern, the baby died in infancy, as had Anne and Thomas before her. Even in an age of precarious births, this was a particularly hard blow. A year and a half later, however, the "Dame Fortune" that Tingey occasionally referred to finally smiled on the couple: Margaret gave birth to a child who would survive into adulthood: Margaret Gay was born in September of 1782, also on St. Croix.

Two years after leaving Philadelphia, however, the Tingeys went back— this time to stay on the mainland. Mary Beale moved back to the city by December of 1782, presumably after having settled her late husband's affairs on the island. It seems probable that she was accompanied by the Tingeys once again. They were certainly in the city by the following autumn, because a daughter Hannah—who, like Margaret Gay, would survive to adulthood— was born and christened in Philadelphia at that time. It was, in a way, a new start for the Tingeys. The Revolutionary War was over, they were finally a family, and they were to establish themselves firmly as residents of the new country's capital city.

Tingey was already familiar with some of the city's merchants from his time in the West Indies, and he would now have the opportunity to broaden his contacts and his dealings to some of the larger and more-active firms. Trade in those days was most generally conducted among persons familiar with each other—personal trust was vital in a time when communication was slow and unreliable, credit was based on reputation, information generally was out of date and incomplete, and instructions often had to be put into effect in totally changed circumstances. Captains of merchant ships were not mere sailors: they also were agents of the owners, with broad powers. They were entrusted with the buying and selling of trade goods for the owners, settling accounts through letters of credit, gauging risk with proper insurance, and even selling the vessels in cases of financial or physical distress. Moreover, they often traded on their own account or managed the property of individuals engaged in "adventures," as speculative trading consignments were called. A reputation for probity was therefore essential, and Tingey was careful to establish his, and then to keep it intact.

The Tingeys began to put down roots in a city where Margaret already had numerous relatives. As good members of Christ Church, they rubbed shoulders with the Anglican merchant elite. But not all their visits to the church were happy ones. In 1785 and again in 1786, they went to the church burial ground to grieve over the infant deaths of two more children, first Phebe and then a second Thomas. The sadness of those occasions was offset to some degree, however, by the addition to their family of a ten-year-old nephew, Robert Thurston, and then, sometime later, his older sister Susanna. The two children came over from England where their mother, Thomas' older sister Susanna Tingey Thurston, had recently been widowed and was having a hard time. Money was short everywhere, and hospitality to the children was easier for Tingey than cash assistance to their mother. Tingey sadly admitted, "My duty to my own family ha[s] prevented me affording her relief but in mere pittances."[12]

Thomas' business, for the next five years, appears to have been mostly in or with the West Indies, although the record of his activities or ships for the period is sparse. In the summer of 1788, he was in St. Croix again, apparently the captain of a vessel called the *Planter*, and in charge of at least some goods from the Philadelphia firm of Tyson and Vaux. His correspondence indicates that he was uncertain as to how long he was to stay on the island, or whether Mrs. Tingey would come out to join him or stay in Philadelphia. (She apparently stayed in town.) At some time in the next months, moreover, his relations with Tyson and Vaux would take a promising new turn, and he would accept an offer from them to be first mate on a much more ambitious trading mission—a trip to India.

CHAPTER TWO

Merchant Captain

Tyson and Vaux's offer would open new horizons for the ambitious thirty-eight-year-old Tingey, who surely knew how the developing India trade offered an exciting growth opportunity for American merchants. Independence had restricted their access to traditional markets such as the British West Indies where, as fellow subjects of the king, they had previously had free access. But independence had also opened up the prospect of Oriental markets that had previously been closed by royal policy. Impelled by buoyant demand for the distinctive and inexpensive fabrics of Bengal and Madras, the first American ships had arrived in Calcutta in 1785. By sending a ship toward the end of 1788, the firm of Tyson and Vaux was going to be among early Philadelphians on the scene, and Tingey would be among them.

The promising new start soon turned sour, however, and the voyage out, on the ironically named *Harmony*, turned out to be a near disaster. Tingey and his captain, Willett, did not get along well during the long southward crossing of the Atlantic, and Willett apparently began to harbor resentment or even feel threatened by his deputy's take-charge attitude. Tingey must share some of the blame for the eventual blowup: his cocky self-confidence shows through clearly in a letter written to a friend in which he tried to exonerate himself. "I have been familiar, in a series of years, to support my authority on ship board with tranquility, not only to my self, but to those under my command," he wrote.[1] He may have forgotten, after having been in charge of ships of his own, that on this voyage he was not in command.

The crucial incident came off the Cape of Good Hope, in late March 1789. Captain Willett had entertained a number of officers from a ship that was sailing in company with the *Harmony*, and had come on deck to see

11

them off. Tingey, as watch officer, ordered an immediate change of course once the two ships separated, in order to safely clear the Cape, but the captain—who had had a glass of wine too many—"abruptly and with no small degree of acrimony" countermanded the order. When his first mate tried to point out the necessity to change course, the captain refused, and continued to countermand any order that Tingey gave. Tingey backed down, but in a subsequent confrontation in the captain's cabin "high words ensued between him and me, he pompously declaring his own importance and that he was Captain of the ship and nought should be done till first ordered by him." The situation between the two had reached a standoff. Meanwhile, on deck a growing storm, adding to the captain's stubbornly held but dangerous course, caused a few of Tingey's fellow officers to fear for the ship's safety. One of them even urged Tingey to "bestir himself"—almost an invitation to mutiny. As Tingey recorded, "I repeated my uneasiness at being so critically situated, saying I would not till the last moment use coercive measures—but assuring him that I would not remain an idle spectator and suffer either the Ship or our own selves to come into imminent danger."[2]

The crisis eventually passed, and the ship was not driven onto the rocks, but Thomas' relationship with his captain was irreparably damaged. His subsequent anxiety over the affair and the damage it might do to his career is evident in the memorandum he wrote up in his copybook at the time—his usual neat handwriting replaced by an untidy scrawl, with uncharacteristic strikeouts. "In short, in the whole course of my existence I never experienced so much chagrin, so many uneasy hours," he confided to a friend some months later.[3] And the uneasy hours would last for seven long months before the *Harmony* arrived in Calcutta, during which he and Captain Willett were constrained to observe a kind of icy truce. Tingey came to the conclusion that he had no choice and could no longer, under the circumstances, serve on the ship under Willett. When the ship arrived at Calcutta, he informed the captain that he was resigning, and went ashore.

Attempting to justify his action to his old Philadelphia friend, Tingey wrote, "I found myself subject to a capricious and unstable mind, where systematic rules, or knowledge gained by experience, had no influence." He was afraid that he might have lost the confidence of his employers by his resignation, but pride, stubbornness, a bit of self-pity, and a lively concern for his reputation seem to have driven him to persist in leaving a good position for a situation that had no immediate prospects. "I pretend not to perfection, or an exemption from foibles," he wrote, "but I dare boast of my integrity and of an unremitted strict attention to the interest of all those who have conferred on me preference in their service. I have ever been prompted by a solicitude to gain the esteem of all and every worthy member of society, even of those of inferior rank to myself—And the first wish that animates my heart is that I may ever sustain my character unimpeachable, and immaculate if 'twere possible."[4]

Against the odds, the three months that Tingey spent in Calcutta turned out to be fortuitous. Although no longer a ship's officer, he still had responsibility for a number of consignments or "adventures" left to his management, and as a result had an opportunity to familiarize himself with the Indian market. He worked closely with Graham Mowbray and Co., the English firm that provided local support for Tyson and Vaux, and gained their trust in his attention to business.

If Tingey was at all typical of other early American traders in Bengal, he lived frugally, avoiding luxuries such as the horses, lavish quarters, and mistresses to which the longer-term British residents treated themselves. The American traders, it seems, had already gained a reputation for speedy turnarounds, careful attention to market prices, and almost total lack of interest in the local society or politics beyond the bazaar.[5] Tingey's letters indicate that he may have fit within this stereotype, at least in his preoccupation with his business. But he did have some colorful experiences. For example, one day he came to the rescue of his Hindu banyan (a local buying

CALCUTTA'S NATIVE OR BLACK TOWN, C. 1794

(By Balthazar Solvyns, in Les Hindoûs *[Paris, 1810], from the collection of Robert L. Hardgrave Jr., Austin, Texas. Reproduced by permission.)*

assistant) who had been attacked by a Muslim mob and was in fear of his life.[6] Thomas' few written comments on his surroundings show that he did develop some level of understanding and tolerance toward the complicated racial interactions of the trade between East and West. Although he regularly called the local laborers "black men," he lived in what was called the Black Town, and advised a friend who had married an Indian woman that she would face social difficulties in America because of the color of her skin, but that she could overcome them. "It is no easy matter to overcome our *own* prejudices," he wrote, "but when they are the prejudices of a public, or a community at large, most people of sense see and condemn them, tho they themselves are irresistibly impelled by the torrent around them."[7] All in all, though, the few letters that date from this period give the reader an impression of a well-schooled, disciplined, pragmatic, and optimistic family man, but one without much humor or intellectual curiosity. Calcutta was just another port.

But even though he may have lacked sensitivity to local political conditions (they are almost never mentioned in his correspondence), Tingey was effective in his business. He concluded the "adventures" that had been entrusted to him with evident success, sending the proceeds back—not, however, by Captain Willet and the *Harmony*, but on another ship. And his relationships with Graham Mowbray and Co. became so close that their English headquarters promised him the command of one of their ships, if he could get to London in time. The terms of the promised employment are interesting. He was to get a salary, plus twenty tons of "license" for free cargo—either his own or that consigned to his care by adventurers—and could retain any income from carrying passengers. Without a job and perhaps uncertain as to exactly how he stood with Tyson and Vaux, Tingey agreed to take up the offer, and to travel to England rather than home.

But the most fortuitous, and important, gain from his stay in Calcutta was personal: the forming of a new, close, and valuable friendship, one that would help him not only to overcome his present difficulties, but to expand the horizons of his possibilities. This new friend was Thomas Willing Francis, some seventeen years his junior. The two young Americans hit it off from the start. Francis, in Calcutta for the second time as a supercargo (a passenger put on some ships to take responsibility for managing the owner's business), quickly became both guide and host to his newcomer friend. Tingey, alone and in trouble, was grateful, writing enthusiastically to his Philadelphia sponsors, "I cannot close without taking notice of the particular attention paid me here by Mr. T. W. Francis; his house has been mine from my first arrival—nor have we been separated but only when obligated thereto—my pen would lose itself recounting his goodwill and merit."[8] Part of Francis' merit, of course, and in addition to his personal virtues, was unquestionably his sterling connections—his relatives ran two of the preeminent American merchant houses. His brother John was partner to John Brown in the large Providence, Rhode Island, firm of Brown & Francis, the firm that Thomas Francis was representing in Calcutta. But through his uncle, Thomas Willing, he was also connected to Willing and Morris, one of the premier Philadelphia houses. Thomas Willing was, in fact, so rich and influential that both his vote against the Declaration of Independence and his fraternization with the British while they occupied Philadelphia had subsequently been overlooked—particularly after he and his partner, Robert Morris, became the primary financiers of the perpetually penniless Continental Congress. He had emerged from the revolutionary period as president of the Bank of North America, while his daughter, Anne, would soon use her husband William Bingham's great wealth to become the queen of Philadelphia's high society. Thomas W. Francis' friendship was definitely worth cherishing.

Friendship and commerce, of course, were intertwined. Tingey entrusted some of his trade goods (as well as that of a few of his adventurers) to Francis to take onward with his vessel to the West Indies, where they both thought the market for Bengal goods might be better than in Philadelphia. Any proceeds were to be credited to Tyson and Vaux in Philadelphia, but the firm was not to be fully informed of Tingey's plans. "You knowing my destination as well as I do myself and [the] circumspection necessary thereon, you will please communicate as much thereon to Mrs. Tingey as may dispel her doubts and fears—and to no one else," Tingey pleaded with his new friend. The secret they were concealing was not just the promise from Graham Mowbray and Co. that would or would not become a reality before Francis could arrive in Philadelphia. It seems, instead, that they had devised still another project: Thomas Francis was going to try to have Tingey employed as captain of one of his uncle's ships.[9]

In late January 1790 Tingey set sail as a passenger on the ship *Maria Antonio*, headed for London via Ostend in the Low Countries (now Belgium). But events at the Cape of Good Hope (misnamed, it seems, for Thomas Tingey) would again upset his plans. The *Maria Antonio* reached the Cape without incident, and paused at Table Bay in mid-April to replenish her water supplies. One evening, however, a violent north wind came up, and before long most of the seventeen ships anchored in the bay were in trouble. Seven of them lost their anchors and were driven onto shore. The *Maria Antonio* was among the wrecked vessels—her hold and 'tweendecks entirely under water, the sides and bottom holed, the cargo of saltpeter destroyed, and one seaman drowned. Fortunately, Tingey, his trade goods, and even some important parcels he was carrying for Graham Mowbray and Co. were all saved. But the wreck had left him without passage to London, and by the time he was able to play out his role in the legal inquiry on the wreck and then get passage on a Dutch vessel, he was seriously behind schedule, and Graham Mowbray's ship would sail with a different captain. His passage to London and stopover there were uneventful, but it took almost seven more "tedious to the extreme" months—until early November 1790—before he finally arrived home, via New York.

Tingey had been gone two years, his plans had twice been dashed, his trading ventures were incomplete, and he was in debt to Tyson and Vaux. But the failed voyage had not entirely been lost time. He had been tested, and had shown the strength of his character and his resourcefulness. He had learned, and new possibilities were now open to him. But that was for the future, and for the present it must have been good simply to be home again, in the bosom of his family. Nine months later a new young Tingey, Sarah Ann, would indeed enliven the family house at 16 Union Street, but Thomas would not be at home to enjoy the event.

He was, in fact, already at sea, on the way back to Calcutta. He and Thomas Willing Francis had seen their scheme succeed. Tingey had been entrusted by the firm of Willing, Morris & Swanwick to command the *Baring* on a voyage to India. He had learned the news shortly after arriving from London—good news in that it gave him prestigious employment shortly after his mishaps on the *Harmony* and the *Maria Antonio*, but bad news in that he had to go to work immediately, fitting out the ship for an early departure. Ice on the Delaware River detained the ship for a few days, giving him opportunity to report to his employers that he was "blessed with a crew of officers & Men in health, High spirits, Sober, Diligent and Attentive."[10] But by the end of January 1791, the *Baring* was at sea, enjoying an unexceptional crossing to India.

Serious trouble, however, met them on their arrival in Calcutta. A local financial crisis had resulted in the failure of Graham Mowbray and Co., which also was used by Willing and his partners as their local agency. Worse yet, Willing owed the company a considerable amount, and as a result much of the *Baring*'s cargo was subject to seizure by creditors of the failed firm. The *Baring* had no supercargo on board, so Tingey was responsible for clearing up the situation with minimal damage to his new employers' interests. Reporting that the creditors somehow knew that his instructions from Willing, Morris & Swanwick gave him broad authority, he was obliged to work out the best deal possible or "stand the test of litigation." The value of the cargo, however, would not cover his employers' debts, and Tingey had to negotiate yet another deal: he mortgaged the *Baring* to raise the necessary cash. Within a few weeks, he had succeeded in paying off the debt, which amounted to more than £16,400 Sterling. "I have not accomplished all this without much fatigue of both body and mind," he somewhat boastfully wrote back to his employers, "however I feel a satisfaction in having done the best possible and assure myself (I will repeat it) your approbation."[11]

His problems, though, were not yet over. He had neither cash nor credit with which to buy a return cargo of Bengal goods, and no one wanted to book space on his ship for American destinations. So he hit on the expedient of offering to carry goods to Europe, and advertised his eventual departure for Ostend. To his satisfaction, the business was available: he succeeded in almost filling the *Baring*. He also had to renegotiate insurance coverage for his own goods. It only remained to settle the various "adventures" that had been entrusted to his management. He succeeded in selling most of the American goods, and then turned to local middlemen for return products. (His preference for dealing with middlemen is clear from this account he gave to one investor, whose goods "were bought of an Armenian Merchant here, noted for the freshness and quality of his goods. . . . [I]t seldom occurs that every color of silk is to be found with one person, and to purchase only 10 or 12 pieces of each colour from different hands would greatly enhance the price. Even now I was necessitated to have recourse to the Bazar for the low-priced Taffoties.")[12] Since he would be headed to Europe, most of the venture cargo, including his own, was entrusted to Captain Ashmead of his old ship *Harmony*, which happened to be in port at the same time and not apparently caught up in the bankruptcy of Graham Mowbray. The *Harmony* was headed to the West Indies, where Bengal goods might make a good profit, before returning to Philadelphia.

The *Baring* sailed at the beginning of 1792, spending a few days at Madras before continuing to the Cape. It appears, though, that just before departure from Calcutta, Tingey had the pleasure of a short reunion with Thomas Francis, who had been sent out by his firm to protect their interests from the failure of Graham Mowbray. This time, Tingey could be of help to his friend. He and Joseph Brown, the senior partner in Brown & Francis, soon began a lengthy correspondence, in which Tingey gave some advice, but more emphatically tried to convince the cautious Brown that Francis was capable of handling the situation.

> I know the magnitude of the Property you have under his care and therefore cannot doubt of your anxiety, that the safety of so much should depend on one single life, which at all times and places, we hold on such a precarious and slender thread. . . . If ever virtue and integrity, with an indefatigable and unremitted attention to the business and interests [of] others were

contained in one man, that man serves you in the person of
Thomas Willing Francis—for his mental and corporal abilities
are devoted to your service and strenuously exerted for your
advantage.[13]

The *Baring* arrived safely in Ostend but, still encumbered by the mortgage placed on her in Calcutta, was almost sold. Tingey managed to convince his firm that the ship was worth keeping and, in London, succeeded
in the maneuver of putting her up for auction and then buying her back for
the firm for just £100 above their ceiling. Once again, he felt confident that
he had managed his employers' business with success. He brought the ship
back to Philadelphia by September, with a cargo—much of it apparently
brandy—picked up in Ostend.

His correspondence with Brown & Francis had continued, and deepened
into a sort of unspoken business relationship. He had become familiar with
Thomas' brother John Francis, who was the partner in Brown & Francis,
and also with Thomas Mayne Willing, son of Thomas Willing. There was
no disloyalty in this: the two firms were linked by family and cooperated
regularly, but Tingey was sensitive to the possible conflict of interest. While
still in Europe, it seems, he had declined to discuss an offer to command one
of Brown & Francis' ships while he was still in the employ of Willing, Morris
& Swanwick. "I am truly thankful to you for the wishes and desire you had
that I should have accompanied my friend and commanded your Ship," he
wrote to John Brown, "but to have accomplished it I must have deviated
from a previous positive agreement. And surely the man who could reconcile
himself to such measures will never be worth your employ."[14]

By early 1793 the relationship had finally flowered into the offer of a
new command. Tingey, from hints contained in his correspondence, had
been hoping for this, and apparently John Francis had given him reason to
do so while they were both in Europe. When he received an invitation to call
on the firm in Providence to discuss the matter in person, he was on the first
available coach to do so. Those discussions went well, and culminated in the
offer to command a Brown & Francis ship, the *President Washington*, on
her next voyage in the autumn—to India, of course.

In Philadelphia, her husband's successful return encouraged Mrs. Tingey
to look for a new home, and in the spring of 1793 they bought a brick
house on Third Street, between Walnut and Spruce—just around the corner from the mansions of Thomas Willing and his nephew and son-in-law
Thomas W. Francis. It almost surely was a happy and busy time for the
expanding Tingey family—baby Sarah was two, while the two older girls
and the Thurston children (his niece and nephew) were reaching their teen-

age years. The Tingeys were now among the prominent citizens of the city who contributed to public causes and had the respect of their fellows. The captain's connections to the Willings and other prominent merchants provided him a foothold in the Anglican merchant aristocracy, where important decisions were made. It is doubtful that the Tingeys mixed socially with the wealthy and politically active Willings to any great degree, however. The Tingeys always professed disdain for what they called "ostentation," which certainly could describe the style of Philadelphia's high society led at the time by Thomas Willing's daughter, Anne Bingham. The Tingeys were close to Margaret's more modestly placed relatives, the Murdochs, and their social circle was probably largely family-centered.

Business called, however. The house needed to be paid for, as did schools for the children, and Captain Tingey consequently was anxious to nail down his new prospects with Brown & Francis. Having turned down other offers of employment, he wanted to get things moving; his letters to Providence are full of questions as to whether he should start procuring cargo or supplies, suggestions for financing the trip, and so on—so much so that he finally realized that he was being pushy. "I hope you will consider my views herein chiefly impressed by attention to your interest—say at most mutual benefit," he wrote after a long exposition on finance, "and are with deference to your judgment only submitted thereto: that you will not impute to me the arrogance of dictating." John Brown, however, seemed to be more cautious and less committed to the project. He evidently wanted Tingey to report on official views in Philadelphia about the international situation, to aid his company in decision making. Thomas' letters at this time, at least, contain an unfamiliar—and not very useful—smattering of political reporting. (His reporting that "both England and France are extremely particular in giving no annoyance to commerce under our flag," for example, was not fully accurate—even if it was his opinion: he wrote the same thing to friends.) Brown's caution was understandable: the *President Washington* was still at sea, and the war in Europe—Tingey's opinion notwithstanding—was beginning to impact neutral shipping.[15]

The caution shown by Brown in Providence outweighed, in the end, Tingey's enthusiasm. Tingey never got a green light to start preparing for the voyage. By May the correspondence was all about transactions that Tingey was conducting on behalf of the firm, and mention of the *President Washington* had disappeared. The deal was off, and Thomas was once again without a ship or a promise of employment.

But there was another prospect. In 1794 the Willings began to build a ship for the India trade. That trade had become even more profitable, from a combination of tariff preferences enacted over the past few years by the

new federal government, and the breakout of war in Europe, which made
neutral American ships the carriers of choice—as long as the major powers
did not hinder them. The ship the Willings had commissioned was sturdy,
built for the long ocean crossings. Although smaller than the larger English
East Indiamen, she was still, at just over five hundred tons, a sizeable ship.
They would call her the *Ganges*. To finance the venture, Thomas Willing had
brought in new partners, Robert Morris being occupied at the time in his
eventually madcap real estate speculations and John Swanwick having taken
a seat in the new Congress. The new partners were none other than Thomas
Mayne Willing and Thomas Willing Francis, plus two other merchants. Not
surprisingly, they offered command of their new ship to Thomas Tingey—
available, trustworthy, familiar with the India market, steady, and, of course,
a personal friend. The ship was launched in April 1795 and rapidly fitted out
and loaded. By early May she was ready for sea, with a last official nicety:
her ownership was registered with the authorities to qualify for customs
preference and other privileges. On the certificates, Tingey was listed as one
of the owners, and also as master and commander.[16]

The *Ganges* had a slow passage down the river, and it was a bit over a
week later that the pilot was sent ashore. As they headed out to sea, Tingey—
in a tradition presumably dating back to his Royal Navy days—immediately
read his general orders to the crew. The occasion was meticulously noted
down in his journal, which, along with the orders themselves, shows evidence
of a methodical, organized mind. The orders begin as follows: "Being now
at the commencement of a long voyage, and experience on similar occasions
having shown me that a well-regulated system of Order, strictly adhered
to and cheerfully obeyed, will to a certainty be productive of Peace, harmony and unanimity both to the officers and men, I have deemed it therefor
incumbent upon me to issue these orders." The orders then proceed to spell
out, in detail, provisions governing rations, ship's watches, regular reporting requirements, sanitation, weekly cleanup, and discipline.[17] The crew of
twenty-six men responded, the journal tells us, with three cheers. Three of
the crewmen, at least, were familiar to Tingey: they were nephews from the
Murdoch family—James, third officer, John, clerk, and William, ordinary
seaman. On the ship also were seven apprentices put on board by the owners
to learn the trade at Tingey's side.

The Atlantic crossing was uneventful, and the ship was "the easiest on
the sea I ever experienced," as Tingey reported to the owners. She did leak,
however, in rough weather—enough to put the men to the pumps every
hour. The first stop was Funchal harbor in Madeira, Portugal, where they
had to offload cargo onto lighters. Tingey, who suffered from a short bout of
fever during the long weeks at anchor, groused that the process was far too

slow—in part because of "the amazing scarcity of slaves on the island," and also because the locals refused to work on Sundays or saints' days. Barrel staves, iron, and flour went ashore, and a new cargo of wine—lots of wine— was loaded for the thirsty English colonials in India. Tingey, whose inquiries showed that a number of other trading ships had loaded similar cargoes recently, worried that the Indian market would be glutted, and tried to reassure his owners that he had taken on only the best-quality wines.[18]

One of the few untoward incidents of the voyage also took place while they were in harbor: a mutiny, of sorts. Tingey was on shore when he learned that a disturbance had broken out on board ship. He rushed back and found that the crew had somehow (the journal is not at all informative on this point) been excited by one of the seamen into a work stoppage. James Murdoch had taken effective action, however, and put the problem seaman under restraint. Tingey acted quickly and forcefully, cutting off a length of rope and giving the offender two blows across the shoulders. With that the mutiny—such as it was—was over. The offender asked for pardon and was threatened with confinement on shore, but Tingey relented readily enough when the crew objected. Everyone returned to work, and there were no further repercussions, at least as reported by the captain's journal.

The only other incident on the voyage occurred as the ship crossed the equator. Captain Tingey allowed the crew to engage in the customary "frolick," but it got a bit out of hand and a crewman—John Murdoch—was bumped overboard. Happily, the crew reacted quickly under Tingey's command; sails were quickly backed, a boat lowered, and both Murdoch and a seaman who had jumped in an effort to save him were soon rescued.

By late November 1795 they were in Calcutta, where they spent a little more than two months. Tingey rented a house on shore to explore market conditions and deal with Fairlie Reed & Co., Willing & Francis' new local agent. As Tingey had feared, the wine had come to a saturated market, but the agents thought it could be sold in Bombay and arranged to ship it around. Sugar, pepper, spices, and consignments for a number of Philadelphia merchants were loaded. The crew was kept busy recaulking the hull, scraping the live works, rerigging as necessary, and taking on water and supplies for the return voyage. This time, Tingey's business in Calcutta was entirely routine.

Another few weeks were spent in Madras, where they loaded still more fabrics, spices, and some tropical plants. By the end of February, the *Ganges* was back at sea, the hull tight from the recaulking and loaded with a valuable cargo. The return voyage around the Cape was uneventful. Tingey occupied himself, as he had on the outward voyage, by taking readings three times a day of the air and water temperature, and occasionally of the heat in the ship's hold. He was either bored, or complacent to such a degree that he even allowed himself to register a few atypical naturalist's observations—noting "vast quantities of birds" off Cape Agulhlas, as well as passage through phosphoric matter "so intensely luminous that common small print could with ease be read by the light from the ship's wake." With no more excitement than that, the *Ganges* was back in American waters in June 1796, just over a year after her departure. It had been a successful voyage from the commercial and sailing points of view, and for Tingey it must have been a welcome change from his two previous, trouble-filled voyages to India.

CHAPTER THREE

A New Naval Uniform

T ingey had come home, a successful merchant captain in a city that appreciated trade and traders. The goods he brought back from India—muslins, silks, taffetas, calicoes, and spices among them— would supply the wardrobes and tables of America's most sophisticated city for months, and would also, of course, supply profits for Willing & Francis. The Tingey family was well, and the homecoming was surely joyous.

But in the city that was also the nation's capital, politics had come to occupy a central and not so happy role in daily life. The air was full of political contention and partisan zeal, exaggerated by both the upcoming presidential election and the presence of thousands of excitable refugees who had fled the violence in revolutionary France and its West Indian colonies. Domestic politics and foreign affairs were intersecting in a virulent manner, and the young government was struggling to maintain its balance in the press of events.

When Tingey had left for India a year earlier, President Washington and his small group of key officials were struggling with a basic dilemma: how to safeguard America's hard-won independence in the midst of a war between the obstinate major powers in Europe. Specifically, they wanted to resolve their county's persistent trade and security disputes with Great Britain and France—at war since 1793—and yet avoid taking sides in the struggle. Washington's chosen policy of neutrality was serving American interests well: Yankee ships were carrying the trade of both combatants, and business was booming. But it was a precarious success. Neither Britain nor France fully accepted the American argument that "free ships make free goods," and both persisted in ship seizures and other vexations that inflamed American opinion, and, with it, domestic partisanship as the various political groups chose sides.

George Washington chose to settle first with Britain, in large part because of the huge importance of American-British trade and the customs revenues associated with it. In the spring of 1794 he sent Justice John Jay to London to negotiate; after long and secret negotiations plus a heated Senate debate, the proposed treaty was finally approved just a few months after the *Ganges* set sail. Another half year of acrimony and debate was consumed, however, before the treaty was finally ratified.

In Philadelphia, the proposed treaty, when finally made public, pretty much satisfied major merchants like the Willings, in whose eyes almost anything was better than a punishing war with England, queen of the seas. But not so for the anti-Federalists, who vociferously attacked the treaty as a shameful sellout and its supporters as British stooges. The 1795 Fourth of July celebrations in the city, indeed, had been punctuated dramatically by a procession of angry treaty protestors from the working-class suburb of Kensington. Their peaceful parade through the city with an effigy of Jay had turned into a nasty confrontation by that evening, when they burned the effigy with such enthusiasm that the authorities felt obliged to send in the cavalry to quiet things down. Facing a barrage of stones thrown from the Kensington ranks, however, Captain Morrell and his men chose instead to retire. The confrontation, verging dangerously on domestic class warfare, only emphasized the extent to which foreign affairs and domestic politics had become inextricably mixed.

The treaty, after still more drama, was finally ratified early in 1796. In March of that year, John Adams succeeded Washington as president. Unfortunately for his presidency, he was obliged to inherit the consequence of the Jay Treaty—namely, a growing confrontation with France. The directorate that ruled France, as well as its sympathizers among the Anti-Federalists and the French refugees, believed that the 1778 revolutionary alliance should give Paris a special claim on American friendship, and saw the Jay Treaty not only as a repudiation of the alliance, but even as a hostile act. In retaliation, the French became the major harassers of American shipping, replacing the British as the target of American ire. With neither European government ready to fully honor American neutrality, the Jay Treaty seemed to have simply traded one major despoiler for the other. The overseas struggle, moreover, had migrated into domestic politics, with poisonous ramifications.

To cap the prevailing frustration, the fledgling United States government had little or no serious means to defend its honor or its rights. The Army was effectively nonexistent, and a Navy existed only in the shipyards—made up of six new frigates that had been authorized in 1794 to combat the troublesome Barbary pirates. And even that program had been slowed down—

virtually cut in half—when a suitable deal was negotiated with the Algerian government in 1796 and Congress deemed that the threat had eased.

In the political drama of the year, however, Tingey played no evident role. After another long trip away from home, his priorities were his family and his affairs. He needed, of course, to settle accounts with Willing & Francis. He sold back to them his interest in the *Ganges*, and began to sell items from the bale of trade goods that he had brought home from Madras on his own account. He had done well. His growing family evidently needed more room, and, moreover, the life of a country squire may have appealed to him after twenty years of merchant travel. Whatever the reason, in October of 1796, some five months after Thomas' return from India, the Tingeys sold their Third Street house in town. The next month, they bought a 330-acre estate some thirty miles away, near Princeton in New Jersey. They moved there later in the year, but their move did not by any means sever their ties with Philadelphia. The captain had regular business in town and the elder girls were enrolled in Mrs. Capron's boarding school in New Market ward. All in all, the move was not a total success, and Margaret Tingey admitted some years later that she had not enjoyed life in New Jersey. She had not felt happily settled "since we left the city," she told her husband, and, moreover, the "barrenness" of life in the country depressed her.[1]

When the *Ganges* sailed for India again, it was John Green who occupied the captain's cabin, and not Thomas Tingey, who was now a country gentleman.

If retirement, complete or partial, was on Tingey's mind, it was not in his cards. Relations with France continued to deteriorate, and by early 1798 they finally plummeted with the disclosure of what became known as the "XYZ Affair." This diplomatic incident was taken by many Americans as an irremediable French insult to their national honor. Riding the popular slogan of "millions for defense, not one cent for tribute," arch-Federalists seized the moment to pass through Congress that spring and summer a series of actions designed to strengthen the national defense and harm French interests. They included the formation of the country's first standing Army, the infamous Alien and Sedition Acts, repudiation of the 1778 Franco-American treaty, and a trade embargo against France and its colonies.

The measures that most surely attracted Tingey's attention were the formal establishment of a new executive department headed by a secretary of the Navy, revitalization of the shipbuilding program, and authorization for the new secretary to procure another dozen smaller warships. The first three of the 1794 frigates, designed by Philadelphian Joshua Humphreys to be the largest and most powerful ships of their class, had already been launched. The other three would soon be rushed to completion, constituting the backbone of a small but potent naval service, now on its own as a separate branch of the nation's defense. Soon, a corps of Marines was established to help man the ships, and private citizens were authorized to build still more warships for Navy service. A fighting Navy was being reborn, and the new ships would provide interesting opportunities for qualified men, well beyond the number of the six captains who already had been selected to have command of the big frigates.

The new secretary of the Navy, Benjamin Stoddert, was a Maryland businessman who claimed to know nothing about maritime affairs, but who nonetheless proved to be a good strategist and an effective administrator. In addition, as a staunch Federalist he had easy access to the leaders of the Adams administration and the merchant community. In rapidly organizing a Navy and its support establishments virtually from scratch, it turned out, he and his immediate predecessor, Secretary of War James McHenry, had to rely heavily on the private sector. And ships were available. Among them, in fact, was Willing & Francis' *Ganges*, recently returned from her second voyage, and desirable as a sturdily built Indiaman. A deal was rapidly concluded, the ship hastily strengthened and refitted for the cannons and much larger crew needed for a man-of-war, and the *Ganges*, rated at 24 guns, became one of the Navy's new vessels. It turned out in fact to be the first ship at sea. She was under the command of Richard Dale cruising off the mid-Atlantic coast even before new official orders, issued in late May 1798, authorized the seizure of any French warships—official or privateer.

The Quasi-War with France had begun, and Thomas Tingey's brief retirement from the sea would soon be over.

The *Ganges*, after an uneventful three months patrolling the coast, put into New York in early August. (Philadelphia was avoided because of the risk to the crew from the usual summer fevers.) Captain Dale informed Stoddert that he did not want to retain command, and by early September Stoddert was recommending to the president that Tingey be appointed in his place: "[A]s Capt Tingey is represented by a great many Gentlemen of Reputation to be highly qualified for a command in the Navy, and has the appearance of being so . . . it appears proper that these Gentlemen should now be appointed, though ships are not immediately ready for them, that they may take the rank of Captains. . . . Dale will not go out again in the *Ganges* . . . which will make a vacancy on the *Ganges* for Tingey."[2]

How did Tingey come to the attention of Stoddert as a candidate for command? The record gives some useful clues. Tingey and Dale were old friends and colleagues at Willing & Francis—indeed Dale's position as commander of the *Ganges* had been arranged as part of the sale of the ship.[3] It is probable that the firm, Dale, or both simply proposed Tingey as a replacement, and that Stoddert, after some checking among "gentlemen of reputation" (who can be assumed to have been good Federalists) went along. But Tingey may have been doing some lobbying of his own. The previous year, he had visited another old friend, Thomas Truxtun, who was slated to become captain of the Humphreys frigate *Constellation*, at the Truxtun home in Perth Amboy, New Jersey. It is entirely likely that Truxtun, another good Federalist, had been asked to put in a good word to McHenry or others when the opportunity arose.[4]

Secretary Stoddert proffered a captain's appointment to Tingey by letter of 15 September, and Tingey accepted, in principle, two days later. Stoddert

CAPTAIN RICHARD DALE
(Courtesy of Naval Art Center, Naval History and Heritage Command)

was anxious to have the *Ganges* back on patrol as soon as possible for fear of French warships off the coast, but Tingey had two reservations: before he could take command he wished to confer with Dale, and he had to tidy up his private affairs. An exchange of letters with Dale assured him that he was not stepping on his old friend's toes in accepting the command, and, by the end of the month, he had visited with Stoddert in Trenton to accept in person. At the time, he expected to be ready for sea in four weeks. But delay, it seems, was inevitable: in addition to a need to refit and resupply the ship, some forty new crewmen had to be recruited. What with one thing and another, the *Ganges* did not leave port until December 1798.

Tingey, as a senior captain in spite of the newness of his commission (but then, almost all the commissions were new), was to have two other ships in his squadron, both of them small revenue cutters on loan to the new Navy. The *General Pinckney*, a brigantine of 18 guns, was under the command of Captain Heyward, while the schooner *South Carolina*, rated at 12 guns, was skippered by James Payne. On the run down to the Caribbean, Tingey found the *Ganges* a bit underballasted in her current configuration as a warship with heavy guns on deck: "too tender to bear a press of sail," as he put it in his report back to Philadelphia.[5] But, during the cruise, he had his crew add and shift ballast until the problem was corrected.

The squadron's orders were simple: to patrol the waters of the Windward Passage, between Haiti and Cuba, in order to protect American shipping in the area, and to capture or destroy French vessels-of-war or pirates (and all armed vessels cruising without official commissions were to be considered pirates). The United States, Stoddert felt it necessary to remind Tingey, was at peace with all other countries. His ships could seize only French armed ships, and could not recapture any vessels unless they were in the hands of French crews. But the simplicity of the instruction hid a tangle of possibilities. Because Navy ships and their crews could win substantial additional income from the seizure and confiscation of ships engaged in illegal trade (in addition to seizing warships), the incentive was always strong to take prizes. But the real ownership of civilian vessels or their cargoes was in many cases hard to penetrate, and individual cases were often further complicated by wily merchant skippers, or even privateers, who happily falsified papers to suit their interests and hide contraband trade.

Contraband there certainly was. American merchants had a long and profitable history of trading with the sugar plantations of the Caribbean, in particular on the French colony of St. Domingue (today's Haiti). But since 1791 the slaves on Haiti had been in rebellion, French authorities had subsequently been expelled, and the colony was poised at the brink of a civil war between the leader of the former slaves, Toussaint Louverture, and a pro-French mulatto leader named André Rigaud. American traders had by no means abandoned their business because of the insurrection and war; in fact supplying the rebels offered them even greater-than-normal opportunities for profit, and justified the risk of capture. The French, furious at this activity, which they deemed illegal, had retaliated by licensing and then unleashing the very swarms of privateers that Tingey's and the British squadrons in the area had been sent to thwart. And now the American government had complicated the situation even further by suspending all American trade with France—while Haiti was still a legal part of France in spite of the virtual autonomy of the territory controlled by Toussaint and his black army.

In the circumstances, almost all American trade with Haiti was suspect in the eyes of one party or another, and document manipulation was even more prevalent than usual. Tingey was new to the situation, and perhaps had not been well briefed before his departure. So when in early January 1799 his ship intercepted a Baltimore sloop, the *Ceres*, off the north coast of Haiti and apparently headed for Cap François under suspect papers, he sent off an indignant report.

> There is one kind of business carried on here at present which I conceive behooves us much to suppress. Many American vessels are said to have arrived here, with provisions, etc. In a day or two their papers are changed by a pretended sale, and they

go off for French ports—in some instances, without shifting or discharging their cargoes—return here with French produce, assume their American papers, and clear from this [place] for home. I shall endeavor to ascertain and identify some of the actors in this nefarious business and give you information.[6]

What Tingey may not have realized was that this sort of manipulation had been going on for years and was more or less winked at by the American government, and that moves were afoot in Philadelphia anyway to make American trade with Haiti legal once again.

Other than the *Ceres*, which he reluctantly had to release, neither Tingey nor his fellow captains made any interceptions of interest during their cruise—no French cruisers, no legitimate prizes. The *Ganges* made a short stop about mid-January at St. Thomas, where Tingey consulted with friendly Royal Navy units and even persuaded the port commander to make a gun-for-gun exchange of 15-gun salutes. During the stop, he also learned that heavy British patrols seemed to have effectively diverted privateers from north Haitian waters, at least for the time being. He nonetheless made another patrol along the northern coast, down into the Bight of Gonaives, and across the Windward Passage to Baracoa in Cuba, all without finding a single French warship, privateer, or prize ship. By mid-February, he was already on the way home, informing Secretary Stoddert that he was suffering from "no small degree of chagrin" at having found no French targets. He informed Stoddert that he was taking advantage of the part of his oral instructions that said, "if I found nothing effective to be done on my station," he could return. He pleaded that, on the next cruise, he be sent to the area of St. Croix, where the prospect of French privateers appeared to be greater.[7]

It was toward the end of this short initial deployment that Tingey and his crew experienced their first nonfriendly encounter with a British ship, one that would give him his moment of heroic fame and become the subject of numerous banquet toasts in the future. Hailed and boarded one day by officers of HMS *Surprise*, a more powerful 44-gun ship, Tingey himself was surprised when the boarding officer demanded that he muster his men to see if any of them were British subjects, and therefore subject to impressment. Tingey stood his ground. "I did not hesitate to say I considered all my crew Americans born or adopted. . . . [T]here was one single protection in the ship—the only one we carried was our flag—the business subsided there," he reported modestly to headquarters. But the story became considerably more dramatic after members of the crew wrote home, and their reports were picked up and embellished patriotically by the press. "A public ship carries no protection but her flag," he was reported to have said. "I do not expect to succeed in a contest with you but I will die at my quarters before a man shall be taken from the ship." The crew, according to the published versions, then gave their "manly and noble" captain three cheers, ran to quarters, and broke out singing "Yankee Doodle," causing the British boarding party to back down.[8]

Tingey, of course, could not have been unaware that a fellow American captain had recently been cashiered for failing to stop a British officer from impressing a number of men from his ship, and that a general order had been issued mandating resistance in such circumstances. His small act of courage, in that light, may have been a simple act of prudence. Nonetheless, it was a successful gesture, and hit the right note to an American public that was sorely in need of reassurance that their venture into hostilities with one of the major powers was worth the gamble. Combined with the almost simultaneous news that Captain Truxtun, in the *Constellation*, had roundly defeated and captured the French warship *L'Insurgente*, it provided a welcome boost to the morale of both the public and the young Navy. Tingey, when he returned to the Chesapeake Bay at the end of February, had become a minor hero.

Tingey and the *Ganges* were at Norfolk in the Chesapeake Bay for a little more than a month, refitting and taking in supplies for a longer cruise. He had no time to go home, a situation that this fond father of a growing family found "in no wise agreeable." Indeed, if a letter to his daughters is an indication of his real frame of mind at the moment, he was not entirely happy with his situation in the Navy. As he explained to them, "in the manner and situation which it has pleased God to place me, I am not at liberty to retract my engagement at present, nor can I even now conjecture the probable time it will take before I can honorably retire from the service."[9]

During the period in port, he received several instructions from Secretary Stoddert as well as an informal commendation for his performance in the incident with the *Surprise*. He almost surely also heard the breaking political news that President Adams—less than a year into hostilities, shortly after the inspiring victory of the *Constellation*, and against the advice of his entire cabinet—had decided to renew efforts toward a negotiated settlement with France. The process of approving the envoys, getting them across the ocean, and negotiating the terms would take time, of course, but the signal was there—the war would probably not be a long one.

His first task on a new cruise, Tingey learned, would be to escort the ship *Kingston* to Cap François in Haiti, where it would deposit a new American consul, Dr. Edward Stevens. Stevens and his party, Captain Tingey would have learned unofficially, were headed to Haiti to negotiate (along with the British) a deal with Toussaint whereby American trade with the island could legally be renewed in spite of the embargo against its mother country,

France. As part of the deal, Toussaint would have to assure the Americans that he would close down privateer operations from the ports his forces controlled. Stoddert told Tingey that, after dropping off Dr. Stevens, he should linger for some time to see if his ship would be invited into the harbor as a goodwill gesture. In that case, Stoddert instructed him to "conduct yourself with your usual prudence and good sense, and should you have an audience with Toussaint, with your usual address. It is our policy to conciliate the good opinion of that General and his people."[10]

The *Ganges* and the *Kingston* left at the end of March 1799. On the way to Cap François, Captain Tingey finally made an arrest. Off Cape Isabella, in what is now the Dominican Republic, he stopped an American sloop, the *Mary*, out of Norwich, Massachusetts. When her documents appeared suspicious, Tingey deemed it to be engaged in illegal trade and put a prize crew on board, even though the cargo's owners, who remained on board, contested his seizure. A few days later, the *Ganges* made another, and this time a more clear-cut, arrest. In this case, it was a recapture, the *Eliza* of Charleston, which was sailing under a French prize crew, having been captured some days before by the privateer *Telemaque* of Nantes. Again, Tingey put a prize crew on board; he then sent both ships back to Philadelphia to be dealt with in the courts there.[11]

Without further incident, the two ships reached Cap François, where the *Kingston* proceeded into harbor to drop off her official party and a cargo they had brought with them. Tingey, though, showed little appetite for the diplomatic exercise that Stoddert had suggested, and wound up waiting offshore for less than a day before deciding to sail off. Perhaps the two small prizes they had finally made had whetted his and his crew's appetite for the richer hunting grounds of their next destination.

Tingey and the *Ganges* had been instructed by Stoddert that, after dropping off Stevens, they were to proceed to the West Indies to join Captain John Barry's squadron there. Secretary Stoddert had determined that the best strategy for defending American trade was to disrupt or preempt potential raiders at their bases. Since the Royal Navy's overwhelming presence had kept most French warships bottled up in European ports, patrolling the American coastline had proven a costly and largely fruitless exercise for the small American Navy. Most French privateers, moreover—smaller vessels with limited cruising range—could be attacked or neutralized at their ports of origin in the Caribbean. American warships also could escort convoys of merchantmen through the most dangerous southern waters. The new strategy meant a focus on the waters around Guadeloupe, Haiti, and even Cuba, where French officials exiled from Haiti had begun issuing privateer licenses of dubious legality but pernicious effect. Guadeloupe was the

BENJAMIN STODDERT,
FIRST SECRETARY OF THE NAVY

*(Courtesy of Naval Art Center,
Naval History and Heritage Command)*

key point in the West Indies, however, because the French governors there had been actively encouraging privateering, in part as a profitable diversion to keep the colony's contesting factions— the military, merchants, freed slaves, and potential counter-revolutionaries— from each other's throats.

Tingey was carrying with him a set of instructions from Stoddert to Captain Barry. But maritime mail in those days was both slow and unpredictable, often sent by separate duplicate copies to ensure receipt, and delivered by whatever means were at hand: official mail by government packet boat, or simply by exchanges of mail with passing ships. The unreliability of the mail, combined with a slow turnaround time on correspondence, made it entirely normal that there could be a certain amount of confusion in matters of command and control. Stoddert had expected Barry, as well as Captain Truxtun who was the next most senior officer in the area, to be on station for some weeks longer. But both captains, for their own reasons (and perhaps taking a liberal interpretation of their instructions), had decided to leave early. As a result, Tingey was surprised when, arriving at St. Kitts (in what is now the Virgin Islands) in mid-May, he found neither Barry nor Truxtun in the area. A quick check of the other American vessels in port or arriving over the next few days showed that he was the senior officer present. The squadron, according to naval protocol and custom, was his to command.

But his orders were not designed with that eventuality in mind. So Tingey did the appropriate thing: he brought together the other senior officers and together they opened the packet of instructions from Stoddert. Finding nothing there that would instruct them differently, they agreed that Tingey should command the squadron, and that it would continue to focus on patrolling the waters around Guadeloupe. (In fact, there was another order from Stoddert that might have complicated the issue had it arrived in time: it was an instruction to Truxtun to send the *Ganges* to Jamaica.) Tingey and his colleagues had done precisely what Stoddert would have wished them to do, but the poor secretary spent some days back in Philadelphia worrying that they might have failed, in the absence of specific instructions, to read his mind on the mission, which was to "restrain the depredations from Guadeloupe."[12]

In addition to the *Ganges*, there were six American warships at St. Kitts. Two of them were slated to return to the continent in a few weeks. Other than the two departing ones, none was a major ship; the *Ganges* was by far the most powerful of the four ships that would remain. But their task was not to fight other warships as much as it was to run down and capture small French privateers, so speed and sailing qualities, including the ability to work close to shore, were more important than the weight of their broadsides. Two of the ships were revenue cutters that had been taken into the Navy; they were the *Pickering* and the *Eagle*, both of 18 guns and commanded by John Ingraham and Hugh G. Campbell, respectively. The remaining two were ships built in Virginia by public subscription: the *Norfolk*, of 18 guns, under William Bainbridge; and the *Richmond*, of 16 guns, under Samuel Barron.

Barron and Bainbridge were the two officers who had assisted when Tingey had opened the instructions from Secretary Stoddert. Barron would accompany a convoy home within the month, but Bainbridge, who would cruise with Tingey for much of the summer, had already had an interesting year. The previous autumn, his ship (the *Retaliation*) had been captured by two heavily armed French frigates, and, in consequence, he had spent several months as a prisoner on Guadeloupe. The French governor there, General Edme Desfourneaux, had eventually released him because he thought it improper to hold prisoners during an undisclosed war. His act of chivalry would backfire: Bainbridge was intent on hunting down the privateers sailing from the island and would soon have some success.

The ships of the squadron spent two weeks distributing goods recently arrived with the supply ship *Florida*. At the end of the month, as John Ingraham of the *Pickering* put it, "The Commodore [Tingey] having hoisted a Blue and White Flag at the Fore, loos'd his fore top sail and fired a gun, we set sail."[13] The *Ganges*, *Norfolk*, and *Pickering* kept loose company as they worked the area, hailing and when necessary chasing down a number of ships, but failing to catch a French vessel. By mid-June, Tingey was again in a blue mood, reporting to the Navy secretary that a combination of gloomy, "unsettled" weather and the unsuccessful hunt were causing him to be "perturbed and full with chagrin—disappointed in having effected none of the purposes for which I was called to the service of my country—while also my private concerns are suffering by my absence. . . . I [do not] enjoy contentment." On the other hand, he was happy with the performance of the *Ganges*, which, as he reported, often outsailed her sister ships, even the reputedly swifter *Norfolk*.[14]

By the end of the month, however, he was able to report home from St. Bartholemew (now generally known as St. Barts) in a more cheerful mood. The *Ganges* had finally seized a French corsair off Guadeloupe, the *Vainquer*, an 8-gun ship that was reputed to be among the fastest of the privateers from the island. The capture had involved an exciting chase of some ninety miles during which some forty shots had been fired before the French vessel finally surrendered. The ship and seventy-five prisoners had been left at nearby St. Kitts, while ten more prisoners had been brought to St. Barts for possible exchange for Americans being held there. The prize eventually was sent to Philadelphia for condemnation, to be handled by Willing & Francis, with Tingey advising his old employers (who were now his agents in prize cases) that it would be best to sell the ship in the islands, where she had such a reputation for speed that she might bring a much higher price than on the continent.[15]

The commodore (an honorary title granted to commanders of squadrons) also had a diplomatic mission, of a sort, on St. Barts. The island at the time was owned by the Swedish government, and was a free port similar to the nearby islands of St. Eustatius and St. Croix. Too small and rocky for farming, the island and its mixed-nationality population of some five thousand had grown quite prosperous during the wars by providing a harbor and a marketplace for all nationalities and any sort of transaction. The Swedish governor ruled with a liberality that made the place convenient to all nations, but also angered them when their particular interests were ignored. And Tingey's objective on this occasion was to vent his anger. He had been incensed when, sitting helplessly downwind at St. Kitts with the captured *Vainquer*, he had seen French corsairs take what he believed to be three American prizes into St. Barts harbor. Job Wall, the American consul in St. Kitts, had urged him to complain to the governor, and the two of them had come across the strait to do just that.

Tingey's effort at diplomacy, however, was more or less a failure. He and Wall tried to convince the governor that his administration was giving undue advantage to the French privateers, to American disadvantage. The governor listened politely but promised nothing. Tingey even resorted to a bit of bluster; threatening to station one of his ships outside the harbor to close it to French corsairs. The governor, undeterred, parried that he would welcome the move: it would "rid him of much trouble and uneasiness." Unsatisfied and annoyed, Tingey wrote to Stoddert that he considered St. Barts to be "a harbour, in my opinion, the most hurtful to our trade of any in the West Indies."[16] That sentiment did not prevent him from stopping there when it suited his purposes, however.

For the next four months, the ships of Tingey's squadron worked the waters of the Leeward Islands with some success. They had been joined by the *Montezuma*, a 20-gun converted merchantman, under Captain John Mullowny; and the *Merrimack*, a swift 24-gun frigate built by public subscription in Newburyport, Massachusetts, under Captain Moses Brown. Brown was a sturdy New Englander who had led a colorful life as an officer in the Royal Navy, and as a merchant sailor, smuggler, privateer, and now a U.S. officer.

The island ports were full of American merchantmen who wished to form a convoy through the dangerous waters on their way home. Some forty-five of them petitioned Tingey to provide an armed escort. He refused, pointing out that a British convoy was headed the same way, and that his orders were to pursue French privateers in the islands. Sensing their resentment and anger, he quickly wrote to Stoddert to explain his action in case they accused him, back at home, for refusing them protection.

By late July, more mail had arrived from Philadelphia, including several letters for Thomas from Secretary Stoddert. (But there was no mail from family members, from whom Thomas had not heard since March.) Stoddert congratulated Tingey on capturing the *Vainquer*, assured him that he and the president approved of the stance taken toward the merchant convoy, and that "no clamor will injure you." He ordered that the *Ganges* stay on station until late October, when the one-year enlistments of most of the crew expired and the hurricane season would put an end to cruising in any event. He at the same time informed Tingey that he would not go out again with the *Ganges*; another assignment was being considered. "You stand fair to be entitled to one of the six Ships of the line, by the time they are ready," he confided.[17] (Congress, still in a war mood, had approved such a building program earlier in 1799.)

But Stoddert's promise—such as it was—was a distant one. The necessary lumber was still being ordered, and it would be a long time before the large ships could be built. The secretary did have Tingey's next assignment on his mind, however. He would tell the president that Tingey "appears to be a judicious, attentive, Active officer . . . I wish his commission was of older date," indicating by that last phrase some doubt as to whether Tingey could be assured of a command as important as one of the planned 74-gun ships. In his letter to Tingey, on the other hand, he expressed no such misgivings, ending with a sentence that may help explain his support: "We are tranquil here and Federalism has gained ground in all the states."[18]

In spite of his complaint that "I seem destined to such continuance of ill luck that I've hardly expectation of meeting success—we seem perpetually to be where the French are not," Tingey and his squadron took a number of minor prizes during the summer months.[19] In early July they recaptured a British ship called the *Young George*, which had been seized earlier by the French. The cargo, owned by Americans, was sold in St. Barts, but the previous British owner was suing in St. Kitts to recover his ship, and settlement of the case would turn out to be troublesome and long. In early August Tingey and his squadron took a less-complicated prize: the *Rabateuse*, a small French privateer armed with 6 guns. The *Rabateuse* and her cargo of cotton and sugar, destined for Guadeloupe, were sent to St. Kitts for sale. A few days later, and acting on a tip from Tingey, the *Merrimack* seized an armed French merchantman with a letter of marque, the *Bonaparte*. She was rapidly sold, but her cargo turned out to have been owned by numerous shippers of various nationalities, and so the claims and counterclaims persisted for years. The next seizure was a recapture—the schooner *John* of Gloucester, Massachusetts, which had been taken earlier by a French privateer. Finally, headed to St. Croix, Tingey captured a small French privateer that preferred to surrender to an American man-of-war rather than to the British privateer that was also attempting to seize her. Tingey did not even dignify the ship with a name when he reported his capture; she had little valuable cargo and was quickly ransomed back to her owners in St. Croix.

The improved weather, the exciting chases, and the prizes seem to have improved Tingey's mood considerably. Success, of course, was a large part of the improvement. Then he was also back in familiar waters, and able to visit with "the first Mercantile characters there [St. Barts], old friends of mine."[20] But one senses that his small squadron had become a team. Hunting French ships with the *Pickering* and the *Merrimack* in the vicinity, and sometimes joining in the chase, was exhilarating, and Tingey's reports give a sense of the excitement he and the crew were experiencing. The capture of the *John* is an example. The three ships had pursued two unidentified ships all through the night, with the *Ganges* finally closing in and making the seizure. The *Ganges* and the *Pickering* immediately set out in pursuit of the French privateer, *Revellieu*, and chased her all the way to Guadeloupe, with the *Ganges* winning the race but unfortunately losing her prey along the coast. Tingey was careful to note each time that the *Ganges* outran her companions; a spirit of friendly competition with the other ships and crews can be noted, along with Tingey's pride in his ship. When Stoddert expressed misgivings about leaving the squadron on duty as hurricane season approached, the revved-up Tingey quickly wrote back, "No ship in the service (I speak from experience) will be found better able to sustain their violence than the *Ganges*. . . . [B]elieve me, Sir, that she has outsailed every ship & vessel of the United States that we have been in company with. . . . [E]ven the *Merrimack* we have passed in full chace."[21]

September passed with no new prizes taken. Tingey learned, in a letter from Secretary Stoddert, that he would be relieved as commodore of

Guadeloupe Station by Richard Morris, commanding the 28-gun frigate *Adams*. "As to yourself," Stoddert continued, "more agreeable arrangements will be made for you than going out again in the *Ganges*—and you have been so long absent from your family that you ought now to spend some time with them. I have the pleasure of assuring you that your conduct has given great satisfaction to the President, and I doubt not your country, and that he joins me in wishes that your commission was of older date."[22]

Tingey had also learned, by earlier letters, that the task of Consul Stevens in Haiti had met with success: trade with the island was once again open to Americans. But the renewed trade had only stimulated French privateers from Guadeloupe and Cuba to prey in the waters off Haiti's north coast, and more warships were needed to protect American ships and crews. So in mid-September, per instructions issued by the secretary of the Navy, Tingey said farewell to Captain Brown and the *Merrimack*, detaching them from what remained of his squadron to patrol the north coast of Haiti. (Tingey himself had orders to take the same route home, when the time came.) Separation from the old sea dog was a bit sentimental. He and Brown had worked together well and now the team was breaking up. "I cannot take leave of you, Sir," Tingey wrote, "without expressing my regret that we are to separate 'ere the complete termination of our cruise, and also to offer you my thanks for the promptitude and alacrity with which all signals and orders have been put in effect since I have had the honor to have you under command of the *Ganges*."[23]

Two weeks later, off St. Kitts, the *Ganges* took her last prize of the voyage—a French privateer called *L'Esperance*. The ship itself having been seized from a British owner who resided on St. Kitts, the attempt at confiscation was immediately contested in the local court. Tingey, who apparently feared that the British judges would show favoritism, tried to use his contacts with the local British military authorities to have at least the cargo—which was clearly French—declared a valid prize.[24] The case, however, would not be resolved on his watch. By 10 October Captain Morris and the *Adams* had arrived. Tingey's turn as commodore of Guadeloupe Station was over, and he was free to sail home. Stoddert had advised him not to arrive before 10 November because of the city's summer fevers. Tingey and the *Ganges* were home in Philadelphia by 12 November.

CHAPTER FOUR

A Shaky Start
to a New Command

The "more agreeable arrangement" that Secretary Stoddert had in mind for Tingey was the promise of command over a major addition to the fleet—one of the 74-gun ships of the line that had been approved by a patriotic Congress at the height of the hostilities. It was an honor indeed. But, unfortunately, it was also more prospect than reality.

The first problem was that the ship had yet to be built, and Tingey himself would have to supervise her construction over a course of many months. Second, the continued growth of Stoddert's Navy itself could no longer be ensured, in light of the changing military and political situations. An end to hostilities had become a possibility. The American peace delegation, after many delays and a fierce rear-guard resistance by the arch-Federalists, had finally left for France. Talks were under way, and even though President Adams had instructed that matters were to proceed "as if no negotiation was going on," a clock was ticking toward a peace agreement.[1] Moreover, Adams himself was in political difficulty, his policies increasingly unpopular and his own party fundamentally divided. It was entirely possible that the Federalists, major supporters of a national Navy, could be defeated in the elections scheduled for late 1800.

But Thomas Tingey was a practical man, not much given, it seems, to conjecture or doubt. Just returned from a successful cruise, with the promise of commanding a prime 74-gun ship, he had probably all but forgotten that, a year earlier, he had talked of retirement from the service. So in late January 1800, when Stoddert informed him that he was to take charge of the ship scheduled to be built in the new federal district of Washington, Tingey did not hesitate or argue for a different posting. By early February—only four months after returning home—he was already reporting from his new command.

The command, of course, like so much else in the struggling community that was to become the nation's capital, was a design waiting to be achieved. The design had lain in the organized mind of Benjamin Stoddert for some time. A successful merchant in the neighboring town of Georgetown and a landowner in the federal district, Stoddert shared George Washington's vision of a vital, bustling, and prosperous, commercial city on the banks of the Potomac. It was natural that the two landowner-politicians would also support the establishment in that city of a major federal military complex, one that would help ensure the capital's future prosperity (as well as, not incidentally, their own). As early as September of 1798, only a few months after his appointment as secretary of the Navy, Stoddert had started to prepare the ground. Writing to ex-president Washington, he had pointed out that the new Navy would need "one navy yard at least," and that several sites identified in Pierre (Peter) Charles L'Enfant's Washington city plan "appeared to me to be among the most eligible situations in the United States for a navy-yard."[2] He went on to point out the advantages of a Washington location: it would be in the center of the Union, under the eye of government, in a position easily made secure from attack, and with good timber and other building materials readily available. Ten days later, Washington replied in a similar vein, reciting all the advantages Stoddert had mentioned and stressing the defensibility of a Washington position.[3] The two letters are indeed so similar that it looks like a political maneuver: Stoddert may have felt he needed a letter from the revered and respected former president to justify steps that would make a reality out of his plan to establish a navy yard at Washington.

Stoddert, in fact, had already taken the first step. When Congress approved, back in early 1799, the construction of the six ships of the line, the creation of two repair docks, and the purchase of timber for the future uses of the navy, the Navy secretary had taken that as a license to proceed. He had hired William Marbury as naval agent in Washington: "Well knowing your ability and Integrity qualify you for a more important service, I have the honor to request that you will undertake the Agency for this Ship—as well as for all other matters belonging to the Navy Department in that quarter," Stoddert wrote.[4] His instructions to the new agent were at first consonant with the congressional mandate. Marbury was told that one of the ships was to be built at Washington, and that he should begin buying the necessary timber. Soon, Marbury's instructions became broader: he was to seek more land for the yard, and to contract for building a wharf. Stoddert, in effect, was broadening the congressional authorization to build a ship into permission to build a shipyard at the same time.

Marbury was an interesting choice for the job of naval agent. Naval agents at the time were paid no salary, but rather took a 2 percent commission on the value of their procurement on behalf of the Navy, up to $2,000 per year. Marbury did not exactly need the money, having made a sizeable fortune as a financial agent for the state of Maryland. But Stoddert encouraged him to take the job, and to set up as a merchant in Georgetown, for a number of reasons that had little to do with building up the Navy. To begin, Marbury held the mortgages on much of Stoddert's property, and the latter undoubtedly had an interest in keeping his creditor happy with a lucrative job. Equally important, Marbury was a John Adams loyalist at a time when the Federalist faction was beginning to tear itself apart, and the rival Democratic-Republican group was expanding in Maryland. Stoddert surely felt that he and the president could use an ally of Marbury's heft and influence.

Marbury had some initial successes. When the chosen plot of land by the Anacostia River, originally designated by L'Enfant as "Exchange Square," appeared to be too small for a construction yard, he was successful in purchasing two adjoining parcels from the District commissioners. In addition, he negotiated contracts with an Arlington constructor and Lewis Deblois, a local merchant, for the lumber and labor to build a wharf that would facilitate the landing of materials for the planned ship. But, while Marbury may have been a good financial agent, bond trader, and loyal political ally, he proved to be a mediocre purchasing agent, at best. By the time Captain Tingey arrived in early 1800, several contracting scandals were looming that would tarnish the navy yard's image even before it was officially constituted.

The first problem concerned the Deblois contract. By summer, Marbury claimed to have discovered that Deblois was padding the bill by overcharging for labor, and pocketing the difference. Marbury published his accusations in the local press, publicly demanding that Deblois refund the overpayment. Although that was done, the resulting public furor, and the appearance of loose contracting and corruption, gave ammunition to opponents of the entire navy yard project. The second problem involved major cost overruns for the supply of shipbuilding lumber, under contracts issued to John Templeman of Georgetown. The complicated scandal and resultant legal case did not break into public view until the end of 1800, and implicated Stoddert as much as Marbury, but its effect was, like that of the Deblois case, to besmirch the navy yard project.

And construction of the ship had still not begun. Tingey's appointment can be seen as an effort on the part of Stoddert to put an experienced hand in charge of the project, and to move things forward enough to create some sort of fait accompli by the time of the elections. Writing to Marbury in January 1800, Stoddert informed him, "Thomas Tingey, of the Navy, an officer of great merit in our service," was to be the yard supervisor and who, "having seen the navy Yards of England, will be able to direct the layings of that in

Washington to greatest advantage."⁵ Stoddert may have overstated Tingey's credentials, but he did so in an apparent effort to sugarcoat the fact that the naval agent was in effect being downgraded; he also assured Marbury that he would continue to be the contracting officer. To Tingey, the secretary gave a clearer directive: he should proceed to Washington "with a view to super-intend the building," and keeping in mind that any arrangements he made should be done with a view toward building a permanent establishment. The immediate task was to cooperate with Marbury on building the wharf and a place for storing timber, but in the longer term Tingey should "suggest a plan of improvement for a complete navy Yard."⁶

Planning for the yard's future may have been the last thing on Tingey's mind upon his arrival in the federal city. The immediate issue was to get work of any kind under way. A major snowfall that had delayed his arrival had also stopped work on the wharf. He and Marbury rode over to the site together on 12 February but there was so much snow on the ground, Tingey reported to Stoddert, that he had not been able to make a proper site survey. The wharf project looked to be "a Colossial and operose undertaking," but the most immediate need was to build a fence to protect the construction materials, which were arriving slowly, from pilferage.⁷ It was not the kind of news to placate the impatient secretary of the Navy.

Tingey was staying in Georgetown, at the home of George Beale, the nephew of his wife Margaret. He and Marbury would most likely have met there before proceeding to the work site. With deep snow on the ground, they must have ridden horseback to the Anacostia River site, a trip that would have taken more than an hour. Their route through the collection of villages that was soon to be the nation's capital is easy to imagine. After leaving the relatively urbane little town of Georgetown and crossing Rock Creek by one of the new bridges, they would have continued into the federal district along the sparsely settled country track that was (hypothetically at least) Pennsylvania Avenue, until they reached the cluster of houses and con-struction yards that surrounded the still-unfinished president's house. From there, they would probably have continued eastward along the slightly more developed F Street ridge, where a gathering of new but substantial brick houses identified the area as a future center of the town's elite. Crossing Tiber Creek at the foot of the hill and climbing up to the imposing but also unfin-ished Capitol building, they would have had a view back over the Tiber's wide estuary, the fields of the still-farmed plantations of the original owners, and the distant Potomac. At the top of the hill, they would have skirted the vast Capitol construction site and the collection of substantial homes and boarding houses that identified this second major pole of the new town. On the final leg, they would have headed across the hill and down to the broad

Anacostia River, also known as the Eastern Branch. There, under the snow and ice, lay the undeveloped plot of riverfront that was their project.

The plot of land originally had been reserved for government use by L'Enfant as the site for an Exchange Square. It had subsequently been identified during the Adams administration as a potential naval hospital site, until Stoddert chose to make it a navy yard. Bordered on the north by M Street SE and on the east by Ninth Street SE, the original parcel was approximately four square blocks of good land, with the possibility of expansion out to the river channel by filling in the mudflats. To the west, the parcel narrowed where the indentation of St. Thomas Bay extended all the way up to M Street. It was near the top of that bay, in fact, that Marbury had bought the two new parcels—one was almost entirely below the high tide line, and the second mostly mudflat. It was a plot of some thirty-seven acres, if the tidal flats could be filled in at the top of the bay, and out into the river as far as the deep-water channel. The immediate priorities were to finish the wharf (jutting westward into the bay roughly south of Eighth Street), to design a

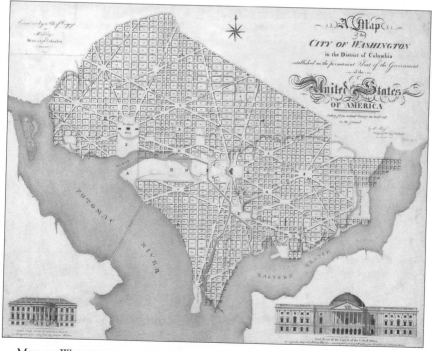

MAP OF WASHINGTON, 1818, SHOWING PLANNED AS WELL AS ACTUAL STREETS.
THE NAVY YARD IS ON THE ANACOSTIA RIVER, LOWER-RIGHT CENTER,
WITH ITS WHARF EXTENDING INTO ST. THOMAS BAY.
(Courtesy of Library of Congress, Print and Photograph Department)

slipway for construction of the ship, and to secure the government supplies in the area from the attentions of the yard's larcenous neighbors.

The neighbors were, for the moment, few. To the west, across St. Thomas Bay and its marshy headwaters, were a pier and a few commercial establishments. From there up to the Capitol along the roughly graded track of New Jersey Avenue lay an intermittent strand of buildings, a few of them the substantial homes of prominent citizens. But around the navy yard site itself were fewer than two dozen houses, most of them wooden, clustered around Seventh and L Streets. However unpromising, however, the neighborhood was where Tingey would have to find a house for his family if he wanted to be anywhere near where his responsibilities lay.

What did Tingey think of this new, raw town into which his professional ambition had propelled him? He knew, at least, that his wife was unhappy over the "barrenness" of her rural New Jersey life, and missed the urban amenities of Philadelphia. But most of all she wanted to be settled permanently. She had very recently written to him to express the anxieties she held for herself and their daughters: "I hope the great God will support me under all the disappointments of this transitory life. . . . You say please the Omnipotent Director that once we are settled in life you are bent on being their [the girls'] tutor." A few weeks later she expressed her frustrations even more dramatically: "Good God are we always to be kept apart and my heart constantly on the wreck? . . . [M]y only wish is to be once more happily settled in life."[8]

A family reunion would probably resolve Margaret Tingey's immediate unhappiness. But the obvious lack of urban amenities in this thinly populated frontier village posed another problem. Would it be a good place to raise a family, or to educate and marry off three budding daughters? Tingey seemed to harbor some doubts on that score, if the unusual tone of irony and even derision contained in a letter to his daughters is any indication. The town, he wrote, was

> a city in an infant state, not yet entirely eradicated from the semblance of Forests! Cornfields! Where abundant harvests have of late repaid the toil of the husbandman! Meadow and pasture grounds, yet replete with wild luxuriant flowering shrubs! Now destined for the seat of Empire—of the Art & Sciences—the Emporium of Wealth & Commerce of your Country—where the deliberative councils of the collected wisdom of our Nation shall henceforth emanate into laws, maturely digested, for ameliorating the state of man in social government, securing equal rights to all our Citizens and disseminating the blessings of uncontaminating Liberty to an admiring Universe.[9]

Whatever reservations Tingey may have had, he had a job to do and a sense of duty that impelled him. Within weeks, he was cultivating the local leaders and their sense of self-interest in making the yard a success. In a letter to an important local businessman (and future first mayor of Washington), he urged haste in getting in the necessary lumber before springtime made it too full of sap: "We have hope by peculiar care in these points to shew a superior ship to those built in the other ports of the Union," he argued.[10] He was anxious that Marines be assigned to the yard rapidly to deter theft, and was looking for a nearby building in which to house them. But work on the wharf was going slowly—and that was Marbury's contract in any case. By the end of March, Tingey admitted to Stoddert that there was not that much to do, and asked leave to return to New Jersey, pack up his family, and move them to their new home.

By early May, Tingey finally had permission to take leave. He made a short trip to Philadelphia to help Margaret prepare for the move, but they decided to leave the girls in New Jersey for the summer. Back in the capital city by mid-month, he wrote to the girls that he and their mother had had a pleasant stop in Baltimore to see friends, were looking for a permanent house, but had offers to stay from both the Beales in Georgetown and Thomas Law. (Law was a prominent investor in Capitol Hill real estate, was married to one of Martha Washington's granddaughters, and had a house near the navy yard site. His welcome was a sign that the Tingeys would be admitted to the best society Washington had to offer.) Tingey wrote that he and Margaret had toured the Capitol building and "on the whole she thinks it all pleasant and agreeable." After staying a few days with the Laws, the couple moved temporarily to the Beale house in Georgetown, and then again to rented quarters nearer the center of town.[11]

The summer passed eventfully for the Tingeys. They made and received the round of socially required calls on the other leading families. At the yard, the wharf project progressed, but slowly, because Marbury was increasingly preoccupied with problems involved in bringing the Navy Department to Washington: finding office space, transporting files from Philadelphia, and so on. President Adams paid a visit to ratify by his presence the transfer of the capital. Secretary Stoddert, too, visited from Philadelphia. Tingey showed him several houses he had identified as possible quarters for the Marines, but the ever-impatient secretary nonetheless grumbled, "the place languishes for want of a little spirit of Exertion."[12] Tingey also enjoyed a visit from his old friend Captain Thomas Truxtun, now a hero after his victories over French warships, who made his calls around town in Tingey's carriage, and undoubtedly complained privately—such was his wont—about the condition of the Navy. Margaret traveled to Philadelphia in late summer and returned with the girls. She and the captain eventually found a suitable house, at Eleventh and G Streets SE—only a short walk from the navy yard site. By late October the family had begun to settle in.

At the same time, things in the broader world were changing dramatically. In France the American negotiating team was making progress toward ending the hostilities, if not in achieving their other objectives. A peace treaty was signed in September 1800, and arrived in the United States in time to be presented to the session of Congress that convened in late autumn. The American political kettle was also at full boil as the presidential elections approached. The opposition Democratic-Republicans were making gains in Maryland, after having won in New York, while the governing Federalists had split irrevocably. If President Adams and the Federalists were to lose the elections, as seemed increasingly likely, the pro-Navy forces would have their backs to the wall.

The issue of standing armed forces had plagued the young republic since its founding. For Washington, Adams, Hamilton, and the Federalists, such forces were an essential element of national sovereignty, pride, and defense. The eastern mercantile and shipping interests, dependent as they were on foreign trade, had naturally allied themselves with that faction, which had now held power for a dozen years. For ardent Republicans gathered around the opposition candidacy of Thomas Jefferson, however, standing militaries were reviled as sources of evil—multipliers of government spending, incubators of aristocracy, and natural generators of war. Jefferson and his colleagues had opposed the mustering of a regular army during the hostilities with France, and would surely dismantle it if voted into office. They were not so adamantly opposed to a standing Navy—"a naval force," unlike an army, "can never endanger our liberties," Jefferson had once said—and he had always supported the use of naval power against the troublesome Barbary pirates. But, fundamentally, the Republicans feared an institution whose traditions and ambitions could provoke unwanted adventures overseas, and they despised the reliance of the eastern seaboard cities on foreign trade, banking, and maritime power. Jefferson—resentful because, as he put it, "we are sacrificing everything to navigation & a Navy" had even proposed an alternative utopia. "What a glorious exchange would it be," he wrote, "could we persuade our navigating fellow citizens to embark their capital in the internal commerce of our country, exclude foreigners from that & let them take the carrying trade in exchange: abolish the diplomatic establishments & never suffer an armed vessel of any nation to enter our ports."[13]

The struggle between the two strategic views—navalist and antinavalist—had persisted since the end of the Revolution, at the end of which the Navy had been disbanded. The supporters of naval power, however, had won the latest round, benefiting from the national indignation against France in 1798 that had allowed Adams and Stoddert to rebuild a respectable, if small, Navy. But the opponents had by no means given up. Indeed, they had never stopped their opposition: the most recent session of Congress had seen calls to reduce the planned number of ships of the line, ostensibly for reasons of economy. Even the granting of an award to Captain Truxtun for his recent victory was taken as an opportunity to criticize the naval establishment— offering battle while negotiations were under way had been a rash act, the critics had carped. They were eager to capitalize on the coming end of a war that they had opposed in order to eviscerate a Navy that they distrusted.

Stoddert and his president, however, could also read the omens, and were prepared with a counter move. They chose to preempt. In early 1801, shortly after the treaty with France was submitted to the Senate for its approval, Stoddert submitted a report to Congress that, in the name of a prospective peacetime "good economy," offered a major reduction of the Navy. The report, and draft legislation that soon followed it, proposed that the majority of the Navy's ships (including the *Ganges*) be sold, scrapped, or returned to the revenue service. The thirteen best frigates would be kept, but only six of them would be on active service at any given time. The rest were to be laid up in a sort of nineteenth-century mothballing, while the number of naval officers and seamen would be drastically reduced, as well as capped. Finally, the program to build the new 74-gun ships would remain untouched.

The move took the wind out of the opposition's sails: it looked as if they had been handed what they were preparing to demand. But Stoddert in fact gained the greater victory. With the support of the still-dominant Federalist faction in Congress, he pushed the bill through the current session, expecting that the next Congress would be more hostile as a result of Democratic-Republican gains in the elections. The Naval Peace Establishment Act became law 3 March 1801, and a parallel act provided money to keep the shipbuilding program under way. Stoddert had succeeded in preserving an active-duty Navy with the best of his ships, the authority and funds to build still bigger ones, and a sort of reserve fleet as well.

The following day, on 4 March 1801, the newly elected Thomas Jefferson took the oath of office as the third president of the United States.

For Captain Tingey, Secretary Stoddert's victory was a personal setback. Twelfth on a list of captains that was now to be capped at nine, he would have to retire from the Navy. So would a number of other good officers, meaning that there would be serious competition among that group of ambitious men for any future vacancies. Moreover, would the new administration, full of opponents of a strong Navy, allow Tingey to stay on as civilian manager of the navy yard? For a man promoted by and allied to the Philadelphia mercantile interests, and holding pronounced Federalist sympathies, he was surely vulnerable. A year earlier, he had suggested to Margaret that he was considering going back into the commercial world, and he might well have been obliged to consider that option once again.[14]

But Jefferson, it was becoming evident, was less hostile to the Navy than his party's statements might have indicated. Rumor had it that James Bayard, leader of the group of Federalists whose abstentions in the House of Representatives had finally led to the new president's victory over Aaron Burr, had demanded as a condition that the Navy be protected. Whether or not that was true mattered less than the international reality. Trouble was brewing with the pirate kingdom of Tripoli, and the Pasha's threats to declare war on American shipping in the Mediterranean gave the new administration a clear choice: it could continue to submit to extortion, or it could use its proven Navy to fight back. Jefferson had consistently favored the use of naval power in that situation, and had come to the realization, perhaps reluctantly, that a Navy was an essential tool, as he grudgingly put it, for "a nation which to a certain degree must be maritime."[15] That meant keeping navy yards, and Jefferson clearly favored Washington for that purpose. Like Stoddert, he liked Washington because all activity would be under the direct and watchful eye of the government. But Jefferson also wanted to make Washington the most important yard—the one where the laid-up ships would be stationed—because he was uncomfortable politically with basing the Navy in any of the seaboard, mercantile cities.

The undeveloped yard at the junction of the Potomac and Anacostia Rivers was thus being chosen for a role that it was not yet organized to play. The new administration would need an experienced and competent hand to put it into order and run it effectively. But their party had few men with maritime experience, much less in running a Navy depot. Tingey was, in spite of his Federalist leanings, not a political man. He might do. Perhaps for lack of alternatives, Tingey was allowed to stay on, neither relieved of his command nor reconfirmed in it.

Jefferson first had to find a secretary of the Navy, a position that proved difficult to fill because candidates seemed to think it would be a dead end, given the Republicans' antipathy to the service. He offered the post to Samuel Smith, a staunch Baltimore Republican, implying that holding the post could be beneficial to his city, but even more so that it was a political necessity. Less than a week after his inauguration, Jefferson wrote to Smith urging him to take the job because, "what renders it a matter not only of desire to us, but permit me to say, of moral duty in you, is that if you refuse where are we to find a substitute? You know that the knowledge of naval matters in this country is confined entirely to persons who are under other absolutely disqualifying circumstances."[16] Smith nonetheless declined, as did several others, until the president finally persuaded Smith's brother, the lawyer Robert, to take the job. Not as effective as his brother, Robert Smith all the same had two qualities that Jefferson valued: he knew something about maritime affairs as part of a merchant family from the busy port of Baltimore, and he was a loyal party man.

Robert Smith took office toward the end of summer; in the meantime, first his brother Samuel and then Henry Dearborn, the new secretary of war, directed the Navy Department. There was much to do. A squadron of ships on active service had already been ordered to the Mediterranean to face down the Pasha of Tripoli: the Barbary Wars had begun. At the same time, the ships that were scheduled for lay-up had begun arriving in the Potomac. At the navy yard, the wharf had finally been finished, but other than that, only the fence and one warehouse had been constructed. The ships were simply parked in the river, exposed to the elements and with most of their supplies still on board. A house for the office was being prepared in the yard, and housing for the Marines was going up at the nearby Eighth and I Streets location that Colonel Burrows had chosen as the site of the barracks. Tingey had requested, and would eventually obtain, money for a second warehouse, but the administration was counting pennies closely and no further expansion was foreseen.

Tingey had his hands full. Five frigates arrived over the summer of 1801. Their officers and crews had to be paid off, the permanent party of some twenty men assigned to each ship enrolled and organized, the rigging taken down and stored, ships' inventories validated and transferred, and rations and other supplies laid in. Tingey could count on the resident Marines to pitch in with the labor of getting things moved around, but administratively he had little assistance other than a few clerks. He also had to supervise the building projects, including a powder magazine at the barracks (and plans for another one to serve the yard). Still another duty was added when William Marbury, the naval agent, was fired in July; Tingey as a result had to take on the responsible and potentially contentious procurement and contracting functions. Rules and regulations, too, had to be drawn up—for the yard as well as for the new system of storing the ships "in ordinary," as it was termed. As was evident from his first, civilian, command of the *Ganges*, Tingey liked system and clarity in command relationships, so this task came readily. He created standing orders for the commanders of ships in ordinary that required watch-keeping, no fires, a weekly situation report, regular maintenance (decks and sides to be washed daily), maximum ventilation, a regularly posted Marine guard, periodic inventories and inspections, and attention to sobriety.

His performance was evidently satisfactory to Secretary Smith, who gradually concluded that this Federalist-leaning officer could serve perfectly well under Republican direction. The men moved toward a mutually respectful, if sometimes conflicted, working relationship that verged on but never reached friendship. At the end of October, Smith offered Tingey a permanent appointment as civilian superintendent of the yard, with responsibility over all public works and property there, and authority over the ships in ordinary and their complements. He would get pay equivalent to that of a captain of a 32-gun ship, but without the ration allowance that had allowed him to set a good table on board the *Ganges* (although a small housing allowance could be seen as partial compensation). His pay came to $1,200 a year before the housing allowance, a modest income for a job with so much responsibility, and while Tingey surely was gratified to have the prestigious employment, he apparently was not entirely happy with the government's parsimony.

Jefferson and Smith, however, were congratulating themselves and their administration on their principled policy of economy. In letters to confidants like James Monroe, the president suggested that even more economies might be made, while in his year-end message to Congress he admitted that the shipbuilding program had progressed very little. (The planned ships of the line in the end fell victim to the drive for economy, and would never be built.) The only relaxation in the economy drive was the request made to Congress by Secretary Smith, early in 1802, for the creation of a position of second in command at the Washington yard, to take direct care of the ships in ordinary. Even then, that position would not be approved and filled for another year.

By early 1802 the initial rush of work and confusion was over and matters had settled down at the yard. A number of the ships were put back into fighting shape, recommissioned, and sent off to the Mediterranean, while others came in to take their place. The future of the yard, on the other hand, was still unclear. The original proposal of building a ship of the line in Washington had not been put into action, even as the necessary lumber continued to arrive. A very basic infrastructure for supporting the ships in ordinary was in place but without a systematic plan, and the continued economy drive—reinforced by strong Republican gains in Congress from the most recent elections—had stopped any further construction and made forward planning problematic. Tingey, in fact, had never drafted the long-term plan that Stoddert had tasked him with producing, and his new bosses had shown no interest in pursuing the idea. The administration had even assigned most new business connected with supporting the ships in the Mediterranean to the navy yards at Boston and Norfolk. Washington's navy yard seemed to be slipping, before it had ever reached maturity, into a secondary role as a harbor for out-of-service ships.

To complicate the situation further, there was growing concern that keeping the frigates in the river was causing them to deteriorate. Exposed as they were to sun, rain, and wind, with little motion to keep them stressed and in shape, the ships' timbers were drying in some places and rotting in others; caulking was heaving out, and mold and decay were setting in. For President Jefferson, this of course posed an intriguing, as well as important, scientific challenge. He read up on the subject and on past European experiences in laying up ships, and began to conceive a solution. Dry storage, he concluded, on land and covered, was the best way to protect the ships' hulls. He even pictured a perfect state of preservation if the right conditions could be achieved. A dry-dock at the Washington yard would be the answer, if it was technically feasible. The main issue, he realized, would be whether there was enough running water available at an elevation that would allow lifting the ships, by a system of locks, out of the river.

To answer the question, Jefferson and Smith turned to Tingey. The captain in turn wisely chose to enlist Nicholas King, a talented surveyor and cartographer then working for the War Department, to help him with the technical aspects of the project. Working together intermittently through the hot summer months of 1802, the two men measured the elevations and the flow of water from the major springs in the general vicinity of Capitol Hill and the yard, and also estimated ways of getting the necessary water from the upstream Potomac. Technically, they concluded, the project was feasible. In his report, submitted to Smith at the end of October, Tingey supplied the necessary information, with some estimates of the cost of buying the necessary land and building water channels and reservoirs; he carefully avoided drawing any conclusions, however. This was, after all, the president's pet project of the moment, and Tingey was not a man to put his neck out when not on familiar ground.

The president had the answer he wanted—it could be done. It seems he had presumed as much, for he had already drafted a proposal for a large dry-dock, covered with a round roof whose design was derived from one of his favorite Paris buildings. But to advance such a proposal to Congress for funding, he needed a more detailed and professional presentation. He also had in mind the man to do it: Benjamin Henry Latrobe, America's first professional architect and a man of many talents, who had previously built waterworks, among his many accomplishments. Only ten days after Tingey had submitted his report, Jefferson sent Latrobe a copy of his own study of a dry-dock, and asked the Philadelphian to come to Washington and prepare a full study. Latrobe, a good republican and ambitious for work of distinction, jumped at the chance to impress his president. He was in Washington several weeks later and had his report on the Navy secretary's desk by early December. Jefferson submitted it to Congress just before the end of 1802.

Latrobe's study was essentially the president's scheme, with engineering details and cost estimates. He proposed that the locks be built on the site of the proposed Tenth Street, where there was a gravel bottom that could support the weight of the necessary masonry. Two locks would bring the ships up the necessary height, where there would be a large turning basin and a round, covered arsenal building in which up to twelve ships—in a second phase—could be stored at a time. The necessary water would come from the nearby springs; the idea of bringing water from the Potomac by a canal was put aside as too expensive. The estimated cost, all the same, was somewhat more than $400,000—the fatal detail.

The now heavily Republican Congress, at the beginning of the new year, made a show of studying their president's proposal. Debate in the House was limited, with only Representative Samuel Smith (as the Navy secretary's brother, not an uninterested person) defending the president's proposal with any warmth. Doubts and objections were raised about the effectiveness of the scheme, and the debate even gave one representative from Massachusetts an opportunity to criticize the very idea of a major navy yard so far from the sea. To counter the point, Representative Smith argued—a statement he may have regretted some years later—"the distance from the sea makes it safe against any immediate or sudden stroke of the enemy."[17] Surprisingly, the debate touched only lightly on the $400,000 appropriation being requested, but that indeed was the real hidden issue. The president, in short, was asking his supporters to approve an expensive and unproven technological experiment at the same time that he was urging them to balance the budget. His own party would not support him, and in the end the bill was resubmitted to committee, where it died of neglect. The ships in ordinary would continue to sit out in the river, at the mercy of the elements.

Shortly after this failure to strengthen the yard and its facilities, Tingey requested a raise. After discussion with the president, Smith agreed to raise his salary to $1,784, a sum still within the range of pay offered a Navy captain. But Tingey held out for more: "I should betray my duty to my family were I to continue for the sum above stipulated," he wrote, "I beg therefore to repeat that I hope for your good offices with the President to augment the sum to $2,500. As for any consideration under that sum, I should reluctantly be necessitated to resign." Smith, it seems, was in favor of calling the captain's bluff. Jefferson wrote back, and while saying he regretted Tingey's position, "because he is a good man," authorized the secretary to make one last offer, and if Tingey would not accept it, "then the office does not suit him . . . and I should be sorry for it . . . because I think him a good officer."

But he warned Smith to be cautious in filling the job with someone else, "for indeed the office is of extreme importance."[18]

Tingey stuck to his demand, and as a result lost his position as superintendent. But not, surprisingly, his job. In April 1803, Secretary Smith finally filled the vacant position of second in charge. He brought in a more junior officer, Lieutenant John Cassin, and appointed him as superintendent at the rank of master commander. But Tingey was also kept on, with the new title of financial agent—presumably still in control of contracting as well as the funds (limited as they were)—and fully engaged in the activities of the yard. It seems, from the president's instructions to Smith, that the two politicians had decided to keep Tingey, and were concocting a legislative fix to the problem. Tingey later called the demotion "a temporary suspension of my power."[19] But, whatever the deal that Smith had in mind, it would take time to work it out.

In the meantime, John Cassin was the new superintendent; all correspondence and orders from the secretary flowed through him, and work went on routinely. Tingey had a secondary role, on paper, but apparently was still very much a presence. Cassin was an excellent choice, as it turned out. He was competent and trustworthy, with a systematic mind that would one day earn him his own command of a navy yard. Tingey and he apparently developed a good professional relationship, in what must have been a somewhat touchy personal situation. Cassin at first lived on one of the ships, but eventually moved into the one new house that had been built on the upper part of the yard.

All in all, 1803 turned out to be a slow year. Even the conflict with Tripoli had devolved into a blockade without any battles. The *Chesapeake* came back from the Mediterranean to be laid up in ordinary, and repairs were made to other ships to prepare them for sea duty. Cassin was sent to Baltimore for awhile to recruit sailors for the frigates fitting out in New York. The biggest problem facing the management was that there were too many idle sailors manning the idle ships; they sometimes were rowdy while on detail outside the yard and caused trouble with the civilian neighbors. The money appropriated for naval yards had mostly gone to the ones serving the fighting fleet, and little new was being ventured in Washington. Money was so tight that when the American negotiators promised the sultan of Morocco that he would receive a hundred gun carriages as part of a treaty renewal package, the decision was made to fob him off with a hundred surplus carriages of the type used on board ships that were lying around the Washington yard. (The sultan, who had expected to use the carriages in his forts, was not pleased.)

Tingey, in his ambiguous role as financial officer, had few clearly visible achievements during this period. Secretary Smith had confidence in Tingey's experienced judgment, and continued to provide him with the occasional special project, such as doing a first draft of the naval regulations.[20] But his work was largely of a mundane administrative nature, with little command responsibility. He was entrusted with routine tasks like chartering the ship that carried the gun carriages to Morocco. One of these jobs, at the turn of the year, was at least enjoyable from a personal point of view: he was tasked to support the work of an old friend, Captain John Rodgers, who had been ordered to the Washington yard to build its first vessel, and then to take command of the *Congress* for service in the Mediterranean. The yard's first shipbuilding project, though, would not be the 74-gun ship that had been on the drawing board now for more than five years, but a humble gunboat.

Gunboats had been found to be useful in the Mediterranean, where such small, shallow-draft vessels could bring their cannon close inshore to work against land batteries. The American squadron had at first leased some from local powers, but now Jefferson and Smith wanted to build their own and take them across the Atlantic. Rodgers' gunboat was to be the first of these, and a testing platform for a different kind of use as well. The president had begun to envision a fleet of small gunboats as a second option to the frigates for naval defense, and wanted to test their qualities. Smith's orders to Rodgers spelled out the new approach: "We conceive that Gun-Boats can be employed with great effect in the protection, in times of war, of our Sea Port Towns, and we are strongly fortified in this opinion by the observations of practical gentlemen."[21] Who the practical gentlemen were was unstated. Tingey might have been consulted by his boss on the issue and, sometime later, would take a public stance on this budding policy, but for the moment he was—at least on the record—quiet.

The policy issue that must have preoccupied him at the time was the fate of a congressional bill—the one that Secretary Smith had proposed to resolve the job and pay issue that had caused Tingey's demotion. With the administration enjoying a substantial majority in both houses of Congress, the bill passed easily. On 27 March 1804, the bill became law, creating the new position of commandant of the Washington navy yard, at the rank of a full captain commanding a squadron on separate service—or commodore's pay without the ships. Tingey was named commandant and reappointed as captain in the Navy, although with a current seniority date rather than that of his old Quasi-War commission. He had prevailed; his bosses had met his terms, and he could take "satisfaction at the discomfiture of a few secret enemies"—persons unnamed, but presumably colleagues who coveted reinstatement in the Navy for themselves.[22] He would once again have full authority over the yard, all its government property, and the ships in ordinary, as well as the contracting responsibility as naval agent. But this time he would enjoy a pay increase, a senior deputy (John Cassin) to whom the management of the ships in ordinary could be delegated, and a permanent staff of division chiefs and clerical workers to assist him in the work.

The yard was emerging from its hiatus. The war in the Mediterranean was creating more work as ships rotated in and out of service, Lieutenant Cassin had already done some good work in creating administrative systems, and Latrobe (who had been brought to Washington by Jefferson to work on the Capitol building) had also been appointed as engineer to the Navy and asked to prepare a building plan for the yard. It was time to go to work.

CHAPTER FIVE

Building the Yard

The next ten years would be, in spite of the ebb and flow of government policy and congressional appropriations, years of steady growth for the Washington navy yard.

Captain Tingey was well past his fifty-third birthday when he was appointed commandant. He still cut a fine, sturdy figure, but his seagoing days were undoubtedly behind him. Younger men, including men who had served under him in the undeclared war with France, now had seniority over him because of his break in service and their heroics, but he did not dwell on it, as some of his rank-obsessed Navy colleagues might have done. Not that he lacked pride or a sense of honor: no Navy officer of the time was shy of those traits. Tingey, though, was a pragmatic man who did not seek confrontation, even while carefully guarding his honor and reputation for integrity. As had been the case at the time of his misadventures on the *Harmony* and the *Baring*, he continued to be quick to defend himself against any hint of impropriety in his work. Absent such insinuations, however, he was a man who could balance principle against reality, and find an equitable middle ground to vexing administrative problems.

Equanimity was a skill he needed to run the yard. Running a navy yard was a complicated and ticklish job at best, but more so when that yard was at the seat of government and subject to close observation from both critical senior officials and political opponents of the Navy. And there were plenty of the latter, as the dispute between the pro-Navy and anti-Navy forces continued unabated throughout the decade. Tingey was both by background and profession committed to a strong blue-water navy. All the same, he was ready to leave the politics of defending the service to his bosses the secretaries of the Navy, rarely taking a public position and sticking to a narrow

ROBERT SMITH,
SECRETARY OF THE NAVY,
1801–1809

*(Courtesy of Naval Art Center,
Naval History and Heritage Command)*

definition of his business as much as possible. Indeed, on several occasions when his bosses demonstrated impatience over his management, it might be interpreted as annoyance over his apparent failure to appreciate the political pressure that they were under from a critical Congress.

Tingey and the Navy secretaries were in daily contact, largely through messenger runs between the yard and the department's offices, situated across town next to the president's house. Notes flowed back and forth, with exchanges often being completed within a working day. Tingey generally corresponded in his own hand—neat and flowing normally, but occasionally rough and hurried-looking—yet always signed with his large, distinctively spiky signature. The majority of this correspondence was about routine matters such as work priorities, contracts, or employment issues. Yet in the flow of those exchanges (complemented, of course, by numerous but undocumented personal encounters), Tingey and his bosses gradually worked out a management system for what was at the time the government's primary naval yard.

Secretary Robert Smith, who served throughout Jefferson's two tours as president, was an effective secretary but also an active political figure, ready to deploy the assets of the department and the yard in ways that would most benefit his party and its supporters. Of course, this was scarcely unusual in the young days of the republic, when there were no conflict-of-interest laws, and the Congress had even declined to pass a bill that would have prevented secretaries of the Navy from engaging simultaneously in commercial activities.[1] Smith's pragmatism in this respect complemented Tingey's, and the two were alike in taking a flexible attitude when their desire for system conflicted with more practical concerns.

That was not the case, however, with Smith's 1809 eventual successor, the South Carolina rice planter Paul Hamilton. The new secretary, Tingey soon found out, was a friendly and generous person, but one who had a strict and moralistic view of his responsibilities. He was openly critical of contracting and other procedures at the yard. Yet Hamilton's management collapsed over time, and he, too, issued some dubious contracts as the combination of personal and financial worries, in addition to the pressures of the War of 1812, overwhelmed him. The office became so slipshod that President Madison was finally obliged to ask Hamilton for his resignation. The next secretary, William Jones, had yet another management style. Previously a sea captain (both in privateers and merchantmen), a businessman, and a congressman, he was a tireless worker who brought great and relevant experience to the job. He was not easy to work with: gruff, sometimes arrogant, and authoritarian, he insisted on greater order and system. His relationships with Tingey were at first difficult, but then, according to Henry Latrobe, "after six months of shyness and aversion, personal and political, our old Commodore has completely conquered the Secretary and they are inseparable."[2]

When Tingey resumed command of the navy yard, it was still in most respects a facility only for the laying-up of out-of-service warships. The grandiose plans for a dry-dock had died, the construction of a ship of the line was on indefinite hold, and only a few warehouses and a residence for deputy commandant Cassin had been built. Necessary repairs to the ships were performed by the ships' skeleton crews, which included carpenters, but there were no permanent workshops on land, and even most of the crews and supplies were still housed on board. In fact, there were too many men assigned to the ships in ordinary, and one of Cassin's management problems had been simply keeping order among the underemployed and overly numerous contingent. His recommendations for a thorough revision of the staffing, submitted to and accepted by the secretary in early 1804, not only reduced the staffing of the ships in ordinary, but also transferred them to a central complement under the direct control of the commandant and his deputy.

Cassin's recommendations were incorporated into the legislation that reappointed Tingey to the Navy and as commandant, and mark the real beginning of the yard's role as a repair, refitting, and shipbuilding facility. The new legislation gave to the commandant and his deputy a permanent staff of thirteen salaried and supervisory employees, plus a hundred seamen. Four of the permanent staff were administrative support: a clerk of the yard to monitor the workforce, a storekeeper to maintain the inventories, a purser to disburse government funds, and a surgeon to run a hospital. Appointment of a sailing master, chief carpenter, plumber, cooper (or barrel-maker), block-maker, sail-maker, gunners, and boatswains presaged the yard's future divisions: riggers, ship builders, metal workers, block-makers, and sail-makers. Men, almost all civilians, soon were appointed to fill the new staff positions, and Cassin's additional recommendations for controlling workforce attendance and pay were put into effect. The organization of the yard began to take real shape.

A little more than a year later, in May of 1805, general regulations for the governing of the yard were approved by Secretary Smith. They had been drafted by Tingey and Cassin, with inputs from key employees such as Josiah Fox, who had been appointed as naval constructor to supervise the ship-building activities. The regulations reinforced Tingey's authority over the workforce, designating the commandant as the sole point of official contact between the secretary's office and the yard staff. He already had been given command over the Navy personnel in ordinary and the Marines assigned to guard the facility, and he now had effective command over the growing civilian component as well. But the new regulations also came with a warning: "It is especially recommended to him to introduce a more careful attention to the property of the public and a more exact economy in all the details of the establishment, as without more care and economy than have hereto obtained at the Navy Yard, neither this nor any Country can maintain a respectable Navy," they read.[3] They also restricted the scope of his authority: he was to enter into no contracts, make no repairs or alterations to ships, build no new buildings, nor hire staff or additional workmen without the approval of the secretary. The regulations, however, proved to be general enough to provide for operational flexibility—such as delegating to Tingey the authority to purchase goods of certain types or values without prior approval by the secretary, or the hiring and firing of most workmen by category rather than individually. In practice, too, mutual confidence allowed Tingey to submit things for his boss' "approbation" that were already all but decided.

The next need was for a long-term plan for the growth of the yard. In his role as engineer to the Navy Department, Henry Latrobe had submitted, by early 1805, a plan that would influence but not dictate much of the construction during the next decade. Because of the site's shallow waterfront, Latrobe identified the greatest need as an extension of the wharf to deep water, so that large ships could pull up and unload or load goods. He recommended that the wharf's perimeter be stone-built on top of deep piles, so as to resist the hydrostatic pressure that was already weakening the wooden sides of Marbury's wharf. The enlarged wharf would extend the yard both southward to the river channel and westward into the mouth of the bay, further deepening the cove where originally there had been a smooth shoreline. On the river side of the wide wharf, he envisaged a row of warehouses serviced by cranes. The various shops were to be at the junction of the wharf and the original shoreline, to which heavy goods could be moved directly from the wharf or by a short canal cut into the yard from the cove on St. Thomas Bay. The wharf project, Latrobe recognized, would require that "an immense quantity of land must be made in order to get at the channel."[4] It could be extended gradually, he suggested, and in phases.

Over the next decade, the wharf did indeed expand by phases, extending in the end more than three hundred feet out from the original shore. It was also more than two hundred feet wide. But it was not built with stone as Latrobe had wished, and consequently the filled land was not sound enough for major buildings or slipways without the expense of driving piles. As a result, the major buildings wound up being behind the wharf or clustered in the southeast corner of the yard, along the eastern wall—an area Latrobe had originally relegated to the "nuisance" activities of the bake-, salt-, and slaughterhouses. Nor was the interior canal built. The workshops, however, did remain in the lower center of the yard as Latrobe had planned, and the whole physical complex that emerged was closely identified with him.

Although his original plan was thus not followed in detail, Latrobe remained closely connected with the work at the yard, supervising the construction of buildings and taking a knowledgeable part in the technical improvements made there. He moved to Washington in 1807, living for several years in a house near the navy yard from which he could supervise both the work at the yard and his major project, the Capitol building.[5] His 1809 report to Congress spells out some of his achievements at the yard: the long timber shed on the wharf started in 1805 and finished in 1807; the M Street gatehouse built in 1806; workshops for the smiths, foundry, plumber, armorers, riggers, painters, and gun-carriage makers built in 1808 and 1809, and additional storehouses built along the way. The gatehouse was his major architectural achievement at the yard: a two-story stone and brick building with Doric columns, and a pediment with a large carved eagle done by one of the Italian sculptors Latrobe had brought to America to work on the Capitol. (Latrobe praised the sculpture as "the most Spirited Eagle I have seen in sculpture either modern or antique," while his detractors claimed it looked "like a good fat Goose.")[6] The multitalented architect also designed an off-compound gunpowder magazine, laid out ship construction ways, designed a patented dredging machine, interested himself in repairs and management of the naval hospital attached to the yard, and supervised the constant pile-driving necessary to underpin the buildings being raised on filled land.[7]

In 1810 Latrobe began to build his favorite installation—a steam engine with a 21-inch cylinder that would be used to drive a saw mill, the machines in the block-maker's shop, and a bellows, a trip hammer, and an iron plate roller in the smithy. The machine was put into operation in late June of the next year, launched, as Latrobe informed the Navy secretary, with "several gallons of whiskey."[8] Although the machine proved to be temperamental, did not have enough power to run all the applications simultaneously, and did not produce all the cost savings he claimed it would, Latrobe remained

very proud of his innovation—and it helped to give the navy yard its growing reputation for advanced technical capabilities.

Tingey and Latrobe enjoyed a close and friendly working relationship
in which the commandant, it seems, generally deferred to the professional
judgment of his brilliant but mercurial (and sometimes arrogant) younger
collaborator. Together, they successfully shaped the town's major industrial establishment and biggest employer. But Latrobe, who was at war
with Congress over his management of the Capitol project and hoping to
recoup his fortunes through steamboat enterprises, was no longer happy in
Washington. In late 1813 he returned to Philadelphia. He and Tingey had
shared many successes, and had built up the infrastructure for a major naval
yard without serious disagreement or hint of mismanagement.

Tingey's other major responsibilities were not so free of discord. The
most sensitive of them was the purchasing and contracting function normally conducted by a naval agent. The Washington yard was for many
years not only responsible for obtaining supplies for the ships in ordinary
and their essential repairs, but was also a major provisioner of the ships in
the Mediterranean and then, as ship construction was renewed, of lumber,

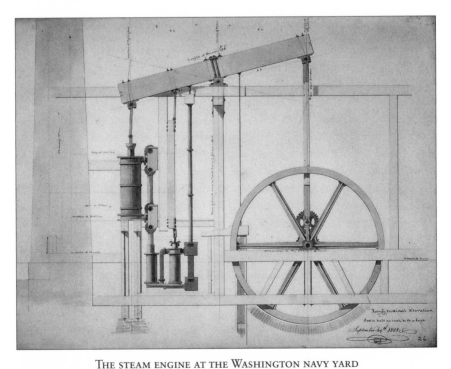

THE STEAM ENGINE AT THE WASHINGTON NAVY YARD

(By B. Henry Latrobe; courtesy of Library of Congress, Print and Photograph Department)

metal, canvas, rope, naval supplies, and other materials. The Washington yard was spending, during much of this period, twice as much as any other yard, and the responsibility was great for spending it correctly. So great was that responsibility, in fact, that Tingey's eventual successor as commandant petitioned (unsuccessfully) for extra pay as compensation for performing "great and unremitting" duties "demanding a large portion of the time of any individual," and which also involved "great pecuniary responsibilities, and therefore attended with great personal anxiety."[9]

Tingey, however, never balked at the responsibility, and there seems to have remained enough of the merchant in his blood for him actually to enjoy it. It undoubtedly raised his profile locally: the yard was a major purchaser of local goods such as lumber, beef, pork, bread, barrel staves, even black-eyed peas, and, as a result, local merchants and landowners sought him out to make offers. A number of industries eventually sprung up locally to meet the Navy's demand, such as Henry Foxall's cannon foundry or Richard Parrott's rope factory. Even though the Navy secretary had to approve any major contract, Tingey's recommendations carried great weight and contributed to his emergence as one of the significant business figures of the new capital. ("We want your name and your influence," for example, pleaded a colleague trying to raise money for a capital project.)[10] And when Tingey could steer a contract to friends or family—as he did, and indeed as was largely acceptable in those days—it was an added bonus.

With the responsibility, however, came risk. The Navy's opponents were ever ready to pounce on any perceived mismanagement, and kept successive Navy secretaries on their toes with regard to the need for both economy and propriety. The secretaries in turn kept a wary eye on their navy yard commandant, through whose hands so much money was passing. Inevitably, they found practices with which they disagreed. Generally, those matters were resolved administratively, but public accusations against Tingey's management were made as well, causing Tingey to defend his honor vigorously. His bosses tacitly supported him, as much perhaps because they could not afford a scandal as out of complete trust in his management. None of the charges was ever proved.

The vast majority of contracts, of course, were entirely unexceptional. But bad contracts were also made, by the Navy secretaries as well as by Tingey. With so many supplies coming in, being consumed, shipped out, or transformed in the building process, large contracts were being written regularly at the yard. The controversial Templeman lumber contract, mentioned in Chapter 4, signed by Secretary Stoddert years before, still lingered as an example of the legal and public relations pitfalls that a dubious contract could pose. And the Navy's critics in Congress, led by John Randolph of

Roanoke, Virginia, were ready to seize on any mistakes or dubious expenditures in order to attack an administration that they felt had abandoned its antispending, antimilitary, republican principles.

There also were contracts that simply went wrong. An interesting case was that of the brig *Huntress*, chartered by Tingey in 1805 to carry gunpowder to the fleet in the Mediterranean. President Jefferson, who happened to be visiting the yard to see a new sawing machine on the day the ship sailed, had bid it farewell with special instructions on how to avoid the pirates and combatants in European waters. He had not expected, evidently, that the ship would instead be seized by a Spanish privateer shortly after leaving the American coast. The capture set off a diplomatic and security stir, with the president debating whether to send a frigate to the Caribbean to try to seize the ship back, or to try legal action. The latter idea was to send a fast vessel to the region to try to challenge any effort to condemn the ship (there being no state of hostility between Spain and the United States). Tingey would have been the government's representative in the effort. The president, Secretary of State Madison, and Tingey (who, Jefferson noted to Secretary Smith, had happened by), debated the issue in the president's office, where Madison's strong opposition—and the captain's concurrence in it—persuaded the president to drop the idea. Tingey was probably relieved that he did not have to go to sea again on such short notice. Moreover, the issue became moot a short time later when it was learned that a British vessel had recaptured the *Huntress*; the problem would be solved in the prize courts.

The ship's charter contract itself was never an issue in the case of the *Huntress*. But other contracts, particularly those to buy lumber—one of the principal products of the immediate area—were a regular source of controversy. They also caused the greatest amount of friction between Tingey and his bosses, the secretaries of the Navy. The secretaries, constantly pressed by congressional critics (many of them fellow Republicans) about alleged waste in the navy yards, wanted minimum ambiguities in contracts. Tingey sought flexibility. For example, he would take raw lumber or finished spars more or less on approval, subject to later inspection and even, sometimes, later pricing. When ship lumber did not pass inspection, he might on occasion agree to buy it anyway, subject to price reductions, and then apply it to a lesser use—even as firewood. On other occasions, he would accept shipments even though no prices had been agreed. Secretary Smith was unhappy with what he saw as loose practice, sending testy requests for information on cases he found questionable, insisting, "[I]t is our solemn duty to observe all the possible economy in the disbursement of the publick monies," and demanding more than once that no lumber be accepted unless it was under firm contract. But at the same time, the secretary, ever the politician, showed that he, too, was flexible: he told Tingey to accept a shipment of unsolicited lumber from one Jonathan Meyers, for example, because "I do not like to disappoint this poor old man."[11]

Whatever the occasional operational disagreements between Smith and Tingey may have been, the two men worked well together, and Smith protected Tingey against outside criticism. When Samuel Hanson, the yard's purser, accused Tingey and Cassin of various misdemeanors in late 1808, Tingey vociferously demanded a public investigation of both his and Hanson's accounts, to clear his name. (The record of Hanson's allegations has been lost, but it appears that Tingey had his own suspicions about his purser's activities, and had refused to endorse his books.) Neither Jefferson nor Secretary Smith wanted the publicity that an investigation would engender, with the president calling the affair a "disagreeable feud . . . at the navy yard & which I would rather allay than foment." Smith pointed out that all of "these unhappy men, Hanson, Tingey and Cassin, in their mutual accusations, have asked for a Court of Inquiry," however, and that, however reluctantly, he had to allow it to proceed.[12] But then he chose as head of the court Tingey's good friend Captain John Rodgers—whose feud with James Barron Tingey had recently mediated, and whose wife was a close friend of Tingey's daughter Margaret Gay. Not entirely surprisingly (Rodgers confided to his wife that he had reason to hope that Tingey's honor would be preserved), the court found Hanson's charges to be groundless. The possible scandal faded away, though it would not disappear entirely, and Hanson managed to remain as purser and a thorn in Tingey's side until the next Navy secretary, Paul Hamilton, fired him in the spring of 1810. Hanson must have annoyed Hamilton as well, for his letter of dismissal was abrupt: Hanson's charges were found, the secretary informed him, "after tedious investigation, to be frivolous and groundless, some of them malicious, and the rest of them of such a nature as not to be entitled to the notice of Government—and for having unnecessarily occasioned great distress to the public."[13]

Following Smith's departure, Tingey found that he had to deal with Navy secretaries who were both more rigid and more insistent on following fixed procedures than Smith had been. The newly appointed Hamilton, in one unfortunate incident, found that Tingey was proposing to accept a shipment of boards, many of which appeared to be substandard. "Greatly embarrassed" by the circumstance, the secretary ordered that the boards be carefully inspected, and that everything not conforming to the contract be rejected and removed from the yard immediately. "That materials thus rejected may be found useful in the Yard for purposes different from which they were intended originally, will form no consideration with me," he insisted, adding acidly, "revocation of the above rule would only tend to encourage in Contractors that carelessness or indifference of which there exists already so much cause to complain."[14]

The secretary's anger can be partly explained by the fact that the contractor was Tingey's own son-in-law, Joseph Wingate—thus compounding the appearance of contracting sloppiness and favoritism. Tingey replied abjectly (and perhaps insincerely, given his normal treatment of lumber at the yard) that he welcomed the instruction, "as it will prevent us frequent importunities and much trouble and tend to keep the Yard clear of Ordinary materials, a very desirable object." He nonetheless persisted in his efforts to make the contract a success, having some of the failed lumber reinspected with the aim of getting its acceptance. When that move was challenged by Charles Goldsborough, assistant to the temporarily absent Navy secretary, Tingey haughtily insisted that he had obtained verbal authority for the step, without which he "could never consent to implicate myself in such a material way."[15] It is not clear who prevailed in the end, but much of the contested lumber, it seems, was eventually accepted. By the following year, though, the son-in-law was effectively barred from doing business with the yard, and the controversy would eventually become public, much to Tingey's discomfiture.

The incident was only one of several in which Tingey and Hamilton clashed over the secretary's desire for firm rules, and Tingey's readiness to bend them for the sake of expediency. Later that year, for example, Hamilton had to remind the captain once again that he was asking for too many exceptions, writing testily, "From this rule I cannot depart and you will be pleased not again to recommend a departure from it."[16]

In this somewhat strained atmosphere, Tingey could not count on Secretary Hamilton to defend him when a second critic publicly alleged corruption in his management of the yard. A shipwright called Joseph Parsons published letters in the Randolph-connected newspaper *Spirit of Seventy-Six* in which he suggested that Tingey possessed "immoral conduct and a deficiency of abilities" as well as "liberality of family contracts." More specifically, he accused his commandant, in the case of the lumber contract entered into with his own son-in-law, of intimidating the inspectors into accepting planks of inferior quality, and then paying too much for them—in short, cronyism, despotism, and fraud. Parsons avoided, however, making a direct libel, as when he spoke of "the profits you [Tingey] could make by family contracts." The word "could" must have been carefully chosen. Tingey struck back. First, he fired Parsons. Then he, too, went public, getting the pro-administration *National Intelligencer* to print an open letter in which he claimed that he had been impelled to defended his honor by "a perfect consciousness of rectitude in my own breast, and the certainty of having during a life of approximately sixty years been guilty of no act in which I have betrayed public or private confidence."[17]

That did not end the matter. Some weeks later, the *Spirit of Seventy-Six* ran another letter attacking Tingey, this time from an anonymous correspondent who alleged that Tingey was also profiting by overcharging the Navy for a house he was renting out for use as the naval hospital. Finally, the recently fired purser Samuel Hanson joined the melee with an open letter demanding a congressional investigation of his and Parson's allegations. Tingey, not at all intimidated, took up the challenge, and sent a memo to Congress absolutely welcoming an investigation. He tried at the same time, however, to mend matters with Secretary Hamilton, writing in a more humble vein, "it is the lot of man to err—and doubtless I have not been exempt—but my errors have never been intentional—and I dare assert my integrity in all matters confided to my trust."[18] His integrity in the end was neither proved nor disproved. Congress refused to investigate the matter, and it simply fizzled out. Such controversies were not at all uncommon at the time; public figures were regularly pilloried in the press or conducted their private feuds through it. And while the accusations undoubtedly were embarrassing for a prideful man like Tingey, they were not without elements of truth. Clearly, he provided official opportunities for profit to his family and friends. His continuing indebtedness to Willing & Francis doubtless also motivated him to do them the occasional favor, including identifying cargo for their ships, steering contracts their way, or lobbying Congress on their behalf. He had a flexible approach to contract enforcement, a businessman's taste for a deal, and an appreciation of and need for money. And he probably was capable of pressuring his employees to see things his way—he was, after all, a ship's captain when it came to exercising authority. None of this adds up to corruption even by the lax standards of that time, but it does indicate that some of his dealings probably fell short of our present ideal.

Tingey's spats with his bosses, and his reaction to public criticism, also cast light on a number of his character traits, not all of them wholly positive. First is his flexibility—he was more a trader than a lawyer when it came to enforcing contracts. Second is a certain amount of timidity when dealing with political authority—an echo of which can be seen some six years later when Latrobe wrote to his wife that he had found Tingey in the office of just-appointed Secretary Benjamin Crowninshield, "sniveling about the secretary."[19] A third trait displayed is the captain's love and support for his extended family, even to the extent of embarrassing himself because of them. And finally is his pride—refusing to take a rebuke from a man of lesser rank, and defending himself self-righteously whenever he felt his honor or integrity to be challenged.

Contracting issues were also the main irritant in Tingey's relationship with the next Navy secretary, William Jones. As a businessman, Jones had the aim of bringing uniform practices to all official transactions, especially at the yards. In the midst of the war in 1813, he had little time to devote to management improvements, but he nonetheless was clearly aggravated by Tingey's unilateral abrogation of a certain lumber contract at the beginning of hostilities. As the contract had been let, once again, to one of Tingey's relatives, Jones seems to have sensed that Tingey had simply let his friend off free when he could not perform. "It may have embarrassed the Contractor, but certainly not the Government," the secretary remonstrated.[20] (Tingey claimed that Secretary Hamilton had approved the contract cancellation, but as that poor man at the time had been overwhelmed by his responsibilities, Jones obviously did not buy the argument.) Jones also criticized Tingey for keeping inadequate record of money received from renting out navy yard machinery to private contractors, calling his procedures "entirely irregular."[21] The hard-nosed Jones tried to resolve the issue the simplest way—by relieving Tingey of the contracting duties. Richard Parrott, the rope manufacturer, was appointed naval agent late in 1813. But that fix did not work. Parrott quit soon afterward, and Tingey was back writing the contracts by springtime.

CHAPTER  SIX

Managing the Work

Next to contracting, the most vexatious problem in running the yard was managing the workforce. Tingey had strong shipboard ideas about discipline, and some of them could be transferred to the uniformed personnel working for him. But he had a different problem managing the now predominantly civilian workforce, where enforcing a military-style discipline was more difficult. Tingey's ideas about discipline can be seen in the advice he gave to a young officer who had just been reprimanded for a too-brutal approach to command: "How rarely it falls to an Officer, to be both truly beloved, and respectfully feared, by those under his command," Tingey advised. He then gave a few basic rules for behavior, and ended with a wish that the young man's further conduct "be exemplary of strict discipline, aided by firmness, and tempered by moderation."[1]

The yard's workforce, and Tingey's management responsibilities, grew substantially over the decade. With the appointment of naval contractor Josiah Fox in 1804 and the beginning of important shipbuilding activities at the yard, the civilian workforce expanded. Tingey and Cassin had a permanent staff of about two dozen largely civilian section heads and clerks. The number of naval personnel assigned to the ships in ordinary was approximately fifty, but fluctuated as ships came in and out of the yard. The yard's military complement also included a small hospital off the yard in rented quarters, a powder magazine farther up the river, and, starting in 1807, a school conducted by the chaplain where training in mathematics and navigation was provided for a handful of assigned midshipmen. The nearby detachment of some 150 Marines also provided physical security for the yard, and its watchstanders were under Tingey's command while they were on the premises.

The number of civilian employees on the rolls expanded and contracted depending on the fluctuations of political and national defense concerns and the resultant congressional appropriations, but the trend was generally up. An 1808 payroll shows about 175 civilian employees, and by 1811— admittedly a busy year—there were nearly two hundred. Many of these were skilled men who had been attracted or even recruited to come to the new capital city, where many settled in the vicinity of the yard and wished to consider themselves permanent residents and employees.

Yet their employment conditions were neither permanent nor secure. All except the section chiefs were on daily pay, checked in and out each workday at morning, noon, and quitting-time musters. They could be laid off—and sometimes were—when work slowed down, congressional appropriations dropped, or bad weather interrupted work. There also were seasonal fluctuations: the number of men on hire went up in summer, and down in winter when the dawn-to-dusk workday shortened the hours they could work. These were conditions, although common enough at the time, that did not promote a happy workplace. And the employees were civilians, neither accustomed to nor accepting of military discipline, and ready, as good Americans, to voice their opinions to authority. In these conditions, Tingey would have a particularly difficult time reaching for his elusive goal of being "truly beloved and respectfully feared." That he to a large degree succeeded speaks well of his management and command skills, as well as of his flexibility.

With one of the biggest payrolls in town, Tingey was petitioned regularly to hire additional hands—even occasionally by the very secretaries of the Navy who were berating him for lack of economy. He was not a hard man; he knew the difficult personal circumstances of many of his employees and empathized often with the plight of applicants; the result was that the rolls of the yard were rarely free of charity or other questionable employment cases. Jobs generally could be found in the ordinary or the hospital for a crippled or destitute veteran, or around the lumberyard for an able-bodied applicant down on his luck, or even for the sons or slaves of destitute widows. These cases generally were not the kinds of inefficiencies that attracted serious political or congressional criticism, nor was another perennial problem at the yard: drunken employees. Although the Navy Department had cut grog allowances from the pay structure at the yard, the custom of twice-daily (or more often) grog breaks continued to be respected, with the men generally sending out for rum or whiskey. The result was often drunkenness on the job, with a substantial number of disciplinary cases as a result.

The major management problem was pay. Sometimes it was about the manner of payment, as was the case in late 1807 when the employees complained that a new pay system instituted by purser Hanson was delaying their monthly salaries. Tingey quickly recognized the importance of the issue to his workers, who depended on regular payment to maintain their vital credit standing with the local merchants. He urged the secretary to scrap the new system, in order to give "relief to the poorer classes, especially those who have large young families," as well as for the "general satisfaction, and to restore the wanted harmony in the Yard." Indicating, moreover, that he already had serious misgivings about Hanson's management of Navy funds, he proposed that the purser's responsibilities be limited to paying sailors at the ordinary, and not to paying the yard labor force.[2] Although Secretary Smith was not willing to go that far, he did agree to roll back Hanson's changes.

More often, the disputes were about the levels of pay. Those were set separately in each section, so usually when a dispute arose it was limited to a particular work crew. That meant that there were no yardwide pay disputes, but on the other hand it meant that the commandant was sometimes faced with complaints from groups of closely knit work colleagues. Tingey had an aversion to such "combinations," as he called them, and his usual response to those challenges was a refusal to deal with the group unless its members respected his authority first. This generally worked because he was prepared to listen if the workers met his condition, and because he had a fairly good record at getting them satisfaction.

The first pay incident came up in 1804. There was not as yet much ship construction in Washington, but a rush to put some of the ships that were in ordinary back into commission had led Secretary Smith to have extra workers recruited from New York. When the handful of shipwrights in Washington learned that the New Yorkers had received premiums to come to work, they grumbled—there is no sign of a formal petition—for comparable pay. Smith and Cassin were able to contain the demand, however, by pointing out that the newcomers were hired only for the season, with no promise of winter or further employment.

Two years later a shortage of funds led to an attempt to cut costs through launching a pay-scale review. Based on a comparison of wages in Baltimore and Alexandria, some wages were reduced. At question in particular was the elimination of an allowance of six cents a day given in lieu of the customary Navy grog ration. The joiners, or carpenters, had agreed to the reduction, but when they found out that the other trades had fought it off, they demanded equal treatment. They did not show up for work one day, but at the same time submitted a petition for redress. Tingey refused to act on their petition until they returned to work—he wanted them to accept his authority over the issue. But once they returned, he recommended to Smith that the allowance be restored, and apparently it was.

MASTER JOHN CASSIN

*(By Charles St. Memin; courtesy of
Photographic Collection,
Naval History and Heritage
Command)*

Two other pay disputes marked the spring of 1807. The sail-makers "submissively remonstrated against the wages paid them," as Tingey put it in a note to the secretary. But because he found their approach acceptable—to petition, not demand—and because he found that a comparison with wages paid in Alexandria justified it, he recommended that their wages be increased. Not so for the smiths, who at about the same time requested an increase in pay, but had the bad judgment to threaten in their letter that they might quit if their demand was not met. This was a red flag to Tingey, who informed the secretary that the raise was not justified by comparison with other wages, and added, "Should we give in to the inordinate request of these men, the precedent will doubtless lead throughout the Yard." Secretary Smith, considering the smiths to be "a dissatisfied set of men," sent off to Maine to recruit a number of "orderly, hard working fellows" to replace the complainers.[3] Faced with Tingey's firm opposition to their tactics as well as to their claim, plus the prospect of the secretary's strike-breakers, the smiths backed down. The would-be strike never took place, but the new Maine men turned out to have their own drinking and discipline problems, and the smithy continued to be a source of trouble.

Tingey's stand against the smiths illustrated his concern to root out any and all "combinations" against the paternalistic order that was his goal. When a black caulker named Henry Adams sent a petition to Secretary Hamilton about wage issues, Tingey apologized to the secretary that he should be "pestered" by such demands, and dismissed them as trivial. But at the same time he saw the incident as a potential challenge, and indicated that he intended to find out "who it is that is thus prone to disturb or destroy the regulations and discipline of this yard by aiding such men as Mr. Adams with their pens."[4] As when he had rope-whipped the rebellious sailor on the *Ganges* years before, he did not take lightly challenges to his authority.

A major pay dispute arose in 1809. The previous summer a total trade embargo had caused a general lack of work and a surplus of workers, which enabled the Navy Department to economize by both a reduction in the number of employees at the yard and an across-the-board pay reduction. But when the embargo was lifted at the beginning of President Madison's administration, Tingey immediately requested that the old pay scale be reinstated because the yard was once again busy. His request appears to have been shelved during the transition to the new secretary, Paul Hamilton. Hamilton was much more interested in saving money than in pleasing the workers, because Congress had once more reduced the appropriation for repairs. He demanded both a further workforce reduction—"every unnecessary person in the Yard must be discontinued and every expense that can be passably be avoided must be avoided"—and a sort of loyalty check, saying, "It is sound policy, it is justice, that men, who receive the money of the United States should be only such as are the friends of our Country and its government."[5] In the middle of the summer, Tingey was obliged to cut wages once again rather than provide the raise he had sought for his men.

As may be imagined, this did not sit at all well with the workers. Their frustration finally surfaced in early November when a group of shipwrights refused to show up at work for a number of days, after having left the frigate *Congress* stripped of her upper decks and exposed to the weather. Although their petition for redress held no further threats and Tingey may even have sympathized with their pay demands, he considered their action a provocation—"a combination to coerce an immediate rise in their wages." He instructed that their names were not to be called at roster (implying that they had been fired) until they reported back. Once again, he was insisting that his authority be respected before he would listen to a complaint. And, to head off any possible intervention by the secretary, to whom the shipwrights had also addressed themselves, he wrote, "I must hope that the Department will support rather than interfere in this business otherwise the authority of the officers and every attempt at discipline must cease in this Yard." By the end of the month, Tingey had had his way. The shipwrights returned to duty, work on the *Congress* continued, and Secretary Hamilton agreed to restore the previous (though not the pre-embargo) pay scale. And yet Hamilton, in a strange communication that probably did little to ease any awkwardness that had built up between him and his navy yard commandant, tried to take credit for what he called his "friendly attention" to the workmen's interests, grandly assuming that his tardy and grudging restoration of their docked pay would earn their gratitude.[6]

The 1808 reduction in the workforce had brought forward one issue that, though not as vital to the functioning of the yard as were the pay issues, was nonetheless controversial. That was the issue of race relations. It had been the custom in Washington, since the beginning of construction on the White House and Capitol, to hire black laborers—slaves and freemen—as well as white laborers on the public works projects. The African Americans provided not only a readily available labor source, but also put downward pressure on wages because they could generally be hired for lower wages. The navy yard had followed this practice, and indeed some of the staff had a vested interest in it: they hired out their personal slaves and pocketed the wages. Tingey was no exception to this practice. His principal objection to the employment of black freemen and slaves, in fact, appears to have been a concern that mixed work crews could create discipline and morale issues. (That, presumably, had been the reason why, back in 1798, he had instructed the recruiting officer for the *Ganges* to hire no "mulattos, Negroes, or suspicious characters.")[7] All in all, though, the yard at this time seems not to have had any serious race-related issues. The workplace was in many respects segregated by trade: the whites monopolized the skilled trades, while the blacks were generally found in the general or seasonal labor force, as servants in the ordinary, or as smith's assistants ("strikers"), painters, and caulkers. A job on the caulking crew, where most of the freemen worked, was as close as most African Americans at the yard could get to a higher-paying job. It was respectable work, moreover, and several of those men became leaders of their community.

That is not to say that race relations at the yard were free of tension. White workers were resentful of the slaves and even of the free blacks, believing that their employment dragged down the general wage level. And where a particular shop or trade was generally staffed with black workers, whites often felt it beneath their dignity to be employed alongside. Finally, there were the inevitable workplace disputes, which could become inflamed if they cut across racial lines. An 1812 incident, if it is typical, shows that Tingey tried to act fairly, and with his habitual flexibility, in these disputes. A white worker in the smithy had struck a black worker—normally, according to the rules, grounds for dismissal. But Tingey ruled that the black worker had provoked his assailant, and the latter got off with a warning. Nonetheless, the white blacksmiths angrily petitioned that they were "subjected to the insolence of negroes employed in the Navy Yard," and that management should restrain "the misconduct of blacks" by "only employing such as are orderly & absolutely necessary."[8] Tingey wisely ignored their request.

This underlying but tangible racial tension was sharpened by the 1808 embargo. That sweeping measure had brought about a collapse of the country's maritime industries, with the result that many destitute seamen and craftsmen descended on the yard looking for work—at the very time that appropriations had dropped and there was need for greater economy. The competition for jobs became much more acute, and Secretary Smith yielded to the pressure for discrimination in hiring. His instructions to Tingey, though somewhat rambling, were clear enough in their intent—slaves were to be laid off in order to open up the jobs for whites.

Our expenses at the Yard must be reduced. They are at present astonishingly great. You will take a particular view of all the different departments & of each class of laborers the work to be performed, and [the] number of the laborers necessary . . . & report the sum to me in your opinion as to the retrenchment which must most economically be made. You will at [the] same time send to me a muster roll of all the persons of every description employed in the Yard designating the monthly or daily pay allowed to each, & in case of blacks whether they be free or Slaves, & where they were Slaves the persons to whom they respectively belong . . . to assist in the retrenching in the most judicious manner the expenses of the yard.[9]

Several weeks later, after Tingey had submitted the requested information, Smith ordered the purser to drop all slaves, with the exception of skilled mechanics, from the payroll. Tingey was not willing to take such a sweeping step, however. He considered some of the slaves to be essential to the efficient working of the yard, and he doubted that they could be replaced easily, or that white men would want their jobs. Noting that severe inconveniences would result from such a blanket dismissal, he petitioned the secretary for the retention of some twenty-three slaves who worked as strikers in the smithy or as caulkers and carpenter's assistants. The secretary relented. The men kept their jobs—and their owners, the slaves' salaries.

But, in the process of looking into that situation, the secretary had spotted another practice that he considered to be a straightforward abuse. In the duty rosters of the ships in ordinary were eleven "servants," or slaves, of officers in the yard, including of Tingey himself. Some of those slaves in fact did little ship duty, working rather for their owners while drawing (for their owners' accounts) a salary from the Navy. Smith ordered the practice stopped. Tingey claimed that this was a customary indulgence for officers in the armed services, and that he was only seeking equal treatment. But Smith had done a study of his own, and rejected that argument. Could Tingey document, he demanded, any "officer in the army or marine Corps receiving pay from the Public for Services of his Slave employed as his Servant?" Tingey could not, and had to comply, all the while grumbling that he had "experienced some unpleasant feelings: at having *asked* an indulgence that cannot be complied with."[10] Abraham Lynson, his slave who had been on the payroll as an ordinary seaman, would as a result no longer be a source of additional revenue for the commandant.[11]

In time, Tingey succeeded in whittling away at both orders. Once the embargo was lifted in the spring of 1809, the merchant marine revived rapidly, and jobs at the navy yard were no longer sought after so avidly. But even before the lifting of the embargo, exceptions had been made at the commandant's request. Two more slaves had been hired for the smithy when white men who wanted the job could not be found, and a slave (who belonged, perhaps not coincidentally, to Tingey's son-in-law) was put on the payroll as cook in the ordinary. By summer, Tingey had received approval to hire twenty more slaves for the ordinary when he and Cassin convinced the Navy secretary, "[W]e are so much reduced as not be able to man a boat or even to wash the Decks of one of the Ships. . . . Seamen cannot be obtained at the present wage."[12] The commandant had shown his usual flexibility in the matter—keeping his focus on the efficient running of the yard, bending to the wishes of his political superiors when necessary, but always looking for an opportunity to bend or reverse a rule that he found detrimental to the happy running of the yard.

Tingey had still another major personnel-related problem to cope with, and that was managing his relationships with a few sometimes exasperating colleagues. He himself was surely difficult at times, in spite of a generally affable character. He believed in military discipline, brooked no challenges to his authority or against his honor, and could no doubt intimidate when he wished to do so. All the same, his geniality, flexibility, and empathy were more often on display, and the yard was considered a good place to work. He also was favored with a compatible and collegial second-in command in John Cassin, and the two men had no serious issues over some ten years' collaboration. But a number of the other senior staff were, quite simply, management problems. Tingey and Josiah Fox, the naval constructor hired in early 1804, simply never got along well. Fox was an experienced and skilled naval architect, a man who had received his training at the Royal Navy shipyards in England and who then assisted Joshua Humphreys in constructing the American Navy's big 44-gun frigates. He had argued against Humphreys' radical design innovations, to the degree that when he was entrusted with building the *Chesapeake* he altered Humphreys' plans—unfortunately not successfully, as the ship proved to be a cranky sailer. He had been recruited by Secretary Smith to come to Washington shortly after the passage of the legislation that put Tingey back in command, and was an essential part of Smith's plan to make the Washington yard the primary facility of the Navy.

Fox's assignment to Washington marked the beginning of serious shipbuilding activities at the yard, starting with repairs to the badly deteriorating frigates in ordinary and construction of the first, experimental, gunboats. Fox, as an experienced builder, appears to have resented Tingey's effort to oversee the work, considering it to be interference. Although he and Tingey both leaned toward the British model in ship design, which put sturdiness and reliability over the American penchant for speed and maneuverability, it is unlikely that Fox had much respect for Tingey's opinions on shipbuilding. Indeed, a few years later he wrote, "It must be obvious to every reflecting mind that Persons of a Military Character are the least fitted for conducting or having in any degree the direction of building, equipping (except the armament) or repairing Ships of any class."[13] While Fox's scorn in this instance was leveled at the ships' captains, and thus was in tacit accord with Tingey's attitude toward their demands, his was a scorn that presumably encompassed the navy yard's commandant as well.

JOSIAH FOX, NAVAL ARCHITECT
(Courtesy of Photographic Collection, Naval History and Heritage Command)

Within two years, Fox was directing the largest and most skilled group of workers at the yard, and had instructions to build the yard's first proper ship, the *Wasp*. Tingey may have had misgivings about maintaining his oversight of such an important part of the yard's work, and those misgivings were in no way lessened when Fox gave signs that he considered that his appointment by the secretary of the Navy meant that he could bypass the chain of command or ignore yard policy when it suited him. Little incidents, it appears, began to accumulate between the two, and employees began discretely to take sides. By the spring of 1806, petty issues were being inflated into written admonitions and each man was complaining to the secretary about the other. Tingey, coming back to the office after an illness, claimed to have discovered that, during his absence, Fox had taken unexcused absences from work. His letter to Fox, threatening to report the matter to the secretary if he did not comply with yard rules on attendance at work, so annoyed Fox that he wrote to Smith instead, saying, "The reason for my not answering Tingey is not from want of respect to him. . . . On perusing his letter, I found my spirit roused above its natural state and thought it would not be prudent to pass it by without making any comment or observation, lest the event might bring on a disagreeable contest no ways pleasing to either, nor profitable to the service in which we are engaged."[14]

What Secretary Smith thought of this squabble between his two valued subordinates is unknown, but it appears that he simply tried to stay out of it to the degree he could. Nevertheless, the complaints kept coming in. Tingey, only weeks later, wrote, "the behavior of Mr. Fox, which I am necessitated to term contumacious, having also a tendency to cavil, and to perplex the orders operations and organization of those particular duties in the Yard," had finally reached the point where Fox had refused to follow a specific order of the secretary's.[15] If Tingey had expected that this incident would result in Fox's dismissal, he was disappointed: Smith also had a letter of explanation from Fox, and took no action. While the two men might continue to complain, it was not affecting the work of the yard.

The next major incident took place almost a year later. It began when Fox complained that one of the carpenters (who was a particular protégé of Tingey's) was taking improper credit for work that Fox had done on the *Chesapeake*. In retribution, or so Tingey claimed, Fox had tried to fire the carpenter for drunkenness after deliberately setting him up with extra grog—an act Tingey described to Smith as "a nefarious project, indeed villainous."[16] Tingey and Fox had an inconclusive confrontation that ended by Fox storming out of the room, but Tingey reported to the secretary that he was not seeking Fox's removal. He had learned, perhaps, that Smith would neither discipline nor fire the valuable naval architect.

When Robert Smith departed to take the job of secretary of state at the beginning of the Madison administration, though, Tingey apparently saw an opportunity. Fox was vulnerable in the eyes of the new Navy secretary, Paul Hamilton, for several reasons. First, he earned a top salary at a time when the secretary was anxious to cut costs. Second, he was an outspoken Federalist working for a secretary who was a zealous Republican. Hamilton, inexperienced in naval affairs, was gradually convinced that Fox was both unnecessary and disloyal. (Fox had indeed been in correspondence with that inveterate foe of the Navy, Congressman John Randolph.) Although Tingey's hand in the affair cannot be proven, it can safely be assumed. Hamilton even asked Tingey to keep an eye on Fox, who he feared was leaking unfavorable information to the press. "There is so much calumny and other wickedness going on against the Government under the guidance of others that it is unnecessary from those who are in the Service & eat its bread," he pleaded with the commodore.[17]

Fox was fired, unceremoniously and perhaps unjustly. Tingey had removed another thorn in his side, but Fox's departure left him with full responsibility for the very important shipbuilding operations at the yard.

Another problem employee was Benjamin King, the master blacksmith at the yard. All the iron fittings for the ships were repaired or made new in the various shops under his control, and the range of work was substantial and technically complicated: mast and rigging fittings, galley stoves (cambooses), chains, anchors, cannon gear, pumps, and so on. The blacksmith operation was, in short, vital to the repair and building of ships at the yard. Tingey respected the work done in the shop, and considered the smiths to be "a valuable set of workers, most of them of extraordinary ability and industry."[18] But the shop was the source of an inordinate number of labor problems, and part of the problem lay with the foreman himself, who drove his men hard and his supervisors to distraction. Moreover, because he owned some of the slaves employed at the smithy, he had a double financial interest in wage issues and played a suspect role in the periodic crises that arose in his shop.

King, a gruff Scots republican, had come to the United States through the unusual route of having served in Napoleon's defeated expedition to Haiti. He combined the qualities of a highly competent mechanic and clever inventor with those of a violent supervisor and scheming and all but insubordinate employee. Henry Latrobe, who worked closely with him on the steam engine project, recognized his technical skills and tried to win his cooperation. But before long he became exasperated by King's impetuous behavior, confiding to his journal, "the strange wildness of his [King's] temper alternately embroils him with everybody with whom he has anything to do." Latrobe eventually took his complaints about King's behavior to Secretary Hamilton, who chose not to fire King but rather to have Tingey warn him that "such conduct repeated will certainly be followed by the most pointed displeasure of the Department."[19]

King was not so easily intimidated, however. According to Latrobe, King then provoked a key mechanic (one whom Latrobe had recruited especially to run the steam engine) into threatening to resign unless he received a raise. Latrobe suspected that King was behind the move so he could get the job himself, although that was never proven because the mechanic stayed on. But King struck back, volunteering to go before Congressman Randolph's Committee on Investigations as a hostile witness against the navy yard management. There, he publicly criticized Latrobe's management of the steam engine, forcing Latrobe to write a long defense of his machine and its management. Hamilton and Tingey, presumably, seethed inwardly at such disloyal behavior.

Tingey, it seems, never took on King directly, and, unlike Latrobe, never complained about him to the secretary—at least not in writing. As to whether he agreed with Latrobe's evaluation that the master mechanic was more a fool than a rogue, the record is equally silent. The reality was that the commandant, like Latrobe and the various secretaries of the Navy, had to acknowledge the value of King's technical skills to the yard's operation. All the same, King's various misdeeds could not be overlooked entirely, and he was threatened with dismissal or actually fired on several occasions. But his dismissals

Benjamin King, the yard's
master blacksmith

*(Courtesy of Library of Congress, Print
and Photograph Department)*

were always turned into suspensions, and he remained on the payroll until well after Latrobe's departure, and even after Tingey's death.

The case of the yard purser, Samuel Hanson, has already been mentioned. Hanson remained on the yard payroll for several years after his charges against Tingey had been dismissed and his appeals to the congressional investigators ignored. Relations between the two men obviously remained strained, to the degree that Tingey—even after he had been cleared by the court of inquiry—wrote to the secretary that "existing circumstances preclude (in my opinion, and consistent with my feelings) any correspondence, or intercourse between Mr. Hanson and my self."[20] This may have been somewhat awkward because Hanson, as purser, was responsible for making all the payments that Tingey authorized, and Tingey had some responsibility for checking his books, even though pursers reported directly to the Navy Department. With no advantage foreseeable from a possible confrontation, Tingey probably preferred to work with Hanson, to the degree it was necessary, through his clerks or John Cassin.

One of Hanson's successors as purser became a problem of a different sort for the captain. The issue, however, was not personal. Far from it, since Tingey and Lewis Deblois had extensive social contacts, and apparently were friends as well. Deblois lived a few blocks from the Tingeys, owned a number of businesses including a tavern near the navy yard gate, and was active in Washington society, apparently well liked and even trusted in spite of his shady transactions on the navy yard wharf contract more than a decade earlier. Tingey had even interceded in Deblois' favor at the time, urging Marbury to show leniency, "with humanity much to his praise," as Marbury then admitted, "on account of Deblois having a large family."[21]

In spite of Deblois' spotty record and opposition from members of Congress, Secretary Hamilton appointed him as purser of the yard in 1812. But Deblois' career as purser turned out to be as shaky as most of his other business ventures. His mismanagement of Navy funds led to his bankruptcy, at which time he was obliged to deed over his home and other property at Pennsylvania Avenue and Ninth Street (later the site of the naval hospital) to satisfy his debts to the Navy. Tingey, unfortunately, also had a stake in his performance, because he and three other prominent citizens had put up the necessary $10,000 performance bond. When Deblois was finally dismissed for cause, the government tried to collect on the bond, but the case went to the courts, ultimately to the Supreme Court in 1831. The court ruled against the government, and Tingey's estate was not required to pay.

Still another troublesome senior employee was the yard surgeon, Dr. Thomas Ewell. Ewell was a well-connected Virginian, married to a daughter of Benjamin Stoddert, Tingey's old boss and friend from the days of the Quasi-War. Possessed of a brilliant but restless disposition and a fondness for alcohol, Ewell was a competent if not dedicated doctor, with an interest in naval hospitals that complemented that of Secretary Hamilton. Almost from the moment he joined the staff in 1808, though, Ewell complained that his salary was insufficient, and sought means to supplement it. This led him into a sort of business as an apothecary, in which he foolhardily mixed the government's medications with his own private stocks, leading to a formal rebuke from Hamilton and an order to get out of the pharmacy business. He was already taking in private patients—not a conflict of interest under the laws, but certainly something that distracted him from his responsibilities to the hospital and its patients. Finally—and this is where Tingey had to become involved directly—he decided that he could make gunpowder to help satisfy the growing needs of the Navy.

Dr. Ewell set up a gunpowder mill and attempted to sell the product to the Navy, through Tingey as naval agent. The problem was simple: the gunpowder was not up to the Navy's standards. When Tingey had the yard's sailing master, Salvatore Catalano, conduct tests on the powder, Ewell complained that Catalano had manipulated the tests against his product, and demanded his court martial. He also decided that his real nemesis was Charles Goldsborough, the chief clerk at the Navy Department, and began a campaign of public invective against him. Dr. Ewell, unfortunately, was acting both unprofessionally and in a way guaranteed to draw unfavorable attention, a point recognized by the new secretary, William Jones. Confiding to Tingey that he was "not at all surprised by any imposition or outrage committed or attempted by Mr. Ewell," Jones reprimanded the doctor, but—this being wartime and the need great—did not prohibit him from continuing his gunpowder manufacturing.[22] After a number of additional failures, Ewell and his employees finally did get the process right; most of their product finally passed the requisite tests, and Tingey duly bought many barrels of his powder for shipment to the frigate *John Adams*. Over the longer run, however, the business was not a success. As a result of its failure, among other things, Ewell left the Navy in 1815. Tingey, who typically had tried to avoid direct confrontation with a man who surely had tried his patience, could not have missed him.

Dr. Ewell eventually moved, as had Henry Latrobe before him, from the navy yard district to the more fashionable area around the president's house. But Navy Yard Hill, as the neighborhood had come to be called, had grown considerably over the years, commensurate with the growth of the yard's workforce and importance. In some ways, it had become a village of its own. North of Pennsylvania Avenue was still open countryside, but the little settlement around the yard combined gardens and orchards with stores, artisans' shops, churches, a market, a Masonic meeting hall, a school for free black boys, boarding houses and inns, the inevitable taverns and grog houses, and a growing number of modest houses—as well as an occasional grander one. And Commodore Tingey, as he was affectionately known, was more or less the chief citizen of the neighborhood.

CHAPTER SEVEN

At Home, In Town

When the Tingeys came to Washington in the spring of 1800, it was to a place only slightly more urban than their country home in New Jersey. The ten-mile-square area had been selected as the site of the nation's capital a short ten years earlier, but the public works were even more recent, and the federal city was still more farm and woods than city. Georgetown, just up the Potomac River, and Alexandria, downstream, were fairly well-established small towns, but the planned capital city was as yet little more than a few hamlets clustered around the main public buildings—the Capitol and the president's house. However, things were looking up. The government had only recently moved down from Philadelphia, and the population of slightly more than four thousand was growing steadily. Moreover, in spite of a poor real estate market, there were still hopes that the city would grow into a major commercial center, based on the Potomac valley as gateway to the west and a good harbor where the Anacostia River, or Eastern Branch, joined the tidal waters of the Potomac.

In this small-town, growth-oriented atmosphere, the Tingeys were a welcome addition. The leading families in town were few, saw each other regularly through a tradition of social visits and invitations, and welcomed the broadening of their circle that the government influx was bringing. Captain Tingey, a senior military officer and a hero of sorts from the recent war, was surely a welcome new arrival, along with his family. Moreover, he brought important business contacts and represented the commercially interesting potential of a major government installation in the neighborhood of the harbor. It is scarcely a surprise in this light that Thomas Law offered the hospitality of his house to the Tingeys. Law was a rich man and a habitually generous host, true, but he also had major real estate investments at the harbor end of town, and Captain Tingey most surely could be a useful ally in promoting the interests of his new neighborhood. It is not hard, indeed, to imagine Law describing to his houseguest the advantages of economic development in the eastern end of the nascent town.

With the hospitality of the Laws to pave their way, the Tingeys had immediate acceptance into the elite society of the town—what came to be known as the "first circle." Thomas' apparent worries that his wife would not like her new home eased, and he was able to write home to the girls that he believed that "Mama will not object to living in Washington."[1] Mrs. Law, who was a granddaughter of Martha Washington, introduced the Tingeys to additional members of her illustrious clan as well as to other old Virginia and Maryland families. After leaving the Laws' home, Thomas and Margaret spent a few days with her cousin George Beale and his family in Georgetown, where they met the leading families of that town. They then took up rented quarters near the president's house, where Mrs. Tingey began to pay the regular daytime calls on her neighbors that so lubricated social relations in the new community. Anna Maria Thornton, who as wife of a city commissioner was one of the leaders of the community, noted in her diary that summer a series of calls and dinners—formal and informal—with the Tingeys. In short, by the time Margaret returned to their New Jersey home in early August to gather up her family for their new home, the couple was already well-introduced into the Washington community.

While Mrs. Tingey was off in New Jersey, the captain could concentrate on finding a home for his family. His official business was slow; work on the wharf at the yard was dragging. (Mrs. Thornton commented that when she visited in spring there was very little done, and only six men at work.) Fortunately for his house search, Tingey had influence in the Washington real estate scene. His connections with the Willings in Philadelphia had brought him, years before, into contact with their old partner Robert Morris, who had since become a major player in Washington land speculation. A partnership of Morris, James Greenleaf, and John Nicholson had contracted with the Washington city commissioners to buy and develop thousands of lots, but had eventually failed, dragging down real estate prices with it. The failed partnership was in the hands of trustees, but still an important (and even respected) factor in the new city. Tingey's old Philadelphia friends had asked that he help represent them, and he had agreed. It was a position that gave him access and influence.

Unfortunately, Tingey, like the partnership, was in financial difficulty. Exactly what had gone wrong is not clear, but it must have involved a speculation with Willing & Francis because his account with the firm was seriously in the red, and they were the only ones who knew the extent of his problems. He had sold his New Jersey farm (though not the house), although he had not realized much gain from the sale because he had carried a substantial mortgage. The prize money from the four ships seized by the *Ganges*—amounting to something like a half a year's salary—apparently had also been spent or badly invested.[2] Appealing to Willing & Francis for relief, he urged them to keep the matter private. "I have endeavored to appear chearful under the heavy pecuniary disappointments which *you know* I have suffered," he wrote, "and no other persons know their extent or has heard me complain. It can be of no service to you to let a knowledge thereof escape you—it cannot possibly do me any good but might possibly do me some injury."[3] Continuing, he suggested that the firm recheck the books to be sure that there was no error in the amount he owed, credit him promptly with his share of the sale of the *Ganges* cargo, and give him favorable terms for the repayment of his debt to them over time. A settlement was reached, but Tingey would in one way or another remain in debt to the company—morally as well as financially—for many years.

It appears that Tingey hoped to ease his financial situation by investment in the speculative Washington real estate market. The idea of investing in rental properties had intrigued him from his arrival—even though his wife had tried to dissuade him. ("In my opinion it is an extravagant idea that people should go to a new settled place and pay such high rents," she had advised him back in January.) Perhaps he intended to use the Morris, Greenleaf & Nicholson name for this purpose, because he had bought forty lots worth $6,000 at public sale, having "no idea of purchasing on my own account when I bid for them," as he admitted to Willing & Francis.[4] In any event, and although he eventually came to own a number of properties in the city by more routine purchases, he seems to have disposed of the forty lots rapidly and avoided becoming either a major landlord or a speculator.

Among the properties owned by the receivers of the failed partnership was a two-story frame house near the navy yard, which was an area with relatively few large properties. As the company's agent, Tingey had been advertising the house for sale since June, but had found no takers. The house was spacious: forty-two hundred square feet, with a large kitchen, its own well and pump, and a separate stable and carriage house with a huge hayloft. On the corner of Eleventh and G Streets SE, on a block with no other houses, it combined availability, space, and convenient distance from the navy yard in an area where there were few equivalent choices. Somewhere toward the end of summer, Tingey reached an agreement with the partners to rent the house as his own family dwelling. The family moved into their new home in October, and over the succeeding years they would buy not only the house, but also the adjoining lots along G Street, giving their home both privacy and a large garden and orchard.

Tingey was once again surrounded by family, a situation he obviously relished. Fatherless, then separated from his own family as a child, he had grown to be not only a gregarious and company-loving individual, but also a doting father and attentive husband. He was already an active and trusted member of Margaret's extended family in Philadelphia, and now in this new setting he had the opportunity to create his own family circle. From the family letters that have survived, it is evident that Margaret and the girls loved and admired him, and that he in turn was deeply involved in their lives and moral education. The girls were growing up: Margaret Gay was already seventeen years old, Hannah sixteen, and young Sarah eight. The Thurston children—Thomas' niece and nephew—had remained in Philadelphia, where they already were living independently. Susanna was twenty-eight and Robert was twenty-six.[5]

Another member of the household had come down from New Jersey with Margaret and the girls: Surrey Dean, the cook. Sukey, as she was called, was a slave, perhaps the same one who had been registered in the 1790 census in Philadelphia as part of the Tingey household, and almost certainly the same Sukey who was with the Tingeys some twenty years later. She was obviously a strong character. When Mrs. Tingey had suggested that she would sell her rather than take her to Washington, Sukey had resisted. According to Margaret, Sukey had retorted, "I won't go anywhere but where I chose a master, and you cannot oblige me." She had prevailed, and she and her daughter would remain part of the household and feature occasionally in the family correspondence over the years. Assuming that she was the same Sukey whom Tingey advertised as a runaway in 1821, she had become even more of a character—he advertised that he would almost rather not have her back because of her troublesome behavior.[6] But in 1800 she was only the first of a number of household slaves eventually kept by the Tingeys, who before long had at least one other housemaid plus several coach, stable, and garden men. Six slaves were registered in the 1810 census as part of the household. How humane the Tingeys were as masters we do not know. We do know that they were people of their time, in that they apparently saw no contradiction between aspiring to lead an honorable and moral life while at the same time buying, selling, and keeping slaves in order to live a life of comfort.

They had, indeed, a comfortable life. Even before he achieved his income aspirations through his 1804 reappointment, Tingey's salary, investments, and prize money should have ensured the family a good standard of living at a time when $1,500 a year provided a reasonable level of comfort. They kept a carriage and a number of horses—status symbols it is true, but also necessities for a family that needed mobility for work, shopping, and social intercourse in a town where the distances between houses was often substantial.

And while the Tingeys also entertained regularly, they put on no show—in fact, they professed to scorn any display of wealth. As Margaret put it, her ambition was simply "to live genteel, and [to have] something clever for our dear offspring when we are silent in the grave. You know, my love, I abhor pride and ostentations." This is not to say that they were oblivious to the benefits of money, and Tingey was assiduous in increasing the family wealth. But all with moderation, as he advised a daughter contemplating marriage: "A sufficiency is more likely to produce happiness than great riches—yet real poverty is a sure bar to it."[7]

When they arrived in Washington, Margaret Gay and Hannah had reached the age at which young ladies were introduced into society and, it was hoped, met eligible young men. They had already had some exposure to the fashionable world in Philadelphia and Trenton, providing an opportunity for Thomas to provide fatherly advice about benefiting from the "pleasures of society" while avoiding the "levity of the giddy." Washington as yet had a small social circle, though it was growing rapidly—particularly after the inauguration of Thomas Jefferson as president in 1801 brought a change in administration and many new faces to town. The young women and their mother lost no time in making the rounds, where they made a favorable, if not glamorous, impression. Neither Margaret nor her daughters were beauties, it would seem, but they did have an openness that could charm. As their recently arrived neighbor Margaret Bayard Smith (a woman with a discerning eye) expressed it, the Tingey women were "most truly friendly," and the girls "good natured." But the pious and serious Margaret Tingey she found only "a good sort of woman, tho not very agreeable; yet she appears very worthy."[8] Faint praise indeed. One suspects that the intellectual and politically astute Mrs. Smith had found Margaret Tingey just a bit dull.

In spite of Mrs. Smith's dismissal and a dearth of good information about Margaret Tingey's character, it would be wrong to consider her little more than a worthy cipher. She was surely a strong and capable woman who had raised her own and two adopted children while her husband was often away, who enjoyed his confidence to the degree that he entrusted her to sell the New Jersey house, and who was a hub of her extended Philadelphia family. Though she lacked a passion for intellectual or political discourse, at least it was a trait she seems to have shared with her husband and passed on to their children. Assuming that family correspondence and its library can provide us with indications of the family's intellectual life, that life was without much animation. Readings or ideas are rarely mentioned. Although the library contained a fair number of books, the titles are prosaic—reference and travel, classic English works of poetry and history, but no political philosophy and no novels later than *Don Quixote*. As for politics, Margaret

Gay may have captured the family attitude when she wrote home—in an election year to boot—that a dinner party she had attended had left her wishing she were at home, where she would not have had to "listen to the jar of politics."[9]

What the Tingey women may have lacked in flair and color was provided by Thomas. He was not a physically impressive man. Short and sturdy—indeed plump, weighing two hundred pounds in his later years—he was also gregarious and garrulous, and enjoyed a good time. He had a fine singing voice, was an enthusiastic dancer, and had no objection to raising a glass or two—in short, the sort of fellow who could be counted on to enliven an evening. It is no surprise, then, to find that he was enlisted, shortly after his arrival in town, to be one of the organizers of a dancing assembly—a series of evenings at a local hotel where he could both enjoy the dance and show his daughters to society. Or, again, that he and Thomas Law were chosen to preside at the first Fourth of July banquet under the new Jefferson administration. There, at an event punctuated by numerous toasts and music from the new Marine Corps band, the jovial captain sang, "with happy animation," a patriotic verse composed by Law:

> *Immortal be that glorious day*
> *When first we cast our chains away*
> *Let Independence be our boast*
> *Ever mindful of what it cost*
> *Ever grateful for the prize*
> *Let its altars reach the skies*
> *Firm united let us be*
> *Rallying round our liberty*
> *As a band of brothers joined*
> *Peace and safety we shall find.*[10]

Over the years, Tingey would be a regular performer in the roles of banquet and dance organizer, and a mainstay of the festive side of Washington life. From the beginning, he also made the navy yard and its facilities part of the social fabric of the community. National holidays were invariably begun with a sunrise salute from the guns at the yard, and large patriotic assemblies also were held there, enlivened with music by the Marine detachment's band. The 1802 Fourth of July dinner and ball, for example, was the first of many such celebrations at the yard. Large marquee tents were erected on the upper lawn, the tables were decorated with ship's flags, the frigates in the harbor were illuminated for the occasion, and the dancing went on until late at night. Tingey also held private events at the yard, such as the ball he held in 1804 in honor of his friend Captain Rodgers and the ships going out for duty in the Mediterranean. The yard and the Marine barracks became, in a sense, leisure-time attractions for the broader community. At the barracks, there were periodic parades and music, while at the yard there were always interesting things to see—including, after 1808, the city's first monument, the Tripoli memorial.[11] Paid for by naval officers in honor of their colleagues who had fallen in the Barbary campaigns, it was erected in a place of honor in the upper yard and visitors were encouraged. Both Mrs. Smith and Mrs. Thornton wrote of passing pleasant afternoons strolling to the yard and barracks, as if they were part of a large public park. Even though he had constant worries about pilferage from the yard—"nocturnal depredations," he called it—Tingey wanted the yard to be a hospitable part of the broader community.

Years later, Latrobe's son would recall how he as a child had seen their familiar neighbor, "a rotund man, with a quarterdeck roll in his walk, a round red face, and a speaking-trumpet voice. His laughing gray eyes and good humor shine through a long vista of memory. A jolly sea dog, but a refined gentleman, Commodore Tingey."[12] Yet Tingey himself might well have preferred the characterization furnished by the portraitist Charles St. Memin, who engraved a profile of him in 1806. There, he appears sturdy and resolute, a handsome military figure whose balding pate is artfully disguised by a wispy combover. The portrait proclaims him to be less the jolly sea dog, more the distinguished leader. But, in fact, he was both.

It was, indeed, Tingey's combination of the fun-loving and the practical that made him such a recognized figure in early Washington. With power and authority from his position at the yard, and a solid and unimpeachable family life, he rapidly became a pillar of the community. He had been a regular member of the Church of England congregation on Capitol Hill since his arrival, and in 1805 was elected to the vestry of Christ Church, a responsibility he would keep until his death. He was chosen to head the fundraising efforts for a new church building, a role that also became a familiar one over the years, as other organizations asked him to take similar responsibilities. Thus, he was an organizer of a subscription drive for a theater in 1803, a trustee and fundraiser for a municipal school system in 1805, fundraiser for his church and its cemetery from 1807 on, and, of course, a key member of many an organizing committee for civic and patriotic events over the next quarter of a century.

Tingey was also involved, in that day of minimal conflict of interest laws, in a number of purely commercial enterprises, where it seems his political neutrality and business judgment were valued by his fellow citizens. He was appointed as one of the directors of the local branch of the Bank of the

CAPTAIN THOMAS TINGEY, 1806
*(By Charles St. Memin; reproduced with
permission of the owner, Eben W. Graves)*

TINGEY'S DISTINCTIVE SIGNATURE

United States. (Willing & Francis, not unmindful of the possible advantages of having a friend on the board who had promised to "be responsible to you," had actually put up the money to buy his nominal share.)[13] When that bank's charter expired in 1811, Tingey was asked by the founders of the privately held American Bank to help them raise capital, but he did not become an officer of the bank. But he did become, as Thomas Law probably had wished, a supporter of efforts to develop the eastern end of the city. In 1802, for example, he was among the prominent Washingtonians who pledged to raise money for Latrobe's scheme of a canal to link the Potomac to the Eastern Branch. (This was the project, mentioned in Chapter 4, on behalf of which Latrobe some years later urged Tingey to exert his "name and influence.") Starting in 1808, he was also on the board of the Washington Commercial Company, a business set up to promote trade in the eastern end of the city; the company's warehouse and store were at Brady's wharf near the navy yard. He also invested in a number of more speculative affairs, such as Dr. William Thornton's alleged North Carolina gold mine, as well as less-dramatic ventures such as building lots, houses, wines, horses, or whatever struck his merchant's instinct as a good deal. Finally, he also used his commercial skills to help the members of his extended family make their way in the difficult business climate of the time. And while there is no evidence that he made much money from any of these projects (certainly not from the gold mine venture, which failed to find any gold), over the years they must have brought in something. The Tingey family lived well, perhaps better than his government salary alone could manage, and Tingey eventually left to his children an estate greater than the "something clever" that his wife had wished for.

In the early years of their stay in Washington, however, the Tingeys had to live with a number of uncertainties. They were in a rented house that was still technically for sale, the navy yard was underfunded and under attack in Congress, and the captain himself was suffering a "temporary suspension" from his job, was still financially strapped, and had yet to establish a comfortable working relationship with his new Republican bosses. Nevertheless, they settled in well, and made many friends in the new administration. One of the most significant of those was the new secretary of war, Henry Dearborn, who had been a member of Congress since 1793 as one of the rare Democratic-Republicans from New England. In the small town that was Washington, the leading families saw each other regularly, of course, but in some manner the Dearborns and Tingeys established a particular bond of friendship that would deepen over the years. Dearborn had brought along to Washington as his aide and secretary a young New Hampshire fellow, Joseph Ferdinand Wingate, who was a brother-in-law to Julia, the Dearborn daughter. As the Tingey and Dearborn families became close friends, Wingate was naturally included in the circle, and gradually he and Margaret Gay Tingey began to be more than just friends.

A business relationship was sprouting as well, probably initiated by Dearborn but certainly supported by Secretary Smith and Captain Tingey. In early 1804 the Navy was charged with buying a cargo of lumber and ship spars for the Dey of Algiers, part of a "gift" that the American government was presenting to that ruler to keep his corsairs from seizing American ships in North African waters. The contract was given to the Wingate family lumber firm, without their even bidding on it. In fact, Smith approached them, writing coyly, "it had been intimated" to him that they could supply the necessary lumber, and asking them to do so "on the best terms in your power."[14] It was all very cozy: a no-bid contract worth in the vicinity of $7,000, granted to a good Republican family in Federalist-leaning New England, with the supplier free to vouch for the quality of his lumber and set his own price and shipping terms. Tingey contributed to the process by shipping five brass cannon and a bag of coffee to New Hampshire to be added to the gift to the Dey. The fact that the transaction was done under a special appropriation, not closely monitored by Congress, made it pass virtually unnoticed, but it is an indication of the contracting standards of the time, and the strength of political as well as family ties in business.

The first Tingey daughter to get married, however, was not Margaret Gay, but her younger sister Hannah. The groom was a handsome young government clerk, Tunis Quick Craven, whose family came from Hunterdon County in New Jersey, not far from Philadelphia. While New Jersey and family connection presumably led to their introduction, we know little of the young couple's courtship except that they were married in September 1803 at Christ Church's original building on Capitol Hill. The wedding was just in time, it would appear: their first baby, Margaretta, was born just six months later, in March. A second girl, Anna Maria, was born in October of 1805.

TUNIS AND HANNAH CRAVEN
(Courtesy of Naval Art Center, Naval History and Heritage Command)

The first family wedding and the birth of the Tingeys' first grandchild were, however, the good family news. There was also tragedy. In June of 1804, Mary Beale, Margaret's older sister, at whose house in St. Croix she and Thomas had been married, passed away. Margaret had been close to her sister, and she and Thomas hastened to Philadelphia to share their grief with her large and closely tied family. Thomas, by now a respected elder of the Murdoch clan, was appointed coexecutor of Mary Beale's will. Because Tingey also continued to have investments and business connections of his own in Philadelphia—as agent of Morris, Greenleaf & Nicholson as well as his continuing connection with Willing & Francis—he and his wife were back in that city in the autumn of 1805. The visit itself was uneventful, but on their return to Washington Thomas fell seriously ill, and was all but incapacitated in bed until the turn of the year (he kept up his official correspondence, though). Margaret, too, was ill: "suffering under her old complaint," as her husband wrote to a Philadelphia friend.[15] (What the illness was, or how long she had suffered, we do not know.) And then, while both parents were thus under the weather, Margaret Gay was severely injured in a carriage accident, and was brought home nearly lifeless, according to her father. But she was young and healthy, and recovered early in the new year.

Throughout 1806, however, Margaret's debilitating illness continued to pull her down. By October, when Tingey wanted to take her to Philadelphia and to visit the Rodgers at Havre de Grace, the doctors advised him that travel of more than a dozen miles a day would be "more than her weak frame will bear." The trip was cancelled, as was much social activity that winter, while Sarah, and particularly Margaret Gay, nursed their mother through an ordeal that included "spasms and pains almost all over." By February, Tingey had become resigned. Margaret, he confided to his old friend Rodgers, "continues to grow weaker and indeed is almost spent—and so emaciated that I entertain very little expectation of her recovery." She finally succumbed in April of 1807, after "a long, lingering and often excruciating illness," which, her obituary in the *National Intelligencer* read, "she bore with more than ordinary fortitude, and with a cheerfulness superior to what, considering her emaciated frame, her friends could have conceived her capable of supporting."[16]

The town rallied to support the family—Mrs. Thornton noted with some amazement that twenty-seven carriages had brought mourners to the funeral reception. But for Thomas, the archetypal family man, it was a hard blow. Only a few a few days after their thirtieth wedding anniversary, his confidante and support, the woman who had lost six of nine children prematurely and yet remained to their friends "one of the most amiable women I ever knew," had passed from his life.[17]

His daughters were somewhat of a consolation. But Sarah was away for several months at a boarding school in Baltimore, which she attended along with one of the Latrobe girls. And Hannah was living in Alexandria with her husband, who had left his government job to try his hand as a merchant and hardware store owner in Alexandria. Tingey's eldest daughter, Margaret Gay, was also away from the family home—off on a trip to New England with their friends the Dearborn family. A busy year at the navy yard kept their father at his job, and his evenings must have been particularly lonely that late summer and fall as he dined alone in a house that had once been full of commotion. In his letters to Margaret Gay, he sounds a bit depressed: complaining that he was suffering from his usual autumn cold and that he had lost his appetite (yet he asked Joseph Wingate to send some pickled fish!).

Margaret Gay herself was at a turning point in her life, and her father was trying to guide and support her though his letters. She was enjoying the social life and other excitements of visits to Philadelphia, New York, and New England in the company of the Dearborns, who had apparently taken it upon themselves to give Margaret Gay a change of scene as an antidote to the distress of her mother's death. But one of the company, it appears, was the attentive young Joseph Wingate, who was creating a different kind of anxiety for Margaret Gay, as he was emerging as her suitor. The courtship was by no means a whirlwind one, moving slowly and not reaching a climax until the following summer. Margaret Gay at the time was once again in New England with the Dearborns, while the captain's two other daughters were visiting the Craven family in New Jersey. Father and daughter, it seems, shared some reservations about the potential marriage, because Margaret Gay offered him an opening to voice any objections he may have harbored. "You know my happiness is too much concentrated in yours ever to refuse my assent to a prudent union," he wrote, but he also pointed out that he wanted to see her married to "a partner fully worthy of you." Moreover, his simultaneous advice about the need for "a sufficiency" of money in a marriage implies that he had some doubts about Wingate's earning potential. He urged Margaret Gay to open her heart; her secrets, he said, would be "locked in the impenetrable secrecy of my bosom," and his advice would be that of a friend, not "the authoritative dictum of a parent."[18] Whether Margaret Gay did open her heart to her father we do not know, but we do know that in the end he accepted her decision. Margaret Gay and Joseph Wingate were married on 27 November 1808 in the new building of Christ Church at Sixth and G Streets, the building that senior vestryman Tingey had raised much of the money to build.

And it was, indeed, a happy occasion for him, as we know from his friend and neighbor Henry Latrobe. Latrobe's daughter Lucy had been married just two weeks earlier to Nicholas Roosevelt, and Latrobe admitted that he was feeling blue at the time about his daughter's departure from the family home. Yet the mood was reversed by the good humor of the other father of a bride: "Captain Tingey, who is a very lively man, made this evening, to us a moment of a very distressing separation, very cheerful."[19]

His eldest daughter's departure for Maine nonetheless must have been difficult for Tingey, now fifty-eight years old and a widower. He and Margaret had raised a close and loving family, whose surviving letters are frequent and more than routinely sentimental, and speak regularly of desire to renew the family circle. Sixteen-year-old Sarah now was the only one of the womenfolk at home with whom the genial captain could sing of an evening, or read to from the works of his favorite author, Dryden. Sarah sometimes had friends come to visit, which must have added a welcome air of femininity and even drama to the house. Such was certainly the case when, toward the end of 1807, Evalina Anderson of Chester, Pennsylvania, was the family's houseguest. David Porter, recently promoted to master commandant in the Navy and between assignments, called on Tingey at home, was introduced to Evalina, immediately became smitten, and set about to win her heart. Tingey, probably embarrassed at being in loco parentis in this ticklish situation, shipped the young woman back to her own parents (we can imagine the scene), but the impulsive young Porter followed her there and soon enough won over her parents. They were married in March 1808.

There was also some compensation in the fact that Tunis and Hannah Craven had moved back to Washington and taken a house around the corner. That this led to much family visiting and welcome commotion, there can be little doubt. Tunis Craven would in the next year join his father-in-law on the church vestry, and even (unlike his father-in-law) dabble in civic politics as a member of the Washington city council. Moreover, the family was once again growing: Hannah gave birth to their first son, Thomas Tingey Craven, at the end of December.

Another factor that may have compensated for potential loneliness was the fact that the Washington social scene was becoming considerably more lively. President Jefferson had followed a routine that included few public events, preferring instead to entertain with small but regular dinners, at which Tingey—neither a leading political nor intellectual figure—was rarely included. But James and Dolley Madison showed, as early as his inauguration, that they would follow a different model. They allowed a ball to be organized in their honor to celebrate the inaugural—Washington's first such event. It was held at one of the local hotels and organized by the dancing assembly, which meant that Captain Tingey had the honor of leading the resplendent new First Lady into the dance hall. But he did not have the honor of the first dance with her; she excused herself as a Quaker from participating in that part of the evening. Captain Tingey, we can assume, did not decline to dance the evening away with other partners. We can also assume that he was a fairly regular attendee at Dolley Madison's other social innovation: the weekly White House reception, a no-invitation event for the Washington gentility that became so popular it came to be called the "squeeze."

As this more-festive entertainment climate permeated Washington society and the growing diplomatic community, the navy yard and the Marine barracks were by no means excluded. Indeed, during the years in which America prepared to defend its rights against the warring European powers, patriotism was greatly in favor. The Marine officers gave occasional balls at their quarters to repay the hospitality they had received from the town's citizens, and Tingey as well as other officers from the ships entertained at the yard to mark special events. (Mrs. Latrobe wrote home about one such ball, held in the yard's sail loft by the officers of the *Enterprise*, at which she developed a headache from the "great smell of tar.") And sometimes the yard's facilities were simply used for pleasure, as was the case of a boat excursion to Mount Vernon and Fort Warburton organized for Mrs. Madison. The large party, which included Secretary Hamilton, filled two boats accompanied by a tender for the food, drink, and dinner equipment, plus a boat full of Marine musicians. The evening ended, Tingey wrote to Margaret Gay, "in high glee" with after-dinner songs at the fort.[20]

There was also reason for gaiety at home. Hannah gave birth to another boy, Alfred Wingate Craven, at the end of October 1810, and shortly after that Margaret Gay came back to Washington to have her second child, Virginia Ann, born at the end of January.[21] In addition to the two new grand-children, Tingey also gained another son-in-law during this period. Sarah Tingey, now almost twenty years old, had met and become engaged to Daniel French Dulany. Dulany, the third son of a well-connected local family that, unlike many in those days, had both land and money, owned a farm in nearby Falls Church, Virginia. He and Sarah were married in April of 1811 at Christ Church and began their life together across the river in Virginia, where she soon gave birth to their first child—and Thomas' fifth surviving grandchild.

Beyond the joy of these new additions to the family, however, there was an undercurrent of unease about the finances of the young women's husbands. Joseph Wingate was having financial difficulties. It was he who had sold to the navy yard the shipment of defective lumber that had so angered Secretary Hamilton, and Tingey's protracted efforts to protect his son-in-law's interest in the affair, over those of the Navy, were a blot on his record. Tingey, appar-ently unabashed, even tried to get Wingate appointed as storekeeper at the Washington yard, but Hamilton would have none of it, pointing out that it created an open conflict of interest.[22] While some observers seemed to con-sider Wingate rather unstable and the match unfortunate, Tingey remained highly supportive and actively involved in his son-in-law's business affairs, offering him advice and perhaps occasional investment opportunities.[23]

In the summer of 1811, Secretary Hamilton, showing that he, too, could on occasion take a flexible attitude toward government regulations, autho-rized Tingey to take an extended trip up the East Coast, ostensibly to exam-ine some captured French guns in Baltimore and gunboats constructed in New Hampshire. It was, of course, cover for a family trip: though the cap-tain dutifully sent back reports on his various tasks, his real pleasure came from seeing Margaret Gay in her home in Maine, and, perhaps, from taking the opportunity to size up his son-in-law's prospects more closely.

Joseph Wingate and Tunis Craven also corresponded on possible business deals, and in some ways the family was a loose business partnership. Craven, however, was in financial difficulty, because his business in Alexandria had never done well. Tingey had tried to help his son-in-law by proposing him (unsuccessfully) as a fellow member of the bank board in 1808, and in 1812 had been obliged to come to the rescue in a major way when Craven went bankrupt. He sprung the fellow out of debtor's prison, paid off several hundred dollars of immediate debts, and then talked Secretary Hamilton into appointing him as a Navy purser. That did not resolve Craven's problems, however. The following year, he could not pay off a $900 note that Tingey had endorsed—thereby burdening the captain with the debt. (Once again, Willing & Francis provided the loan that enabled their colleague to overcome his difficulty.)[24] And then Craven lost his purser's position when the new secretary of the Navy, William Jones, cancelled the appointment in objection to the suggested nepotism and conflict of interest involved. However, and once again with his father-in-law's help, Craven wound up with an appointment as storekeeper at the navy yard in Portsmouth, New Hampshire. There and subsequently in Brooklyn, New York, he had a successful career, but at a personal cost to Tingey of losing the young Cravens as neighbors.

Tingey's interventions on behalf of his two sons-in-law were not the only examples of his readiness to advance family interests. He had obtained for James Murdoch, his Philadelphia nephew, a job on a Willing & Francis ship back in 1801, though he had been careful to say that Murdoch's lack of experience disqualified him from being hired as navigator on the India-bound ship. George Beale, Margaret's cousin, also received help from time to time, particularly after he moved to Washington permanently in 1809. He went into the nail manufacturing business, in a house owned by Tingey, and soon was selling the nails to the navy yard. And in 1812, at the beginning of the war with Great Britain, Tingey let him get out of a lumber contract on which he could not deliver—a cancellation that Secretary Jones thought both ill-advised and improper. Tingey, who was acting without today's more-explicit instructions about conflict of interest, never seems to have considered it unusual to put his family interest almost on a par with that of the government.

One family member who, it seems, neither asked for nor received help from Tingey with respect to government business was Daniel Dulany. He and Sarah and their growing family were living a rural life at their farm, Oak Hill, in nearby northern Virginia. It was far enough from the city to make casual visits difficult, and Tingey never seems to have shared the kind of relationship with Dulany that he had with Wingate and Craven.

But the new connection between the Tingey and Dulany families produced, instead, an unexpected result. Ann Bladen Dulany was a younger sister of Daniel's, and she and the elderly widower are likely to have met at the wedding or its preparations. What kind of courtship followed we can only guess at. In any event, Ann Dulany became the second wife of Thomas Tingey on 9 December 1812, at a marriage ceremony held in Christ Church. Tingey had become the brother-in-law of his own son-in-law, and Ann Dulany became the first Tingey wife to manage the commandant's house on the navy yard grounds, where the captain had moved only in August.[25]

Ann Tingey was young, a mere twenty-seven years old, "a comely, youthful, and genteel woman," according to secretary of the Navy designate William Jones, who unfortunately had few such compliments for the captain who was soon to become his subordinate, and whom he called a "withered, tremulous old man." (Jones had Tingey wrong, of course; the captain still had many healthy years ahead of him and died only eighteen months before Jones himself.) But the spring-autumn match clearly gave some amusement and titillation to Washington society, including to Henry Latrobe, who noted the interesting fact that Tingey, since his wedding, had "become a reformed man; never tipsy either before or after Supper."[26] In those days, of course, everybody drank, naval officers perhaps more than others, and Tingey may well have had a drinking problem in the years following Margaret's death.

Ann Dulany Tingey, sad to say, had little opportunity to share her new life with the captain, for she sickened and died after only sixteen months of married life. She was buried in Christ Church cemetery, where the man who had briefly been her husband would one day join her, Margaret Tingey, and the two grandchildren who had died on Navy Yard Hill. When she died in April 1814, the country was at war, and her husband would soon have a catastrophic decision to make.

CHAPTER EIGHT

Ships or Boats

The first vessel to be built at the Washington navy yard was finished in June 1804. This modest item, Gunboat Number 1, was a far cry from the 72-gun ship of the line that Secretary Stoddert had envisaged as the yard's first ship. The new gunboat had started off as a special project, an auxiliary vessel for the American flotilla in the Mediterranean, requested because her shallow draft and powerful 32-pound long cannon could be employed against local harbor defenses. Number 1 never served in the Mediterranean, however, and only a double handful of the gunboats crossed the Atlantic in 1805 and 1806. All the rest of the 166 boats built over the coming years were designated for American coastal and harbor defense. Captain John Rodgers' experimental craft had become the prototype for an entirely different naval strategy.

Even before Number 1 was laid down, President Jefferson and Secretary Smith had begun to focus on gunboats as a solution to a strategic dilemma. The war between the European powers was intruding into American waters and threatening American commerce. Foreign warships patrolled outside American harbors and on occasion brazenly entered the ports to search American ships for contraband or deserters. Moreover, trade from the western territories also was vulnerable to disruption or blockade. The Louisiana Purchase had given America control over both banks of the Mississippi River lifeline, but not of the sea beyond. Westerners had joined Easterners in concern that America's vital trade was vulnerable.

And yet, in the face of the threats and insults from the European powers, America was virtually defenseless; its harbors were unfortified, and its tiny Navy either on duty in the Mediterranean or laid up in Washington. But Jefferson and the Republicans continued to reject the idea of a blue-water navy to defend the nation's commerce and sovereignty. They did agree to additions to the fleet necessary to complete the task against the Barbary states, but they had begun to envisage and articulate a policy of passive defense for American waters. Harbor defenses and a fleet of gunboats, equipped and manned by local militias, they thought, could protect America against insult. As Jefferson saw it, "every [port] into which an armed belligerent ship can enter ought to be furnished with boats to preserve order."[1] American ships at sea, however, would be on their own.

A bill before Congress in early 1803 set the direction of policy. The original bill called for the construction of four new brigs of sixteen guns each, to be used in the Mediterranean. It passed the Republican-controlled body with minimum debate—but an important change of direction. The administration capitalized on the current anxiety about defense of American interests on the Mississippi to change the authorization for two of the brigs into authority to build the first fifteen gunboats. The act passed at the end of February, and suddenly a brown-water navy was born.

Captain Rodgers had built the first gunboat, a routine boat-build, with the assistance of the Washington yard's chief carpenter. By the time the boat was commissioned, however, the yard's capacity had been substantially increased. Josiah Fox, a man whom Secretary Smith considered "a scientific as well as a practical man, [who] stands high among the first in his profession," was brought on as naval constructor.[2] His talents would be deployed at first in creating designs for other gunboats. The yard's management also had been strengthened by the legislation that had created the position of commandant for Tingey, providing him with an enlarged staff that could offer the necessary support to an expanded building campaign. Finally, the Jefferson administration had decided that the Washington yard—close enough that Secretary Smith and the president could always keep a sharp eye on it— would be at the center of their developing naval policy. Accordingly, Smith informed the president that he had instructed Fox to go ahead and build two more gunboats at Washington, because, as he put it, "I am persuaded they will be built here better than at any other place. . . . With the advantages he will possess here he will necessarily build boats that will answer our purposes better than those that may be undertaken at a distance from us."[3] Fox also lobbied Smith successfully for the chance to build one of the newly authorized brigs. When President Jefferson agreed, Fox began to plan the 16-gun *Wasp*, which would be the first ship built at the yard. The Washington yard was finally becoming the shipyard it had been intended to be.

But a Washington location for the country's major naval yard had already come under attack from the champions of various seaside locations, and since the federal city had no congressional supporters of its own, it fell on the president and Smith to defend their choice. Addressing objections from fellow Virginians who were encouraging an emphasis on Norfolk, Jefferson asked, "Is it the interest of that place to strengthen the hue and cry against the policy of making the Eastern branch our great naval deposit? Is it their interest that this should be removed to New York or Boston, to one of which it must go if it leaves this place?" He tried to convince the Virginians, too, that they should support the gunboat program rather than hope for a Navy, "which will not be built in our day, and would be no defense if built."[4]

Tingey's navy yard, while by no means the "great naval deposit" imagined by the president, had certainly become a more busy and productive place. In the first part of 1804, five of the frigates that had been languishing in ordinary for the prior three years had been reconditioned, fully refitted, and sent off to relieve the ships currently in the Mediterranean. The process was not without its difficulties, unfortunately, and mistakes were made. The sails, for example, were uniformly condemned by the skippers of the departing squadron as badly cut and sewn, earning a rebuke from Secretary Smith. And Captain Rodgers, on the *Congress*, was so unhappy with some of the ironwork done—or not done—by newly hired (and typically troublesome) Benjamin King, that he threatened him with assault on his return.[5]

There was also indication of a more distant difficulty for the yard: the rivers were beginning to silt up as a result of intensive farming upstream. The Potomac port at Georgetown was already becoming shallow from sediment, and the town's merchants were losing business. Discussion of means to solve Georgetown's problem only pointed to the disturbing fact that any scouring of the channel there would simply lead to more silt being accumulated at the mouth of the Eastern Branch, just outside the navy yard.

In addition to the continuing task of supplying the fleet in the Mediterranean, work was under way on the *Wasp*, the gunboats, and the two major frigates remaining in ordinary. To meet the need, the workforce expanded rapidly during 1805, with roughly a hundred men added to the rolls. Priorities changed confusingly during the year as the situation in the Mediterranean changed and the crisis surrounding the capture of the supply ship *Huntress* by privateers just off the American coast distracted the president. When President Jefferson toyed with the idea of armed intervention to rescue the *Huntress*, Tingey and his men rushed to get the *Adams* into seagoing shape, but then the crisis eased and priority was given once again to the *Chesapeake*. Then, shortly after the *Huntress* affair had played out, in midsummer, word came across the ocean that the Pasha of Tripoli had finally agreed to terms, and the war in the Mediterranean was ending. Although it took months for a treaty to be ratified, major elements of the Navy were once again scheduled to be deactivated, and a cap placed on the number of men in uniform. Indeed, by the beginning of 1806 the yard at Washington was once again host to the major part of the fleet. The frigates *United States, President, Constellation, New York, Congress, Adams, Boston,* and *John Adams* were stripped down for a period to be spent in ordinary, while only the *Chesapeake* continued to be fitted out for possible sea duty.

The end of the Tripoli campaign, to some degree, reignited the old argument about the need for a Navy. Proponents of a blue-water navy, including a number of the commanders of the Mediterranean flotilla, came to Washington to argue that the Navy should be kept at full strength. The European wars, they held, required America to take an active defense posture, with warships patrolling the coast to protect American shipping from arbitrary actions by the belligerents. But Jefferson did not want a debate on that subject. Ever leery of the Navy, and trying at the same time to negotiate with the British about their aggressive patrolling tactics outside American harbors, he deftly changed the subject. In his annual message to Congress, he framed the discussion as one about how to defend American ports. An active defense was not placed on the table; the congressional discussion was to be focused instead on how much money, if any, to spend on harbor fortifications and gunboats. The blue-water U.S. Navy was to be reduced by a new Peace Establishment Act, and the president made only a vague promise about building the oft-promised ships of the line. The loyal and economy-minded majority in Congress followed the president's lead. Even when the British warship *Leander* killed an American sailor during a boarding-and-search operation at the very mouth of New York harbor, the resulting popular indignation was channeled into support for purely defensive measures.

Congressional parsimony, in any event, resulted in appropriations that were inadequate for even the modest aims Jefferson had defined. In the appropriation act of April 1806, only $150,000 was allocated to harbor defense, while $250,000 was allocated to the building of fifty more gunboats. At the same time, the Naval Peace Establishment Act of 1806 once again reduced the size of the Navy. In theory, Congress approved the eventual construction of up to six 74-gun ships of the line with lumber and money left over in the Mediterranean war fund, but Smith and Jefferson, who had been arguing all along that gunboats were more cost effective than men-of-war, of course never exercised the option.

This time, passage of a Peace Establishment Act did not affect Tingey. His position as captain and commandant was secure, even though the administration had to cook its books in order to stay under the general naval manpower ceiling mandated by Congress.[6] The legislation even left enough space in the officer ranks to allow for the overdue promotion of John Cassin to master commandant that year. While activity at the Washington yard dropped somewhat, there was enough work to keep most of the workforce busy. The *Wasp* and the two gunboats were completed by mid-summer, and the focus of major work then shifted to the frigate *United States*, which required a major rebuild. Tingey and Josiah Fox collaborated constructively—in spite of their personal disagreements—on the problems involved, which included raising the gun deck and repositioning the foremast to correct a problem of excessive pitching.

Tingey was involved in another clash of personalities that summer and autumn of 1806, this time between two fellow naval captains. His friend John Rodgers and James Barron had had a number of set-tos during their service in the Tripoli campaign, which culminated in a confrontation that resembled a challenge to a duel but fell just short of the reality. Rodgers chose Tingey as his second,

CAPTAIN JOHN RODGERS

(By Gilbert Stuart; courtesy of Naval Art Center, Naval History and Heritage Command)

while Barron chose the Marine commandant, Colonel Franklin Wharton, who lived at the barracks just outside the yard. Those two neighbors kept up a slow-motion negotiation on behalf of their principals for months, and also, it seems, on behalf of circumspection. Tingey tried to keep his more excitable Navy colleague calm during the long process, which coincided with Rodgers' wedding to a close friend of Margaret Gay. "Let me now my friend advise you to be tranquil," Tingey pleaded, "and make yourself happy. You have certainly, in my opinion, gained advantage thus far in the controversy, and that it will terminate in your honor." After many months, a "highly laudable mediation" on the part of Colonel John Stricker, the naval agent in Baltimore, enabled Tingey to nudge Rodgers into agreeing on a (not very sincere) reconciliation with his rival. It was much to Tingey's relief. "You will make us all happy by being thus rid (in a manner truly honorable) of a situation which could not but excite extreme anxiety among the breasts of your friends," he wrote his old friend.[7]

In a service full of personality feuds or arguments about rank and precedence between prideful and ambitious officers, Tingey stands out as one of the few officers who remained on reasonable terms with virtually all his colleagues. Perhaps Tingey's relatively short period of high-tension sea service, and the relative insulation offered by his separate command, contributed to this, but it also can be seen as a tribute to a flexible and friendly personality.

All the same, for the next months Tingey and Barron were obliged to work side by side in what must have been a somewhat awkward personal relationship. Captain Barron had been assigned to Washington to oversee the fitting out of his new command, the frigate *Chesapeake*. The *Chesapeake*, designed by Fox a decade earlier, had been in and out of repair status at the yard for several years, alternately made almost ready for sea and then put back into ordinary in response to the ever-changing priorities of the president and Secretary Smith. That the process had become a nuisance to Tingey is clear from a rather testy exchange he had in early 1807 with Smith. Smith had complained that work on the ship seemed to be lagging, and requested a report "in detail, of the cause of this great delay, that I may know where the blame attaches." Smith may have had Fox in mind as the responsible party, but Tingey apparently took the criticism personally. He introduced his report on the ship with an unusually sharp reminder—"without aiming at or being in the least desirous of the shelter of subterfuge"—that the problem lay in the off-again, on-again nature of the orders received. Now, he added, Captain Barron was insisting that the already finished lower rigging was inadequate. He was working with Barron to resolve the issue and approve the sails as well. But, he concluded, the whole process was in need of revision. "I hope that this business may lead to a permanent regulation [as to] how far we shall proceed [in] fitting or refitting a ship" prior to the arrival of her new captain. "If we are ever to be subjected to alterations in finished work, when a ship is nearly ready for sea, our exertions and labor must become nugatory and our most strenuous endeavors for system will be entirely paralyzed." If an inquiry was considered necessary, he concluded, he would welcome it, because he expected that he would be held blameless.[8]

Tingey and Samuel Barron, James' brother and also a Navy captain, were already involved in another project. President Jefferson had persuaded both men to write short papers on the usefulness of gunboats for harbor defense, which he then attached, as a sort of expert evidence, to his own report to Congress promoting the gunboat policy. Neither paper exudes enthusiasm or conviction, and both captains were careful to limit their claims for the supposed advantages of gunboats to the narrow issue of harbor defense. By making no claims that the boats had any broader utility, they may have dodged at least some criticism from their colleagues for allowing themselves to be used in undermining the frigate program. Tingey's three-paragraph paper, indeed, provided only tepid support to the administration. It commended the agility and flexibility of gunboats, but concluded rather weakly with, "[I]t is believed that they would essentially assist in the defense of all the principal ports in our country."[9]

This document is a rare example of Tingey's having taken a stance, ambiguous as it may have been, on an issue of public policy, and raises the question of his political opinions. There is little doubt that he wrote the paper because Jefferson asked him to; Barron's paper, submitted a day earlier, even states that it is in response to a presidential request. A presidential request, of course, is hard to turn down. Tingey did have an interest of sorts in the gunboat program: building them was better than building nothing at all, which seemed the likely alternative in the political atmosphere of the moment. But did Tingey also need to curry favor, or to prove his loyalty? While that is possible, it scarcely seems to have been necessary. Although Tingey had Federalist leanings like most naval officers at the time, he was never a partisan. The only other time he took a public position on a policy issue had been back in 1801, when he was a member of a committee of citizens chosen to draft a petition to Congress promoting some form of home rule for the federal city. In fact, he was considered to be enough of a republican (with a small "r") to have been proposed as a candidate for city councilman in 1804, an honor he declined.

Tingey's promaritime and moderately Federalist views were well known to the administration. Secretary of War Henry Dearborn, a staunch Republican, knew Tingey intimately, and acknowledged that the commodore was "a person whose opinions are contrary to [my] own."[10] But Tingey knew that any uneasiness that the president or Robert Smith may have had about his views, or his loyalty, had been resolved years ago when they had sought special legislation to make him commandant of their principal naval yard. He felt secure in his position.

Secure enough, indeed, to invite Thomas Truxtun, an outspoken critic of Secretary Smith and under suspicion, in addition, for a purported role in the highly sensitive Aaron Burr conspiracy case, to stay with him when his old friend planned to come to Washington. Truxtun delicately declined the invitation, but did come to dinner, writing afterward, "[Y]ou must have felt awkward at having had me, a *conspirator*, at your house—but I will not put you in jeopardy again." Tingey shrugged off such fears, writing to his daughter that his friend "would not stay with us on his way through—fearing his intimacy would endanger my situation. I myself have no such fears—such illiberality does not I am convinced inhabit the breasts of those who have the power to affect my appointment."[11]

On balance, then, it seems that Tingey wrote the gunboat paper out of a sense of confidence, not insecurity—that he felt he could be responsive (even if minimally so) to the president's request without harming either his position or his reputation among his naval peers.

CAPTAIN THOMAS TRUXTUN

(By Charles St. Memin; courtesy of Library of Congress, Print and Photograph Department)

And yet he was by no means happy with his situation in a cash-starved and disrespected Navy. He and John Rodgers had apparently talked about retirement, but had agreed that to do so would be a very difficult step to take. Tingey nonetheless encouraged his younger colleague to ask for a year's furlough so as to take command of a merchant ship to China, and perhaps earn some good money. "Congress," he complained, "has in my opinion done nothing that has the least tendency to promote the navy. . . . I feel, or think I see, daily approaches in a majority of Congress to wipe off even the little respectability that is considered here to be attached to us."[12] It was, indeed, an appropriate time for him to be depressed: his profession was under attack and in apparent decline, and his wife was dying. On the other hand, he had a decent salary, a busy job, the trust of his superiors, daughters to be married, and (to be honest) few other options. He—and Rodgers too—hung on.

Tingey's gunboat screed, in any event, had little impact on Congress, inasmuch as no new money was appropriated. The focus once again was almost entirely on port defense, specifically that of New York, and was interesting largely for the evident animosity held by many representatives against that bustling commercial center. The only voice raised in defense of a blue-water navy in the House was that of George Clinton of New York. "Because we cannot meet the whole navy of Great Britain on the ocean," he asked rather plaintively, "is it a reason we should have no navy at all; that we should have no force of that kind to chastise marauders and pirates, to protect our commerce and defend our ports?" At the other end of the spectrum of opinion was the statement by John Smilie of Pennsylvania, who "believed there was no country on earth whose commerce would justify the creation of a navy merely for its protection. I would rather give up the whole trade than protect it by a navy."[13]

James Barron and the *Chesapeake* finally departed the yard in May 1807. The ship was not yet ready for sea duty, because her passage over the bar at the entrance to the river had been made possible only by withholding her full complement of weighty cannon. As it headed down the Potomac for her final fitting out at Norfolk, a topgallant yard hitch gave way, killing two sailors and contributing to the ship's growing reputation as a bad luck ship, or a "Jonah." The ship's departure allowed Tingey and Fox to concentrate on the other work scheduled for the yard that summer. The frigate *United States* still needed work, the *President* was to be repaired and fitted out for sea duty, and the *John Adams* was being cut down to a flush-deck corvette. The schooner *Nautilus* was in to be converted into a brig, and several other small ships were expected for rigging or other repairs. Once again, it was necessary to hire new staff to take care of the sudden increase in work. In addition, the frigate *Essex* had come in needing major repairs; Tingey and Fox surveyed the ship with an eye to starting the repairs later in the year.

Just weeks later, the sad and alarming news arrived that the *Chesapeake* had continued her run of bad luck. Shortly after leaving Norfolk, and while still in U.S. waters, the ship had been ordered by HMS *Leopard* to stand by for search. When Captain Barron refused, the British ship opened fire, causing three deaths and eighteen wounded. The British then seized four seamen from the *Chesapeake* as deserters from the Royal Navy. The incident, the latest of many such insults by the British, inflamed public opinion, but by no means helped the Navy's cause. To the contrary, opponents of a blue-water force seized the incident to argue that the Navy had shown itself incapable of defending the country's commerce or its honor, and should simply be abandoned. Poor Captain Barron was sent before a court martial (Tingey was excused as a potentially unfriendly member), and suspended for five years.

Indignation ran high, but the country was not ready for war. As a precaution, the Navy was put on alert, and efforts were made to procure supplies that might become short if hostilities broke out, but there was no effort to mobilize. The president declared American territorial waters closed to British warships, but—knowing he had no ability to enforce such an order—called an early session of Congress to consider what actions might be taken in response to what Congress rapidly chose to call "outrages committed by British armed vessels within the jurisdiction and within the waters of the United States."[14] The debates covered the usual arguments for and against a blue-water navy, coastal fortifications, or the efficacy of gunboats, but also focused on an idea that had long been near to the president's heart: a trade embargo. The European powers and their colonies, Jefferson maintained, were highly dependent on American exports and shipping, and the best way to get their attention and make them honor American maritime rights was to deprive them of American trade. Previous partial embargoes had not worked, he reasoned, therefore the only choice was a total suspension of trade. Congress, frustrated and loyal to the president, went along. By early 1808 Congress had approved, by large majorities, an additional $1 million for fortifications, and the construction of up to 188 additional gunboats. It had also approved, almost without debate, a total stoppage of foreign trade—an action that would cripple the country's commerce and maritime industry.

The Washington navy yard was assigned responsibility for building ten of the new gunboats. It meant work for Tingey and Fox and their men, even if it gave less professional satisfaction than work on the frigates. (Fox commented that the gunboats might someday, at least, make good oyster boats.) By summer, work on the *United States* was completed and the crews were shifted to the *President*, while material was procured for the extensive repairs required on the *Essex*. The latter job became a problem for Tingey when it turned out that some of the lumber used in the repairs had been condemned by the inspector, but had been installed anyway. Fox, picking another fight with Tingey, blamed the problem on the yard's lack of system: "I never found any difficulty in implementing and receiving timber in public works, and I see no reason for its being otherwise here were it not to create trouble and confusion," he groused.[15] Eventually a board of inquiry had to be established to look into the matter, but its members, Captains William Bainbridge, John Rodgers, and Isaac Chauncey, found no serious deficiencies that needed correction.

The yard, over the years and in the absence of any other official scientific establishment, had become a sort of technology center for both the city and the government. The Navy had equipment, skilled mechanics, and talented technicians otherwise unavailable in Washington—men like Josiah Fox the naval constructor, William Small the instrument maker, or Benjamin King the smith, who had several inventions and patents to his name. Requests were made regularly to the Navy secretary for loans of equipment or technical assistance, and the secretary was inclined to respond favorably to such requests as long as the costs would be reimbursed. As a result, the staff was regularly involved in a variety of outside tasks, ranging from lifting sunken ships to helping out at the perpetual construction site that was the U.S. Capitol, and even to fixing the clock in the president's house or manufacturing hookah pipes for the visiting Tunisian minister and his exotic retinue. Fulfilling those requests diverted effort from the staff's normal responsibilities, of course, even as the administration pushed for greater economy.

The yard, in similar fashion, had become the testing ground for inventors who could convince the administration that their gadgets had a potential military application. Thus, in the first few months of 1808 alone, Tingey was asked to provide men and testing facilities for three inventors who had convinced the secretary that their ideas had merit. In some cases, it seems that the secretary was even a bit unsure of exactly what he was promoting, as in the case of a Dr. Wallace, who, Smith said rather vaguely, "has invented a Machinery which he confidently states will prove of great benefit and I wish to give it an experiment. You will therefore put any of the men that can be best spared to making this machinery."[16] Other instances were more precise, as when Benjamin King (going outside the chain of command, probably to Tingey's annoyance) persuaded the secretary to have a prototype of his mechanical range finder produced at the yard, at government expense. The yard itself originated technical advances as well, and produced some complicated mechanical devices, such as pistols.

The most prominent of the outside inventors was Robert Fulton, the well-connected entrepreneur and inventor. Since his return from a long stay in Europe, where he had tried to sell his concepts of the steamboat and naval torpedo to both the French and British governments, Fulton had been actively promoting them to American authorities. In the climate of intense concern about the nation's defenses caused by the *Chesapeake* affair, he had quickly received a favorable hearing, and had proven at least the first step— that a properly placed and detonated mine (or torpedo, as he called it) could easily sink a sizeable ship. The test had taken place the previous July in New York harbor. (Margaret Gay and the Dearborns had been able to see it from their temporary lodgings.) It had taken three tries, but it had succeeded, and Fulton followed up rapidly, aiming for a full-scale demonstration in Washington before congressmen and the administration. He wrote to the president who, happy to find another cheap means of defense against naval vessels, gave his secretary of the Navy the go-ahead. "This means of harbor defense," Jefferson wrote, "has acquired much respectability from its apparent merit, from the respect shown it by other nations, and from our own experiment at New York, as to entitle it to a full experiment from us." Tingey, instructed by the secretary to support the trial, did not share the president's enthusiasm, however. Like most other naval officers, he was unhappy with still another weapon system designed to neutralize or defeat naval power, and "sneered," according to his friend Latrobe (who was also a friend of Fulton's) at any suggestion that the weapon could be successful.[17]

Fulton came to Washington at the end of the year and conferred at length with Tingey; the two came to agreement on a plan of work. Aiming at a spring 1808 demonstration of a torpedo attack against a ship, they agreed that Benjamin King would make the torpedoes, and a navy yard boat and crew would be trained in methods of attack. (Fulton's plan was to get small boats close enough to the target to attach the torpedo to her hull by means of a harpoon gun and ropes.) But then the project languished. King, it seems, did make the torpedo bodies, but Fulton did not produce a successful harpoon gun or instructions for the boat crew in time, and the test, when it finally did take place, was in 1810, and once again in New York harbor. Tingey may well have been relieved not to have to support a trial that he secretly wished would fail.[18]

The Jefferson administration was drawing to a close in an atmosphere of disillusionment. The embargo policy had not worked. It was detested at home, where the maritime and commercial sectors had collapsed without a corresponding increase in domestic manufactures. The European powers had simply tightened their belts and shrugged it off; Jefferson had overestimated American ability to influence their policies while they were locked in a vital struggle for survival. Jefferson, however, still believed that the real interests of the nation were being held hostage by its maritime towns. Even as he was about to leave for retirement in Monticello, he was writing, "With respect to the interests of the United States in this exuberant commerce which is now bringing war on us, we concur perfectly. It brings us into collision with other powers in every sea, and will force us into every war of the European powers. The converting [of] this great agricultural country into a city of Amsterdam—a mere head-quarters for carrying on the commerce of all nations with one another, is too absurd."[19] And yet he could no longer defend the embargo, and the general expectation was that, when the administration of James Madison took over, the policy would change.

At the navy yard, a change was eagerly awaited. The embargo had meant a very painful cut in pay for the employees, a loss of work and jobs, and increasing competition for the remaining situations. The embargo also had allowed the Navy's opponents in Congress—in particular the eloquent, irascible, and feared John Randolph of Roanoke—to argue that a country without trade had no need at all for a Navy. So it was with relief that Tingey and his colleagues learned that the winter session of Congress, even before the inauguration of President Madison, had finally begun to pay attention to the need for a blue-water navy. The debate had been typically confused, and the result less than hoped for, but the ice had been broken on naval deployments. The president was authorized, by an act of 31 January 1809, to immediately deploy four of the frigates: the *United States, Essex, John Adams,* and *President,* and to station them in the nation's harbors or on patrol off the coast.[20] The change in mood also made it possible for the president to exercise the flexibility he had been granted some two years earlier, and bring more ships out of ordinary "as in his judgment the public service may require."[21] Finally, as a sort of final act of his departing administration, Jefferson signed the Non-Intercourse Act, in which the total embargo was greatly relaxed with a view to its eventual lifting. The days of gunboat mania, it seemed, were ebbing, and Navy ships were back at sea, defending America's shores and trade.

President Madison, as secretary of
state for the past eight years, had taken
few identifiable positions on the issue
of naval power. As a good southern
Republican, he naturally favored the
agricultural interests of the country
over the maritime, and resisted large
military establishments or government
expenditure. Yet he understood the
use of naval power to protect trade
or back up diplomacy, and was aware
that the embargo, even though he had
supported it originally, had failed. His
secretary of the Navy, Paul Hamilton,
came to the job with little experience
in naval affairs and no preconceptions.
His first presentation to Congress,
indeed, even critiqued the cost of the
gunboats and entertained the possibility of deploying the frigates again to
protect American trade. Tingey soon

PAUL HAMILTON,
SECRETARY OF THE NAVY,
1809–1812
*(Courtesy of Naval Art Center, Naval
History and Heritage Command)*

was confiding to his friend John Rodgers that he saw the new secretary as
"an ardent advocate and friend to the service, and have much hope and
expectation that his representations to the Congress will be productive."[22]
Moreover, a strong contingent of the new administration's supporters, the
western "War Hawks," wanted expansion to the west and north, which
implied at least some credible naval presence to protect the eastern seaboard
in case of hostilities. In short, the new administration had a more open mind
about naval power; even if the Navy's opponents in Congress could continue
to find grounds to criticize and attack, they were not ensured of an acquies-
cent administration.

In Congress, debate centered again on the need for fortifications. No
new gunboat money was approved, and an effort to reduce the Navy to its
1806 levels was defeated. The focus of criticism switched, at least to some
degree, to the shipyards. Congressmen claimed, with some justification, that
the yards needed more-systematic management. Representative Randolph,
always ready to push a thorn into the administration's side, singled out the
Washington yard as the chief culprit, because it had "eaten up half of all
funds for yards." "Sir, as long as a single [wood]chip remains in that yard,
you will never see anything like reform," Randolph declaimed in his ver-
bose, high-pitched and yet compelling manner. "You will have a man riding

in his carriage, with a long retinue and deputies and clerks to take care of
it. . . . [U]nquestionably every material of ship timber and naval store has
repeatedly been brought from Norfolk to this place at immense cost, worked
up here by men collected from Baltimore, Philadelphia, etc, in order that, so
worked up, it might go back to Norfolk, there to remain."[23] But the debate
was without result; enough congressmen defended the yards, or commended
the Washington yard in particular after paying it a visit, that no action was
taken on an effort to strike Washington from the list of approved naval
yards. Not losing, in a way, was a victory.

At the yard, the immediate job was to get the ships in condition for sea
duty. Congress had authorized almost eighty new hires to get the work done,
but not all the repairs were funded. Tingey had reported in January that three
frigates would be in good shape for sea duty once they were resupplied and
rerigged; one was nearing the end of a major repair program, two could do
harbor patrols but could not stand up to heavy seas without repairs, and the
remaining two needed major repairs. This meant that there was an impressive amount of work to be done if the money was made available for it.

In this light, it seems a strange time for Tingey to have maneuvered
Josiah Fox out of his job as naval constructor, but that is exactly what happened in August. It is true that there were no new ships or gunboats to
be designed and built, and hence no demand for a naval architect of Fox's
caliber, but some of the reconstruction jobs were going to be substantial and
could benefit from close supervision. A case in point had been the problem
of the defective lumber installed in the *Essex*—somebody had not been paying attention. (Of course, it is possible that Tingey thought that Fox had
been part of the problem there, rather than part of a solution.) In any event,
for the next four busy years, Tingey would work without a naval architect at his side. Sometimes, the design issues would be referred to a survey
board, as was the case when a panel of captains Tingey, John Rodgers, Isaac
Chauncey, and William Bainbridge (the assigned commander) had met to
determine the armament of the *President*. Most of the time, though, Tingey
alone made recommendations to the new and inexperienced secretary, who
rarely had reason or enough background to question them.

Mistakes, inevitably, were made. Not all commanding officers were in
agreement with all decisions made about their ships, and some of Tingey's
recommendations may have been open to criticism. Every captain thought
he knew better, and the yard's work certainly had its critics: Barron, for
example had adverted, "[I]t is certain that the ships that have been repaired
in the city (the *Chesapeake* excepted) have rather been injured than ben-
efited." Nonetheless, the few mistakes that are documented seem to have
been due to haste as much as anything else. Newly appointed captains, tak-

ing command of their ships, were impatient and demanding, and put uncomfortable pressure on the yard staff to have things their way. When it was discovered, for example, that some supplies for the *Essex* had wound up on the wrong ship, Tingey tried to put the misadventure in perspective in his explanation to the secretary's office. "Such has been the hasty and extreme importunity we have experienced from the officers lately fitting out at this yard, from their laudable zeal for every possible and practicable dispatch, that it will not be surprising to me if many more extraordinary mistakes or errors shall appear."[24]

A few months later and true to his prediction, a similar incident occurred. Captain Bainbridge, in checking out the *President*'s gear, had found that one of her main twenty-inch cables was sadly defective. He complained strongly to Hamilton, who in turn berated Tingey for such a "monstrous outrage to every principle of good conduct and humanity" that could have resulted in the loss of the ship. Bainbridge, it seems, had already tried Tingey's patience, as can be seen from Tingey's comment to Margaret Gay that he was being subjected to the "more than ordinary solicitude of Capt. Bainbridge to get his ship off."[25] His self-righteousness aroused by the secretary's scolding, Tingey began an exhaustive investigation with the rope contractor, Richard Parrott, and the yard staff, and memos flew back and forth between the yard and the secretary's office. A month later, it was discovered that the wrong cable had been put on board. The good cable, which was fully up to the contract standards, was found in the warehouse. It was quickly put on the ship and the incident was put to rest.

Stephen Decatur, the hero of the Tripoli campaign, also had a complaint. Looking over the work already done on his new command, the *United States*, he decided that her lower rigging was too weak. Once again, a complaint went to the secretary, and then back down to Tingey. But this time, Tingey believed, there was no mistake, just a difference of opinion about how to rig a ship when there were no fixed standards for such a job. He responded to the secretary with his old plea—ignored previously by Secretary Smith— that the Navy needed such standards. "There will be no remedy," he wrote, "until a systematic scale is devised and approved, for all the Spars, Rigging and equipment of the several rates and sizes of the Ships, from which no officer shall deviate. We are guided each by his own opinion, and I cannot hesitate to say mine is that the lower rigging of the *United States* was made sufficiently large."[26] To back up his argument, he enclosed a letter from Captain John Rodgers, who made the same points—even more strongly.

Secretary Hamilton, it turned out, found the argument sound, and by March of 1810 a classification system had been put into effect that was at least a beginning of systematizing the process of rigging, fitting out, and supplying the ships. It was tested immediately, when the *Congress* was being rigged for service. The formulas used for establishing the mast and sail configurations for each class of ship had been devised with Tingey's conservative input: as a product of the Royal Navy, he had always preferred sturdy ships over the sleek, tall-masted American models. John Rodgers, the ship's new captain, disagreed with the formula—he wanted more sail, taller masts, and longer spars. Tingey, who could scarcely deny his old friend, proposed a revised formula, which the secretary accepted. Flexibility and compassion had once again trumped rigid adherence to a system for Tingey, even when it was partially his own system.

Of the five frigates laid up in the yard, a major rebuild of the *Congress* was already under way and would last well into 1811. The *Adams* was being used as a receiving ship as she awaited her turn for a major rebuild. The *Constellation*, *Boston*, and *New York* were in ordinary awaiting decisions, although preliminary surveys indicated that the hulls of the latter two were so rotten that repairing them might not be worthwhile. Between 1810 and mid-1812, a number of smaller ships also came into the yard for repairs or rerigging. The brig *Vixen* was hauled up on the wharf, given a new copper bottom, rerigged, and much of her interior and exterior carpentry renewed. The *Hornet*, another brig, had so many rotten timbers in her hull that her rebuild took nine months. The schooner *Enterprise* came in for a short cleaning of her bottom, repainting, and some rerigging, then returned six months later to be hauled up on the ways; her hull was rebuilt and then she was launched and rerigged as a brig. Finally, the *Wasp* came back to the yard where she had been built, but she was in good condition and needed only cleaning, painting, and new sails. Tingey and the men of the yard took considerable pleasure in contrasting her sound condition to the decrepit state of her sister ship, the *Hornet*, which had been built in Baltimore.

Getting the ships ready for sea duty was, increasingly, a program that had the support of Congress as well as the administration. While John Randolph's committee on investigations continued to find fault with the expenses, administration, and indeed the entire concept of the Navy, and created a continuous demand for reports and justifications, the mood had changed as it became clearer that America might need to fight to defend its maritime rights. By the winter 1811–12 session, the administration was finally ready to propose an actual expansion of the Navy, suggesting an appropriation for ten new frigates. That was too much of a stretch for the congressmen, however, in spite of Henry Clay's efforts to find a middle ground and to convince his colleagues that a Navy was as vital to the economic interests of the West as to the Atlantic seaboard cities. The act that emerged at the end of March was scarcely a ringing endorsement for the

Navy, but it was at least another step in the right direction. Congress authorized the immediate repair and putting into service of three more frigates: the *Constellation, Adams,* and *Chesapeake.*

The year 1812 began in a flurry of activity. A major reconditioning of the *Constellation* began in February. She was stripped to her ribs and retimbered, broadened a bit, then careened and her hull recoppered while her rudder was repaired; she was then refinished and refurbished inside, and finally given new masts, spars, rigging, and sails. The *Constitution,* which had come in during April, fortunately needed less work. Her hull was recoppered, some of her masts and spars replaced or altered, and her rigging and sails brought up to standard. The captains of both ships—Charles Stewart of the *Constellation* and Isaac Hull of the *Constitution*—of course complained regularly that the work was taking too long. They were joined by Secretary Hamilton, who began to urge increased haste as spring came around and war with Britain loomed. The *Constitution* was at sea by July, and had her great victory over the *Guerrière* a month later. The refitting of the *Constellation,* on the other hand, would take until the new year, and she never went to sea—spending the war bottled up in Norfolk by the Royal Navy.

Work on the *Adams* began in mid-summer, after the declaration of war in June and even as the pace of other work in the yard had to be stepped up to meet the demands of combat. The *Adams* had a badly rotten hull—so bad that Tingey had initially recommended she be scrapped. But Congress had appropriated money for a rebuild and not a new frigate. It was decided to pull the ship up on the slips, cut her in half, add a new central section that would lengthen her by some fifteen feet, and cut her down to a one-deck sloop of war. This major project would take the rest of the year. In addition, work would go forward on putting into shape the nine gunboats assigned to the yard, which were roughly finished but had never been equipped or manned. It was a major program of work, even for a peacetime environment, and Tingey was short-handed. John Cassin, Tingey's long-time right hand, had recently been promoted to captain and transferred to head his own naval yard command at Gosport Shipyard, near Norfolk. Tingey had a wartime press of work to do without the assistance of either a naval constructor or an experienced deputy.

CHAPTER NINE

War and Disaster

The war with England came as no great surprise. American public opinion, in spite of fierce partisan disagreements on many other issues, had been agitated for years over the high-handed naval tactics of the warring European powers. And even as the American merchant fleet was growing and prospering, Americans were united in resenting the perpetual harassment of American ships, in particular the perceived insults to the flag arising from searches of ships in American waters and impressment of American sailors. Since the *Chesapeake* affair, that resentment and anger had been focused largely on the British, but the French were equally active in harassing American trade. The Madison administration had tried to straddle the issue with legislation that gave both belligerents a chance to withdraw their infringements on America's neutrality, but when the British did not react favorably, opinion turned decisively against them.

By November of 1811 the climate had deteriorated to the extent that President Madison was advising Congress it needed to begin mobilization for a possible war. "With this evidence of hostile inflexibility in trampling on rights which no independent nation can relinquish," his message urged, "Congress will feel the duty of putting the United States into an armor and attitude demanded by the crisis, and corresponding with the national spirit and expectations." Among the various specific recommendations he made for military and financial preparedness, however, his naval policy was left unclear. He gave no more specific guidance as to the administration's naval strategy than to urge Congress to turn its attention "to such provisions on the subject of our naval force as may be required for the services to which it may be best adapted."[1]

The Navy was already about as prepared as a money-starved, undermanned force with fewer than twenty active ships could be. Over the preceding three years, the steady return to active service of the seaworthy ships had been paralleled by increased training through regular patrols along the coast, as well as by a more resolute stance concerning potential incidents at sea. As early as the summer of 1810, for example, Secretary Hamilton had been instructing captains of ships on patrol that they were not to back down. As he instructed Captain Rodgers, "[I]t is therefore our duty to be prepared and determined at every hazard to vindicate the injured honor of our navy and revive the drooping spirit of the nation. . . . You are to maintain and support at any risk and cost the dignity of your flag, and [while] offering yourself no unjust aggression, you are to submit to none."[2] Naval officers, long muzzled by lack of money and Jefferson's preference for questionable gunboats and the feckless embargo, finally saw that the new rules might provide a chance to earn respect for their service, and even honor for themselves.

Too old for active combat, Thomas Tingey still had a vital role to play in the war effort: to help prepare, supply, and support the ships at sea. What he thought of the war policy, we do not know; there are few discussions of politics in the rare private letters of his that survive. But he was no war hawk. Even at the height of public outrage over the *Chesapeake* affair, he had been ambivalent about going to war against the greatest Navy in the world. "I hope war will be averted," he had written at the time to his daughter, "but I am not to be understood that we are tamely to submit to such varied aggressions."[3] Nor was he a partisan about the war, which was being promoted largely by Republican politicians—many of whom had for so long heaped scorn on the Navy. Most of his old Federalist friends were opposed. But Tingey by this time had worked successfully with Republican administrations for more than a decade, and no doubt was pleased that they (if not necessarily Congress) had finally come to realize the potential value of a Navy able to defend the nation's commerce and not just its harbors. Here at last was a chance to earn a meaningful role for the service, and Tingey must have been eager to see his younger colleagues succeed. He was a patriot, and would do his job.

Getting the remaining frigates to sea was the first priority, and indeed was well under way even before Congress appropriated the necessary money at the end of March 1812. The *Constitution* had been fully fitted out for sea duty by July, work on the *Constellation* was proceeding as rapidly as possible, and the *Adams* was up on the wharf for her extensive rebuild. Congress had authorized money, over the previous three years, to bring the *New York* and *Boston* back into service—work that Tingey considered of little or marginal benefit, however. His survey, some months earlier, had considered the *New York* too dilapidated for sea duty and the *Boston* only slightly more worthy of saving, because she was a fast sailer. Neither ship, in the end, would be brought back into service, although serious consideration was given toward the end of the year to the proposal by a Baltimore shipyard to rebuild the *New York* under contract.

The most important function of the yard during the first months of the war was the job of trying to satisfy the suddenly greatly increased demands of the ships already on duty. Washington, in spite of the perpetual shortage of funds, was still the Navy's largest and most fully stocked supply yard; as the demands came in from the ships at sea, they were regularly referred to Tingey and his staff for satisfaction. Not surprisingly, the supplies on hand dwindled rapidly. By July Tingey was reporting to the secretary that he was short of spars, shot for 18- and 24-pound cannon, muskets, pistols, and even gunpowder. (This was the shortage that encouraged surgeon Thomas Ewell to get into the business of making gunpowder.) Resupply shipments, moreover, were subject to disruption because of the risk of capture by the British warships patrolling American waters. For example, a supply of Virginia spars from George Beale, Tingey's relative by his first marriage, was cancelled—in spite of the great need—because of the risk. Tingey began to worry that, when the existing supplies were drawn down, the yard might not be able to obtain new ones.

The uncomfortable fact was that the Potomac River location of the Washington navy yard had begun to represent a disadvantage. The frigates on patrol at sea could not afford the long trip up the Chesapeake Bay and then the river for resupply; their captains and the secretary of the Navy were anxious to keep them at sea as much as possible. As a result, supplies were flowing out of Washington to Boston, New York, and Norfolk, cities that soon became more central to the war effort. Tingey had been correct to worry: once its initial stocks dwindled, Washington rapidly lost its central position as the main naval arsenal. It was still purchasing large quantities of supplies, but often having them shipped elsewhere. By autumn of 1812, when Captain Isaac Chauncey was assigned to create a major new navy yard at Sackets Harbor in New York, the Washington yard began to lose its trained men as well—they were diverted or recruited away for the increasingly urgent task of building a new fleet on the strategically vital Great Lakes.

The pace of work during the last six months of the year was unrelenting, but Secretary Hamilton—burdened as he was with both the logistical aspects of the war, and its strategic and political complications—unfortunately began to falter in his performance. Nonetheless, Hamilton had the honor to preside over some of the great naval victories of the war, vindicating his earlier effort to restore the frigate fleet to its fighting state. By the end of the year, American ships had prevailed in four individual ship-to-ship combats—the *Constitution* against the *Guerrière* and later the *Java*, the *United States*

USS *WASP* DEFEATING HMS *FROLIC*, 1812
(Courtesy of Naval Art Center, Naval History and Heritage Command)

against the *Macedonian*, and even the little *Wasp* against the *Frolic*. The victories were the cause of great national pride and celebration, putting to rest the British boast of Royal Navy invincibility and even masking, to some degree, the unfortunate blunders of the land war.

Washington celebrated the victories with an end-of-year rush of patriotism and ceremony. The officers of the *Constellation* hosted a major event at the navy yard in celebration of the ship's imminent departure. Their five hundred guests enjoyed an afternoon reception with dancing, dinner on board, and then more dancing into the evening. Equally joyous, if not so grand, was a ball Tingey himself hosted to celebrate his marriage to young Ann Dulany. But the highlight of the season, for dramatic effect, was the gala naval ball offered at Tomlinson's Hotel. (Tingey was, of course, on the organizing committee.) The gay event was made even more brilliant by the simultaneous and unexpected arrival of news of the latest naval victory. As a participant described the occasion, "Lieutenant Hamilton [son of the Secretary of the Navy] arrived in the midst of the dance, bearing the intelligence of the capture of the British frigate *Macedonian* by Captain Decatur, and bringing with him the flag of that ship as a trophy of the victory. Mirth and jollity were suspended, and changed into the glow of patriotism and the rapture of applause. Cheers of welcome were reiterated, Yankee Doodle was played, the colors were exhibited, and finally laid on the floor at the feet of Mrs. Madison."[4]

The "glow of patriotism" was contagious, causing even Thomas Jefferson to write to his old adversary John Adams, "I sincerely congratulate you on the successes of our little navy, which must be more gratifying to you than to most men, as having been the early and constant advocate of wooden walls."[5] More substantively, the sense of pride engendered by the Navy's achievements meant that Congress, in a fit of wartime enthusiasm, began to authorize spending for new ships. In fact, the enthusiasm had been shaped in the preceding months by Hamilton and his captains who had argued not only for new frigates, but also for the relative economy of even larger ships, namely the 74-gun ships of the line so long approved in principle but never fully funded. Congress bowed to the mood of the moment in passing two acts: a first act in January 1813 approving $2.5 million for the construction of four ships of the line and six large frigates, and a second act in March of that same year approving six sloops of war plus ships on Great Lakes "as the public service may require."[6]

Those congressional appropriations were among the last of Secretary Hamilton's contributions to the Navy. Overwhelmed by the pressure of his wartime responsibilities as well as family troubles, he had failed as a manager—a situation not improved by his recourse to drink. Madison finally requested his resignation, and replaced him with William Jones. Jones, as Henry Latrobe described him, was "a thorough man of business. . . . [H]e certainly wants the manners and the engaging frankness of his predecessor, but he is a good man for the public."[7] Jones had been following naval affairs from the outside, including the congressional investigations into the service's management practices, and had come to his new job with a determination to reform and standardize its operations. Commenting to his wife that he found the job before him "Herculean," he went on to say, "The truth is the difficulties I have to encounter are artificial, but they are not the less difficult on that account. They arise from the corruption of self-interested men who have taken root in the establishment, and like the voracious poplar, nothing can thrive in their shade." Contracting and the operation of navy yards were clearly on the new secretary's mind. He instructed the new commandant of the yard at Portsmouth, New Hampshire, for example, to conduct his business with "economical management, to prove to the public that establishments of this nature are not necessarily scenes of extravagant waste and expenditure."[8] It appears that he may at first have considered Tingey to be part of the problem, and their initial mutual suspicion ("aversion," Latrobe called it) meant that it was some months before the two men worked well together.

WILLIAM JONES,
SECRETARY OF THE NAVY,
1813–1814

(Courtesy of Naval Art Center, Naval History and Heritage Command)

Jones' new broom was immediately evident. He reorganized his own office, firing several long-serving clerks who failed to meet his standards. He informed Congress that he planned on a thorough reorganization and would consider suggestions in particular for a reform of the contracting system, suggesting a single purveyor's office might be the answer (and then, without explanation, withdrawing his suggestion). He moved to root out suspected nepotism and conflicts of interest, which in Tingey's case meant that he cancelled Tunis Craven's commission as purser in Portsmouth, and took Tingey to task directly by criticizing his improper cancellation of his nephew George Beale's lumber contract. Tingey, it must be admitted, did not serve his own cause well at this sensitive moment by advocating a lumber purchase from New Hampshire suppliers who were probably his relatives, the Wingates. But Jones left the matter there. He had most of the needed lumber purchased from a supplier different from the one recommended by Tingey, allowed Craven to be kept on in Portsmouth as storekeeper, and limited his criticism of Tingey's performance to the matter of the lumber contract. It was, in his view, the entire system that needed correction.

The secretary nonetheless was not fully satisfied with Tingey's performance as contracting officer. What finally pushed him to take action is not clear—perhaps it was the continual appearance of George Beale on Tingey's lists of potential lumber suppliers—but by November 1813, Jones had decided to appoint a naval agent in Washington to replace Tingey in that function. The new appointee, Richard Parrott, relinquished the office after only several months, however, and by spring of 1814 Tingey was back making purchases for the Navy and writing contracts.

In contrast to the busy first months of the war, the spring and summer of 1813 were a slow period for the shipbuilders at the yard. Following the fitting out and departure of the *Adams*, there was no major ship construction work to be done, and Tingey was obliged to lay off many of his day laborers—more than a hundred. With all the frigates save the hulks of the semiabandoned *New York*, *Boston*, and *General Greene* gone, there were not even enough officers in the ordinary that spring to hold a court martial of a midshipman. Jones had promised Tingey that one or more of the newly authorized ships probably would be built at the Washington yard, but plans and seasoned lumber would be needed before they could be started. William Doughty, an experienced naval architect, was brought on as naval constructor, although he was largely absent because he spent most of his initial months traveling to other shipbuilding sites. By autumn, however, enough material was on hand to begin the construction of both a 44-gun frigate and a sloop. Work was picking up again, as was the relationship between Tingey and his secretary—who seems to have come to the conclusion that reform of the system was a better use of his valuable time than a hunt for past instances of maladministration. He had taken a few firm strokes with his new broom and was negotiating with Congress on a reorganization. Tingey and other Navy administrators could have had few doubts that a new system was coming.

The war by this time had imposed new and urgent priorities, and was no longer an event seen at a distance. The small American Navy's moment of opportunity had passed. American frigates were now unable to roam the seas, as they had earlier against a Royal Navy stretched thin by the war in Europe. Instead, the defeat and abdication of Napoleon in Europe meant that additional British warships had been freed up to impose a rigorous blockade on American ports, leaving many of the American frigates frustratingly stranded in port. Capitalizing on their advantage, the British established dominance over the waters of the Chesapeake Bay and its tributaries during the summer, raiding up the lower reaches of many rivers. In July major elements of the British fleet scouted out the Kettle Bottom Shoals on the middle Potomac and came close enough to Alexandria and Washington to throw the government into a frenzy of defensive preparation. The navy yard and Henry Foxall's cannon foundry in Georgetown, as the primary military targets on the Potomac, had clearly become vulnerable. If the British were to pass the shoals, their only serious defensive obstacle would be the undermanned and undergunned Fort Warburton, about twelve miles downstream from the navy yard.[9]

The *Adams*, back in service under Captain Charles Morris but unable to reach the Chesapeake Bay (much less the Atlantic) because of the British presence, was for the moment a major addition to the defense of the city. Jones instructed Morris to take a defensive position off Alexandria in case of attack. Tingey was instructed to have a number of cannon moved to a battery to be thrown up at Greenleaf's Point, and to

> without a moment's delay have all the force at the Navy yard
> in a complete state of preparation for action. You will moor the

three scows near Greenleaf's Point in a proper position for the
channel and select & organize officers and crews for each from
the best of the men in the Navy Yard . . . as the best means of
defense against the approach of the enemy to the City as well
as the Navy Yard is by proper use of force at Greenleaf's Point,
you will place as many men belonging to the Navy Yard for the
Defense of that position and at the Navy Yard as can be usefully
employed.[10]

Fortunately, the British fleet soon ended their summer campaign and
withdrew from the Potomac. But they now knew the way, and with the
departure of the *Adams* later that year, the city and the yard would be even
more vulnerable to any future attack from the river. Joshua Barney, a colorful
figure who had served consecutively in the Continental and French navies,
as captain of a privateer, and now as a captain in the U.S. Navy, proposed a
plan to defend the Potomac, which Jones approved shortly after the British
withdrew. Barney's plan was to cobble together a flotilla of shallow-draft
gunboats, galleys, and barges, each equipped with a large cannon. These
craft could be sheltered in the numerous creeks along the river but deployed
in large numbers to attack and harass an invading fleet. Commodore Barney
spent the following months, with the assistance of Tingey and the navy yard,
in putting together his Chesapeake flotilla.

While Commodore Barney on the water and the various militia companies on land tried to prepare the city's defenses in case of a British return
the following summer, workmen at the yard were busy on the two new ships
as well as on a number of smaller craft. In February 1814 Tingey reported
to Congress that the sloop of war *Argus* had been launched and was being
masted, rigged, and fitted out, while the hull of the 44-gun frigate, *Columbia*,
was still under construction.

Congress for its part, still in a mood of wartime generosity, had authorized the building or purchase of an additional twenty small armed ships,
but its main focus, under Secretary Jones' not so gentle urging, continued
to be on reform of the Navy Department. A year earlier, the naval affairs
committee had asked Captain Morris of the *Adams*, who at the time was
stationed at the navy yard while his ship was being rebuilt, for advice on
problems specific to the navy yards. Morris, answering with frankness, had
hit on one point that Tingey must have agreed with—the continuing lack of
a regular system for classifying vessels so as to standardize their equipment
and armament. But Morris also made criticisms that Tingey could not have
much appreciated: the entire contracting and naval agent system, he claimed,
provided opportunities for abuse and extravagance.

In the end, Congress did not focus specifically on the operation of either naval agents or navy yards. A special committee was set up in the House of Representatives during the spring of 1814 (the naval affairs committee being swamped with war management issues) to look into "means of retrenchment and economy" for the management of the Navy Department as a whole. The premise of the investigation was not to be fault finding; indeed, congressmen had kind words to say about the cost-saving and other measures introduced by Secretary Jones. The chairman indicated that his starting point would be similar to the secretary's known complaint—that is, "the multiplicity of duties attached to the Head of the Navy Department, and the lack of accountability in the various branches."[11] The committee was scheduled to report to the next session of the House, but—the realities of war intervening— did not report until March of 1815.

As the summer season approached, work at the yard continued on a somewhat normal basis. Work on the ships continued; the *Argus* would be largely ready by late summer and the *Columbia* was ready for her rigging. With the Royal Navy remaining at a comfortable distance, shipments of goods in and out of the yard could be maintained at a good pace. (By mid-summer, however, after the British showed up again in the Chesapeake, it became necessary to improvise new routes to send cargo to Norfolk—such as a land bridge between the Potomac at Potomac Creek and the Rappahannock near Fredericksburg.) But manpower was in very short supply: Tingey complained that his men were too often away on militia drills, and that work was suffering as a result. Neither he nor Joshua Barney had enough sailors to fully man the motley of vessels under their respective commands. Even the yard's Marine guard was short-handed, with the result that theft—"nocturnal depredations," as Tingey called them—was increasing. One night a number of barrels of salt pork were spirited over the compound wall. Tingey, much annoyed, called on the secretary to give him reinforcements, but of course they were unavailable. It was clear that, if the yard were to be attacked by any serious force, there would not be enough men on hand to make a stand.

The yard, in spite of its shortages and operating problems, was still a key military target. It was the prime industrial site of the capital city, a storehouse of valuable naval supplies and armaments that were even more valuable. The two almost-ready ships and the supplies of naval stores, gunpowder, and shot were important to the war effort. It was vitally important to keep them out of British hands.

Yet the site was virtually unprotected. If the British could neutralize or defeat the small contingent at Fort Warburton, the only remaining defense from an attack up the Potomac was the small battery at Greenleaf's Point. The only possible defense from a land attack was to cut off any approach over the Eastern Branch (or Anacostia) bridges, but any approach via the turnpike from Bladensburg and the north was essentially unfortified. The yard's perimeter wall, as Tingey knew, was not even a defense against theft. Finally, the entire complex was extremely vulnerable to fire. Wood chips, tar, canvas, lumber in open stacks or stored in sheds, woodpiles for the machines and forges, oakum, coal, gunpowder, and other flammable substances were all over the site. (Fortunately, the storage sheds and workshop buildings were closely grouped at the lower end of the yard, away from the residential and office buildings.)

The news, then, that the British squadron was once again headed for the Potomac should have been cause for serious defensive preparations. A new military command of some fifteen thousand militia to defend the eastern and northern approaches to the city had indeed been set up on paper, but the call-up of troops was never implemented in full or even in major part. And, for reasons discussed much more thoroughly elsewhere, the British move was considered to be a diversion until too late, with the secretary of war and others insisting that the attack was directed at Baltimore. The capital city's defense, as a result, was organized all too tardily and too ineffectively. The Navy's contribution, apart from Commodore Barney's gunboat flotilla with its supporting Marines, was the loan of a number of cannon to the land forces, and the deployment of available seamen and Marines into mobile land forces under the commands of Captain Rodgers, near Baltimore, and Captain David Porter, on the Virginia bank of the Potomac.

The British ships tested and marked the Potomac shoals in late July, but then turned up the Patuxent River in Maryland to begin raiding the neighboring farms. Their superior force pushed Commodore Barney's gunboat flotilla into the upper reaches of that river, effectively neutralizing it above Pig Point. Then, in mid-August, the British made their move. The fleet, which had been reinforced by ships carrying troops from Europe, now numbered more than twenty-five vessels, including two ships of the line and seven frigates. On 19 August they began to disembark thousands of troops at Benedict, on the western shore of the Patuxent and only some fifty miles southeast of the navy yard. Their destination was now clearer: the capital city was most likely the target.

A disorganized rush to protect the city and its contents began. The militia companies in the city and neighboring states were rapidly mobilized and sent to the front, and very soon those noncombatants who could do so began to evacuate their homes. A young visitor from New England described the scene: "The public officials began packing up the valuable papers to be removed to places of safety," she wrote. "Now all is hurry and panic, armies gathering, troops moving in all directions, the citizens trying to secure such things as were most valuable and easily transported, and flying from their homes to the country."[12] One result was a scramble for transportation: horses and wagons suddenly were in short supply, and the lowly carters, many of them slaves, were placed in unprecedented bargaining positions with respect to the desperate officials and homeowners.

Among the first American units to take up a blocking position between Benedict and the city was Barney's contingent of sailors, most of whom had marched from their bottled-up flotilla as soon as the British landed their troops. They were joined by more than a hundred Marines, with their artillery, sent from the Washington barracks. Secretary Jones, recognizing that the flotilla was no longer of any use, authorized the officers left at Pig Point to destroy it if it came under strong attack—which they were obliged to do on 22 August. The secretary was concerned that the British fleet would turn back, come up the Potomac, and place Washington under attack from two directions—he had already been told that Fort Warburton could not hold the river approach against such a force.

Secretary Jones wanted above all to keep the ships and supplies at the navy yard out of enemy hands. Should the enemy's land and waterborne forces succeed in joining forces at Washington, he later reported,

> nothing could be more clear than that he would first plunder [the navy yard], and then destroy the buildings and improvements, or, if unable to carry off the plunder and the shipping, he would destroy the whole. And if the junction [of the British forces] should be formed, it would be a strong inducement to remain, in order to launch the new frigate . . . he would then carry off the whole of the public stores and shipping, and greatly extend the field of his plunder and devastation. Thus, in either case, whether the junction was formed or whether the army alone reached the city, the loss or destruction of the whole of the property at the navy yard was certain.[13]

Secretary Jones visited the navy yard on 21 and 22 August to see the situation at first hand. He found the usually bustling place denuded of its manpower. Consulting with Tingey, he was told that only four officers and a few civilian clerks remained at the yard: all the rest of the employees—with the exception of a few black servants in the ordinary—were serving in their militia units. Jones was anxious that as much of the valuable goods as possible be removed to a place of safety, and agreed with what must have been Tingey's suggestion that they be taken to Oak Hill, the farm of his son-in-law and daughter Daniel and Sarah Dulany, which was across the Potomac in Falls Church, Virginia. Jones directed Tingey to hire or requisition what labor, boats, and wagons he could in an effort to transport "the most valuable and portable items from the yard, to any place of safety, with any means he could command."[14] Priority would be given to removing the gunpowder, which was particularly valuable for both the British and the Americans.

Getting the goods to his son-in-law's place, however, posed a serious problem for Tingey. He had no wagons and only two of the old gunboats for water transport, with precious few men to crew them. Nor, with so few sailors available, was there any way to sail the *Argus* or *Lynx* (a 6-gun sloop recently built in Georgetown that was being fitted out at the yard), or even the three new barges, out of harm's way. The frigate *Columbia*, still on the slipway and almost ready for launching, was entirely vulnerable. As for the buildings, their equipment, and most of the remaining supplies—canvas, cordage, timber, 743 barrels of beef and pork, and 296 barrels of whiskey among them— they could only be saved if the British were diverted or repulsed.

John Creighton, a master commander who had been acting as Tingey's deputy that summer while supervising the fitting out of the *Argus*, was sent off by the secretary to reconnoiter the British naval forces on the Potomac, leaving Tingey even more short-handed. Tingey turned to his clerk, the fifty-one-year-old Mordecai Booth, to go to town and obtain enough wagons to begin moving the gunpowder. Tingey himself remained at the yard, and during the next day and a half somehow rounded up enough men to load the two gunboats with powder and other valuables. They were held ready to leave at short notice, should it be necessary to abandon the yard.

Meanwhile, Mordecai Booth was having an unaccustomedly strenuous but productive day. After borrowing a horse from a friend's wife, his search for wagons met with initial successes. He met a freeman with a sturdy wagon and a team of five horses and obtained the man's agreement to accept being requisitioned—after he had delivered his cargo to Georgetown and Alexandria. Booth quickly wrote up some documents for him, and was pleasantly surprised to see him at the navy yard that evening. Proceeding on to Georgetown, Booth was able to requisition three more wagons, only to have the Navy Department take away two of them for its own needs and to see the third one run away while he was negotiating with the Navy clerks. He managed to requisition several more wagons, though, and while they were unloading he went in search of more. His efforts to do so got him into a heated argument with men who "made use of such language as was degrading to gentlemen," as he reported later that evening. "I had no one with me to inforce the detention of the Waggon, and it was hurried off, in opposition to my positive command to the contrary, and except that I had used violence could not have prevented it."[15] All the same, Booth was able to return to the yard that evening with five wagons, plus the one he had hired earlier.

Early next morning, Booth saw to the loading of two wagons with provisions for Commodore Barney's men, and sent them off to the front. The remaining four wagons were then loaded with 120 barrels of gunpowder and directed to the Dulany farm. Booth, who in the meantime had managed to requisition and load still another wagon, followed the other wagons across the long bridge to safety in Virginia. Late that evening, the wagon train stopped at Wren's Tavern at Falls Church, just a mile from the Dulany farm. There Booth was joined, much to his joy, by his children, whom Tingey had sent along under escort. Booth, exhausted after a long day but by no means finished with his week of uncommon adventure, closed his report to Tingey that night with a rush of emotion: "And now Sir permit me to pause—until I return to you the warmest thanks of a grateful Heart, for the attention you paid to my unprotected Children in my absence. To your goodness, they owe their escape from a Scene, the Most to be regretted of my life—you can never be rewarded beyond the Sensations of a pure heart, and a sound mind—the Attribute of an all wise being, so bounteously bestowed on you."[16]

Tingey in the meantime was finishing the loading of the gunboats. In addition, a number of rowboats were loaded with gunpowder and inflammables, to be positioned under the Anacostia River bridges so as to deny the enemy those routes either into or out of the city. (John Creighton was put in charge, the next day, of the detachment that would blow the nearest bridge, some ten blocks away at the end of Pennsylvania Avenue.) Because it was still unclear whether the British troops would advance directly from the east to the bridges or via Bladensburg in the north, most of the militia and Barney's men fell back that evening toward the capital to cover both contingencies and devise a strategy. Barney stayed with Tingey at the yard.

On the morning of 24 August, a crucial war council was held near the navy yard, with the president; the secretaries of war, Navy, treasury, and state; and the military commanders all present. With the British now showing that they intended to attack via Bladensburg, the decision was quickly reached to send the bulk of the troops there to block their advance. Secretary Jones, who seems to have had little confidence in the military's chance of prevailing, used the meeting to get approval for a decision that had been on his mind since his last visit to the navy yard two days before. It was a necessary contingency measure—namely what to do, in the event of a British victory on the field, with the vast remainder of the property at the yard that could not be moved to safety. Laying out the situation of the navy yard in the terms quoted above, Jones sought approval of his fallback plan—the yard's destruction. Still hopeful that the British might be checked on the battlefield, and with no other options available, the president readily concurred. "It was distinctly agreed and determined as a result of this consultation," Jones would report later to Congress, "that the public shipping, and naval and military stores and provisions at the navy yard, should be destroyed, in the event of the enemy's obtaining possession of the city."[17]

At about 3:00 that afternoon, with news of a battle at Bladensburg (but not its conclusion) beginning to reach the city, the secretary returned to the yard to inform Tingey that he should prepare to burn everything that he could not move out. In the event of an American defeat, and once Tingey had "satisfactorily ascertained that the enemy has driven our army and entered the City," he had the authority, the secretary instructed him, to set "set fire to the trains and retire in your Gig."[18]

It was a wrenching order and a dreadful responsibility for Tingey. Everything that he, Latrobe, Cassin, Fox, and King had built up over the past decade was at risk, as was his own career if the politicians in Congress chose later to second-guess the decision or his timing. But he was a military officer, and even though he had not seen much combat in his career, he knew that war meant destruction. He would do what was necessary, but only when it was abundantly clear that it was necessary. In preparation for the worst-case scenario, though, he rapidly had gunpowder and inflammables placed where needed, powder trains laid for quick ignition, and all available boats prepared for a rapid evacuation by water. He then began an agonizing wait.

It was not a quiet wait, however. Less than an hour after Jones' departure, word had begun to spread that the Army had been routed at Bladensburg. (In what later became known, infamously, as the "Bladensburg Races," Commodore Barney's men and artillery were indeed the sole unit to distinguish themselves for courage.) Mordecai Booth, who had returned from Virginia, was shocked to learn of Tingey's new orders. ("What was my astonishment!" he wrote some weeks later.)[19] He quickly volunteered to find out what he could about a British advance, and with Tingey's grateful approval rode off for another eventful afternoon. It was not long before he saw signs of the defeat. While still on Capitol Hill, he "passed the commons, and to the turn-pike Gate; commanding a View of the Hills beyond the Gate, I saw not the Appearance of an Englishman—But Oh! my Country—And I blush Sir! to tell you—I saw the Commons Covered with the fugitive Soldiery of our Army—runing, hobling, Creeping, & appearently pannick struck." Returning to report to his commandant, Booth heard and saw the nearby bridge being "Blown, into Splintery fragments, in the Air." Arrived at the yard, excited and indignant at what he had seen, Booth informed Tingey that although the American militia were in disorganized retreat the British were as yet nowhere in sight. He urged delay—in terms, apparently, so strong that he subsequently felt it necessary to apologize.

Tingey had other reasons for delay. Although he had been informed by a messenger from the secretary of war that the Army "could protect me no longer," he was reluctant to take action until he had no other option. There was the hope that the Army would yet rally in the hills north of the city and hold up the British advance. But Tingey was also concerned, closer to home, that the wind was blowing from a direction that would endanger many of the neighboring homes were the yard to be set on fire. Having felt it necessary, as the leading citizen of Navy Yard Hill, to warn his neighbors early on that he might have to set fire to the yard, he had been inundated with pleas not to take the step. A delegation of neighboring housewives, in fact, became so obstreperous that Tingey finally lost his temper. As he later reported, "I found myself painfully necessitated to inform them, that any farther importunities would cause the matches to be instantly applied to the trains—with assurance however that, if left at peace, I would delay the execution of the orders, as long as I could feel the least shadow of justification."[20]

Commander Creighton, reporting for instructions after having blown up the bridge, confirmed Booth's information that no British were yet in sight. Tingey, anxious for news that was more reliable than the wild rumors that were circulating, told Creighton to ride out to see if he could determine the location of the attacking army, and report back. He instructed the Marines in Creighton's party to man one of the galleys and row it to presumed safety in Alexandria. Privately, and hoping for the usual evening drop in the wind, Tingey set himself a deadline of 8:30 that evening for making the fateful decision.

Booth and Creighton, on their separate reconnaissance missions, spent the late afternoon crisscrossing the northern approaches to the city, and then the town itself, without spotting any British troops—or indeed anybody but other information-gatherers like themselves. As Booth put it, "the Matropelis of our Country was abandoned to it's [sic] horrid fate." At twilight, and traveling in company with militia cavalry officer Walter Cox, Booth fortuitously ran into Creighton near the president's house. They agreed that it was time to return and report to Tingey, but that they would do so via Capitol Hill, the most likely route for a British approach to the yard. By the time they reached the hill, it was dark. There, just a few hundred yards from the Capitol and Long's Hotel, what they first took to be cows turned out to be troops. A few shots directed their way convinced them that they had finally encountered the enemy. Needing no further confirmation, they rode with all speed back to the yard and reported to Tingey.

After hearing Creighton and Booth deliver their reports, Tingey looked at his watch and made a record of the time. It was 8:20 at night, and British troops were within a half-mile of the undefended yard. There were no

American troops in the area or, for that matter, in the city. The wind had died down, and with it the risk of unintended damages to the private homes outside the wall. The secretary's conditions, and Tingey's own, had all been met, and to delay longer could risk being overrun and letting the yard fall into enemy hands—surely a court martial offense. Tingey had no choice but to set fire to his yard, his ships—his work of the last ten years.

At least it was quick work. Proceeding systematically, Tingey, Creighton, Booth, and the few remaining clerks, Marines, and sailors first lit the powder trains to the warehouses. They then set fire to the frigate *Columbia*, the fire from there spreading quickly to the storehouses on the wharf and the workshops behind, then to the *Argus*, tied up at the wharf. On what he called a "momentary impulse," Tingey decided not to set fire to the schooner *Lynx*, lying farther down the wharf. Finally, the more distant storehouses and the hulls of the frigates *New York, Boston,* and *General Greene,* at anchor in the harbor, were set on fire. By the light of what had become a towering inferno, the two gunboats set off, and then the commodore's gig, loaded with the remaining personnel and headed for Alexandria.

Mordecai Booth, who had been given leave to join his family by land in order to save his horse, was crossing the long bridge to Virginia when he saw the navy yard begin to burn, followed shortly by the British-set fires at the Capitol, and then the fire of the president's house. He was exhausted, distressed, and yet morbidly drawn to the sight. For the next two hours of that fateful night, he stood with other citizens on the hills of Alexandria to witness what he called a "sight, so repugnant to my feelings, so dishonourable; so degrading to the American Character, and at the Same time, so Awful [that it] Almost palsied my facultyes."

Tingey and his party, rowing down the river to Alexandria, could also see the fires at the yard, the Capitol, and the Greenleaf's Point arsenal—the fire at the president's house was hidden around a bend in the river. The sight of such a disaster must have stirred his emotions as well, and the tension and anxiety of the day might have turned into anger, sorrow, frustration, or other channels. Yet we do not know about his emotions. His official correspondence on the event is entirely businesslike, while to his children he simply noted with pride that he had been the last officer to leave the city and the first to return.

Indeed, he left Alexandria at 7:30 the following morning, arriving at the navy yard wharf shortly thereafter, at about 8:45. The place was a ruin. The British had left only a half-hour earlier, after setting fire to the one storeroom that had survived the night. There were, however, a few bits of good news. Little *Lynx*, the new schooner, had luckily survived. So had Tingey's house, as well as the other dwellings and the Tripoli monument at the upper end of the compound. But Tingey's house was by no means unscathed. Some of his neighbors, perhaps including his employees, had taken advantage of the situation to begin pillaging his belongings. He quickly managed to get some of his more valuable possessions moved to friends' houses in the vicinity, but he did not have enough time to complete the job. Hearing that the British were aware of his presence and perhaps intending to arrest him, he soon reembarked for Alexandria.

He was back at the yard on the morning of 26 August, after a night that had seen both a huge rainstorm and the withdrawal of the British troops from the city. The fires at the yard and elsewhere were out, the enemy gone, but the damage not yet completed. Once again, the neighbors had set to ransacking both the residences in the yard and the cargo of one of the barges, which unfortunately had run aground in the harbor two nights earlier. Though Tingey's report is matter-of-fact in tone, he clearly was furious, both at the behavior of his neighbors and at the loss of his possessions. But he could not control the situation with only the boat crew that had brought him across the river. Sending off to Alexandria for reinforcements, he was eventually able to regain "full control," of the yard, as he put it, later that evening. He was back in charge of his yard, but the nature of his command had changed for good.

Tingey's role in the war effort, in effect, was all but ended. With its inventory destroyed and the workforce scattered into the militia or the various naval units operating under captains Barney, Rodgers, and Porter, his command played almost no role in the efforts to harass the British during their occupation and pillage of Alexandria, nor in the siege of Baltimore. The war, in any event, was rapidly drawing to a close. At the turn of the year, peace terms had been agreed and the Americans under Andrew Jackson had won a great, morale-restoring victory at New Orleans.

Picking up the pieces at the navy yard, however, began immediately. Collecting, cleaning, and securely storing salvageable items was the first order of business. This was slow work, involving picking through the contents of burned warehouses as well as lifting cannon and other items from the wrecked ships, some of them at the bottom of the harbor. Second was rebuilding the perimeter wall where it had been damaged, to limit further pilferage. Then began the slower process of estimating the cost of the damages and reporting to the congressional committee that was set up in September to look into the causes and costs of the capture of the city. While a final estimate of the losses at the yard took some time to prepare—Tingey submitted it, still not complete, only in November—it showed that much had been or could be salvaged. The foundations and many of the walls of the burned buildings, for example, were sound and could be reused. Likewise, the extensive and valuable metal goods could be salvaged, from cannon, to sheet iron for roofs, and even to the fittings from the burned ships and buildings. The steam engine and other machinery could be put back into operation. In total, the value of supplies, buildings, and equipment lost was estimated at almost $800,000, but the value of salvaged or salvageable goods brought the net cost down to about $500,000.

The congressional investigation, in the end, was inconclusive. Under attack himself from Federalist partisans, Secretary Jones stepped forward to defend Tingey's honor in the affair. "The order for the destruction of the Public Shipping and property, at the Navy Yard," he wrote to the committee, "was not issued without serious deliberation, and great pain, by him, under whose auspices and direction those noble Ships had been constructed, and a degree of activity, usefulness, and reputation, imparted to the Establishment, which it had never known before. It was given under the strongest obligations of duty."[21] But the secretary's support was not really necessary: no damaging criticisms were leveled against Tingey—and few, for that matter, against any of the other uniformed officers involved in the debacle. Only the secretary of war lost his job, as Congress and the country chose to ignore the more humiliating aspects of a war that in the end had wound up in a draw.

Jones himself retired soon after reporting to Congress. But he had achieved his main aim: the reorganization of the Navy Department. Early in 1815, it would become law, and the management of the Navy and the navy yards would change markedly.

CHAPTER  TEN

Rebuilding

The Navy emerged from the war with honor, public support, and a mandate for change. Thanks to Secretary Jones' advocacy for reform (a need made all-too evident by the shortcomings of the Navy Department during the war) and a solid Republican majority, the Madison administration managed to steer a reform measure through Congress with no embarrassing investigations or fault-finding. The committee on naval affairs simply accepted that there had been wrongdoing, but brushed aside any investigation by declaring that they did "not deem it useful to report to the House a detail of the various abuses that have prevailed in the Naval Establishment."[1] They insisted, instead, that the legislators should move on to reform a system that had allowed such abuses to take place. Their compliant colleagues agreed: the reform bill was passed on 7 February 1815 with minimal opposition, and signed a week later.

A key element of the reform was Secretary Jones' proposal to establish a board of commissioners that would take much of the administrative load away from the secretary's office. That proposal had already been sent around to senior naval officers for comment. Those were very largely positive, reinforcing the administration's case. Tingey's comments, like those of most of his colleagues, focused largely on the structure and functions of the proposed board. But he also used the occasion to plead once again—largely successfully this time—that the new system should support the builder's decisions. "No officer, whatever his grade may be, shall in any way alter the internal or external equipments of the ship under his command," he insisted.[2]

The Board of Naval Commissioners was thus established, and by the end of April had begun holding regular meetings in Washington. The three commissioners were captains John Rodgers, who as senior officer assumed the chair; David Porter; and Isaac Hull, though Hull, unhappy in Washington, soon left for command of the Portsmouth navy yard and was replaced by Stephen Decatur. These were not timid men, and they were eager to take an expansive view of their new authority—which, according to the new legislation, was "to discharge all the ministerial duties of said [the secretary's] office relative to the procurement of naval stores and materials, construction, armament, equipment, repair, and preservation of vessels of war, as well as all other matters connected with the naval establishment of the United States." Relying on the last clause of this authority, they began to gather information about a range of naval activities, including the deployment of active duty forces.

This presumption landed the new commissioners in that most typical of Washington arguments: a battle for turf. They had not counted, apparently, on the determination of the new secretary of the Navy, Benjamin Crowninshield, to protect his own authority over ongoing Navy operations. Crowninshield was from a prominent Massachusetts family active in merchant shipping and politics, and was, as Tingey reported to a colleague, "friendly to the Board, and I think very much so to the service generally."[3] But friendliness did not necessarily mean acceptance of the commissioners' contention, expressed both in official letters and, somewhat rashly, in an article in the National Intelligencer, that they had an authority parallel to that of the secretary. Crowninshield fired back, informing Captain Rodgers that he considered that the board's position "carries with it an air of hostility," in addition to infringing on both congressional authority and executive authority, "in favor of an institution which was created only to assist in the performance of mere ministerial duties." At the same time, he also wrote to President Madison requesting his support. "Shall the Board, which was created to assist the Department, control the Secretary, or shall the Secretary control the Board?" he asked.[4] The president not unexpectedly sided with his new secretary. The commissioners were put in their place, and very shortly thereafter their daily journal reflected a discussion about how abject an apology and pledge of loyalty they should make to Crowninshield.

The debate was useful in the end, allowing the commissioners to settle down gracefully to the more modest role assigned to them—there was, indeed, enough to keep them busy in executing the "mere ministerial," or administrative, duties of the department. They soon sent a circular to all naval establishments instructing that all correspondence on matters pertaining to procurement of materials and construction, armament, and equipment of warships was to be addressed to them rather than to the department. For his part, Crowninshield gave them a free hand in those areas, reserving for himself authority over uniformed personnel, naval strategy and deployment of active duty vessels, and relations with Congress and the president.

Meeting daily at first, the commissioners began to study and implement a series of measures that would systematize navy yard activities and give both Congress and the commissioners themselves a clearer oversight over expenditures. Within their first week, indeed, they had already reached some sweeping conclusions about the existing navy yards. They found none of them fully acceptable, and began what would be a long study of ideal locations for two major supply depots and repair facilities on the seacoast. Toward the Washington yard, their opinions were decidedly negative: "It is the decided opinion of the Board, that the obstructions and its distance from the sea render it unsuitable for every other purpose" than a building yard, they decided.[5] They were tempted, it seems, to recommend closing the yard entirely but, recognizing its usefulness for the administration and congressional relations, they saw fit to continue it as a shipbuilding center. It was a compromise decision, but one that would, by taking advantage of the yard's skilled workforce and mechanical head start, allow it to pick up other responsibilities over time and eventually evolve into a different kind of establishment entirely.

Even to begin construction of one of the new ships authorized by Congress, however, the yard had to be largely rebuilt. The postinferno salvage process was more or less finished: the place had been cleaned up and materials recycled where possible, the lucky little *Lynx* had departed for Boston in March with twenty of the salvaged cannon, and estimates had been made of the cost and feasibility of repairing the major workshops. Getting started on work was in fact vital to the yard's future: most of the workforce—both salaried and daily hires—had been largely unemployed over the winter, many of them had lost their personal tools and valuables in the fire, and hardship was threatening to drive many of the skilled men away.[6] It was good news, therefore, when the board informed Tingey in mid-May that they would authorize repairs to the blacksmith shop: it meant not only a building project, but also that the skilled craftsmen employed there had a prospect of work in the near future. Other rebuilding projects were initiated during the summer and fall, including reroofing the brick buildings that had survived the fire and construction of a shed to protect salvaged lumber. Money, though, was still tight. The board urged Tingey to make sure that all nails possible were reused, and denied money to set up a shelter for the carpenters—they would have to work outside as weather permitted. All the same, it was a new beginning—not only of productive activity at the yard, but of prospects for rehiring many of the near-destitute workmen who had had no regular employment for almost a year.

The commissioners, however, had made it extremely clear to the commandant that they would not allow him the same leeway in hiring as he had extracted in the past from the Navy secretaries. Only two weeks after taking office, they gave him a blunt warning on the subject:

> It is the intention of the Board of the Navy Commissioners to reestablish the Navy Yard at this place, as a building Yard only, & while stating to you this intention, it may not be improper for them to make you acquainted with their views generally with respect to the establishment. They have witnessed in many of our Navy Yards & this particularly pressure in the employment of characters unsuited for the public service—maimed & unmanageable slaves for the accommodation of distressed widows & orphans & indigent families—apprentices for the accommodation of their masters—& old men & children for the benefit of their families & parents. These practices must cease—none must be employed but for the advantage of the public, & this Yard instead of rendering the navy odious to the nation from the scenes of want & extravagance which it has too long exhibited must serve as a model on which to perfect a general system of economy.
>
> In making to you, Sir, these remarks the Navy Commissioners are aware that you have with themselves long witnessed the evils of which they complain, & which every countenance will be given to assist you in remedying them, they calculate with confidence on a disposition on your part to forward the public interests.[7]

Not surprisingly, Tingey was offended by this virtual charge of improper practices from gentlemen whom he considered to be friends. He waited a few days before replying, but nonetheless could not avoid letting his annoyance show. "The tenor of some parts of the letter might justify me in some comments, upon past transactions relative to this establishment," he wrote in a circumlocutious yet clear manner, "but as a retrospective review thereon might only excite unpleasant sensations in my own mind, without being productive of good, I shall content myself with observing that—being now assured of the countenance of the Board in remedying defects—I calculate on the support of the ministerial officers of the Department."[8]

Nor was this oblique insult his only reason for annoyance with the commissioners. In their eagerness to establish clear oversight over the widespread and disparate activities of the Navy and to establish uniform practices, the board was busy creating complicated new financial and operational reporting requirements. Less than a month after they took over, Tingey had already written to Margaret Gay, "our new Navy Board of Commissioners seems to be cutting out new work for me almost daily," and sarcastically calling them "their lordships."[9] He was, perhaps, overstressed from a year of job pressure, a major transition in his work, and a lonely bachelorhood caused by the loss of his second wife. He must have recognized this himself, because he applied at the same time for a long leave to visit his daughters and their families in the northeast. As soon as Secretary Crowninshield agreed to his request, Tingey was off, informing the board that he would visit other naval yards on the way. His travels lasted from mid-June to early September 1815, during which time his second in command, Lieutenant Nathaniel Haraden, supervised the works under way at the yard.

When Tingey returned, perhaps in a better mood, he also heard some good news. The commissioners had decided that, in view of the yard's known capabilities in ironwork as well as a desire to eliminate duplication in procurement, that all large anchors for the Navy would be made in Washington. This was welcome news: it meant that, in addition to the shipbuilding that had been promised and could begin as soon as the building slips were put back in order, the trained smiths and their helpers would have expanded work. Tingey tried to persuade Benjamin King to return from a job in Norfolk because, in spite of his troublesome nature, the man was a talented mechanic and smith. (He did not return until 1817, however.) Tingey was eager to find renewed employment for his old workforce. When the board gave permission to repair the slipways and extend the wharf and the lumber docks, for example, Tingey argued successfully that rehiring his carpenters for the job would be much more cost-efficient than bringing in a contractor. That not only gave men opportunities for work during the cold winter months, but it also made it possible to lay the keel of a new ship—the long-awaited 74-gun ship of the line—in May of 1816.

That summer was a positive one at the yard, in spite of being abnormally cold because of a weirdly darkened sky caused by the April 1815 eruption of Mount Tambora in the East Indies. The president's annual message to Congress had complimented the Navy in a way that inspired Tingey to call it "one of the best state papers that I have ever read, it is replete with wisdom! It has filled me with a patriotic enthusiasm."[10] Significantly, the president's praise presaged a reversal of congressional parsimony. The Navy was no longer to be starved for funds, as an act authorizing a gradual increase of more than twenty capital ships was passed in April. With that promise of continued funding and an accelerating rebuilding program, the yard was returning to a more normal pattern of life. An imposing ship was taking shape on the building slip, the steam engine and its appendages the sawmill and the blockmaking shop were being rebuilt, and sailmaking and rigging lofts, a mold

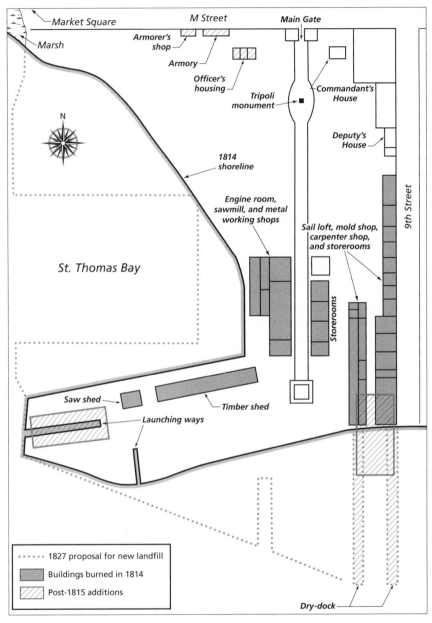

Market Square

M Street

Main Gate

Armorer's shop

Marsh

Armory

Officer's housing

Tripoli monument

Commandant's House

N

Deputy's House

1814 shoreline

Engine room, sawmill, and metal working shops

Sail loft, mold shop, carpenter shop, and storerooms

9th Street

St. Thomas Bay

Storerooms

Saw shed

Timber shed

Launching ways

····· 1827 proposal for new landfill

▨ Buildings burned in 1814

▨ Post-1815 additions

Dry-dock

PLAN OF THE NAVY YARD, SHOWING BUILDINGS EXISTING IN 1814,
DRY-DOCK, AND OTHER POST-1815 ADDITIONS,
AS WELL AS 1827 PROPOSALS FOR LANDFILL EXPANSION.

(or pattern) shop, and new timber sheds were being readied. Cannon and ballast were being pulled out of the burned and sunken hulk of the *Argus* at the wharf, and the commissioners were even authorizing occasional shipments of supplies to the squadron once more in the Mediterranean fighting corsairs. By the time the first of the new anchors was finished at the end of the year, the yard's future was ensured.

The resumption of shipbuilding, however, had created a new yet familiar headache for Captain Tingey—a sort of turf battle between himself and the naval constructor, now William Doughty. Doughty had been employed in that capacity since 1813, but most of his work during the war and immediately thereafter had been in designing ships being built elsewhere, with the Washington yard administration simply providing him with the necessary materials and tools, workspace, personnel, and financial services. Now that one of the new ships of the line (to be called the *Columbus*) was on the ways at Washington, however, the overlap of Doughty's responsibilities and those of Tingey, as commandant of the yard, began to provide a source of friction. Doughty as constructor, like Josiah Fox before him, was responsible for designing the ships, preparing patterns for their component pieces, and—in Washington—supervising the actual construction of ships on the ways. The commissioners had determined that, in Washington, the constructor should also supervise work at the shops that directly supported shipbuilding, such as the sawmill and the block and pump makers. But, of course, other parts of the yard needed the services of those shops as well, and those overlapping needs created confusion.

The problem in this arrangement, from Tingey's point of view, was that a substantial portion of the work being done at the yard was no longer under his direct supervision and control, if at all. By now enough of a bureaucrat to have learned to live with overlapping areas of authority, he was still at heart a naval officer with a clear preference for unity of command. The issue, presumably, had festered in the background before it came to a head over a repair necessary to a pump at the Marine barracks. When Doughty refused to let the mechanics at the pump shop make a piece ordered by Tingey, the commandant lost his composure. Writing to the commissioners in an uncharacteristic state of high dudgeon, he demanded a clear answer: were "the powers of the naval Constructor such, as to counteract at his will my orders relative to the duties of this yard? If they are, I am surely not Commandant of it."[11]

He received an answer the very same day, but not the one he wanted. The commissioners supported Doughty, while letting the ambiguities of the situation stand. First, they reminded Tingey that he had seen Doughty's letter of instruction, "which was sent under cover to you unsealed, that you might observe its constraints." Then, they pointed out, "All the mechanics and laborers belonging to the Constructor's Department were placed under his [Doughty's] exclusive control, and he was instructed not to undertake any operation whatever in his Department without first his first consulting, and obtaining the approbation of, the Navy Commissioners."[12] Tingey, in short, could not direct the work of any of those employees working in Doughty's division, and Doughty did not have to inform Tingey of his dispositions. The phrase "any operation whatever" was a particular blow—it meant that Tingey would have to ask Doughty whenever he wanted services from shops in the yard—ones that the commandant had almost surely considered at his own disposal as well. The commissioners tried to sugarcoat the pill a bit by suggesting in later communications that Tingey "consult" with Doughty over issues of this nature. But the issue, it seems, persisted, and even though the two learned to work well enough together (better certainly than had been the case with Fox), Tingey, over the years, occasionally let his resentment show.

But what he resented most of all, it would seem, was the constant stream of reporting requirements put in place by the commissioners. In a desire to rationalize and systematize procurement, use the lowest-cost option, and track expenditures according to the relevant congressional appropriations, the board and its clerks created over the years an increasingly complex web of periodic reports that had to be submitted on a timely basis. The list grew to include complex weekly and monthly payrolls, monthly materiel inventories, reports on supplies expended, reports on contracts and purchases, and of course many ad hoc reports, all of them necessarily broken down according to the appropriate budget line. At first, Tingey, his foremen, and his clerks provided suggestions for the content and format of the reports, but as the workload increased the dialogue with the board became more petulant on both sides. Polite but slightly acid comments were made, from Tingey's side, on the intricacy of the requirements, the difficulty of assigning some expenses, or the time consumed in preparation ("a great proportion of my time is engaged, that ought, in my opinion, be employed to more useful purpose," he complained). The commissioners and their clerks, on the other hand, carped about late reports, inaccuracies, or "irregularities" (such as Tingey's tendency to charge anything questionable to the contingency fund), and occasionally sent back reports for correction along with snide exhortations "that similar departures from the regulations and orders which have been given upon the subject may not again occur."[13]

Such squabbles, of course, are endemic to any multilayered organization, and the commissioners, to their credit, were attempting to put in place some basic tools of diligent management with which Tingey, on reflection, could not disagree. But Tingey's complaints, beyond that dynamic, can probably be seen as reflecting regret at being forced, after years of relative operational freedom, into a much more constrained mode of doing his work. His reference to the commissioners—his colleagues—as "their lordships" seems, in this context, more than simply an amusing aside in a private letter. And the workload caused by the commissioners' reporting requirements was indeed punishing, as well as new and annoying, for an increasingly elderly man. His letters to his daughter Margaret Gay return to the matter with a tinge of real exasperation. "The cry is always for Reports, Reports, detail Reports, and thus my time is employed in perpetuo," he wrote in late 1820. A few months later he complained that he has so many demands from the commissioners that he was "almost sickened at the sight of a pen."[14]

The reporting requirements were only one constraint enforced by the commissioners. They also were much more rigid than the Navy secretaries before them in enforcing control over both procurement and employment. Tingey had almost no discretion, under the new system, in signing contracts—each one had to be approved by the commission. When the commissioners were away on their periodic inspection tours, he could sign them only within carefully defined price and quality parameters. Tingey, it would seem, had no serious problem with his reduced influence over contracts. He and his colleagues could still recommend suppliers and still conducted the crucial quality-control inspections, so he still played a vital if not determining role in the process. And if he could no longer steer sweetheart contracts to friends and family (though George Beale still won the occasional contract to supply lumber or coal), he was by the same token insulated from charges of corruption. For a man as anxious to protect his reputation as Tingey was, learning not to stick his neck out may have been a good lesson learned from the charges of self-dealing leveled against him by Parsons and Hanson back in 1810. Within a few years, the court martial and conviction of the commandant of the Brooklyn navy yard would serve as a forceful reminder that he and the yard were under constant scrutiny from the press and congressional opponents.[15]

This is not to say that he did not bridle, on occasion, at what he considered to be micromanagement by the commissioners, whose proximity in Washington could sometimes make them intrusive. Called to task by them on one occasion, when he had made a spot purchase of a quantity of oakum and "junk" (rags for oakum and gun wadding) without their permission, he drafted a lengthy reply that combined a bit of humor with self-righteous resistance. Saying that he was not aware of any specific orders regulating such purchases for operations at the yard, he had indeed filled an urgent requisition from his men for work under way—and, moreover, had negotiated a good price. "I am not conscious therefore in this act of having sinned against Heaven, and before the Board," he quipped. "But if it is deemed otherwise! Some mitigation (in judgment) may be admitted, inasmuch as it was unknowingly committed, and the error (if any) unintentional." But, he pleaded in closing, he would hope for continued flexibility rather than more controls: "It will I conceive be very complex and almost useless work to refer every requisition (made on me) to the Board—I hope therefore that the subject will have due consideration and a regular mode devised for obtaining our necessary supplies—which I repeat, I shall strictly attend to."[16]

The commissioners, however, did not buy his argument, and their reply shows clearly how their systemwide view differed from that of Tingey, who wanted only to get on with his work. Admitting that their guidance had been incomplete, they now made it specific:

> A due sense of economy forbids retail purchases and the intention of the Board is to avoid them whenever it can be done. They expect that you would authenticate the wants of the yard, and make your recommendations so as to give time to procure the supplies in sufficient quantities & on the best terms. They request that you will in future take this course. With respect to the Oakum & Junk purchased by you of a person in Alexandria, had the Board been apprised in season of these articles being wanted, they would have added them, on the Junk to make Oakum from the other yards—where they had an abundance— and have saved the expense of purchasing it. This is mentioned to show the necessity of your making known to the Board the wants of the yard, and the impropriety of making any purchases without their knowledge & consent.[17]

Tingey's colleagues on the board had the broad aim of creating a service administered on a rational, cost-effective basis. Moreover, they wished to instill a climate of probity and internal security that would convince Congress that the public's funds were being well spent. This inevitably meant more reports, controls, and prohibitions, some of them irksome. Access to navy yards was decreed limited to strangers and particularly foreigners, yard employees were required to be or become American citizens, and yard employees were not to hold civic office or engage in any business transaction with the yard, nor to engage in business outside that in any way used yard facilities. Although the Washington yard's technical capabilities continued to inspire requests from other government agencies for special services, the controls over such work also were tightened. Yard employees, for example, built boats for the Army and the customs service, repaired chandeliers and set up flagpoles for Congress, and even installed the first flush toilet in the White House—but each job required the commissioners' explicit approval, and prompt reimbursement. Very occasionally, the commissioners would deign to bend their own rules, but even so made sure that everyone understood that the event was exceptional. Thus, when they instructed Tingey to have his mechanics repair a press for the influential publishers of the *National Intelligencer*, they let him know they considered it "unpleasant to impinge upon a rule, and they consent reluctantly, [as] it is serving gentlemen whom they are disposed to serve."[18] It is almost amusing to see how, in a most political town, they felt they had to justify letting politics sneak into a management decision.

Employment was the process at the yard that was most markedly influenced by a range of essentially political factors—connections, nationality, empathy, ethnicity, or even partisan considerations. The commissioners, from the beginning, had indicated that they intended to keep a tight control over the process—and had reminded Tingey forcefully that the payroll was not to be used for humanitarian purposes such as resolving hardships. None must be employed but for the advantage of the public, they had instructed, perhaps with a view to convincing congressional critics that a page was being turned. Who was to be employed, and how the public interest was to be defined, were on the other hand open to interpretation and negotiation.

Tingey had always deferred outwardly to ministerial authority over employment, even while striving (and often succeeding) to influence the decisions of the Navy secretaries. That would continue to be his practice, with the secretary as well as the board. An example will illustrate how some of the elements of a negotiation could work out. In early 1816, facing a second winter of unemployment and great hardship, some of the laid-off employees began to petition or even sue for what they saw as their rights. One of these was the yard's former cooper or barrel-maker, Thomas Murray, who had approached members of Congress for relief. When his case came to the attention of Secretary Crowninshield, he—finding no paper trail justifying Murray's earlier termination—asked Tingey to explain the situation. Tingey replied that salaried foremen like Murray had been laid off by an "imperative and positive" oral order of Secretary Jones shortly after the fire, but that he had managed—again with Jones' authority—to hire them back from time to time on a daily basis in the yard clean-up and salvage effort. "I have never considered," Tingey added, "that it was the intention of the Department for a total and final dismissal of the head mechanics from the service, but only a suspension."[19] Indeed, Tingey was looking for opportunities to bring his old men back onto the payroll, and saw this inquiry as an opportunity. Shortly afterward, he fortuitously discovered that a shipment of beef needed inspection, and recommended that Murray, "whose experience is not excelled," be rehired to do the job.[20] By this maneuver, the congressional inquiry was satisfied, the secretary's authority respected, and Tingey's restaffing objective served. But, by a strict definition, the "public interest" could have been better served by employing Murray on a daily basis, because the need for a full-time cooper was not yet pressing.

When it came to salary negotiations, Tingey generally took a less active role toward the commissioners, whose primary objective he knew was not to protect their workers, but rather to cut costs and establish a systemwide pay scale as far as possible. The commissioners most often took a tough line with any worker demands that they considered at all out of line, as was the case when a delegation of Washington mechanics came to their office to protest an early 1817 pay cut. The board journal notes (there apparently was no correspondence with Tingey on this issue) that the delegation was bluntly informed that they "received the same wages given at the two greatest ports of the United States, and even greater, and that those who were not satisfied were at free liberty to go elsewhere, and seek employment."[21] Tingey often pointed out to the commissioners that, as commandant, it was his duty to forward all legitimate and respectful requests for pay adjustments to the board for their decision. Still, his role was not entirely neutral. He could—and often did—give signals of his support (or lack of it) for the employees' petitions, while still satisfying them that their demands had been heard. It is hard to believe, for example, that an October 1815 petition from the joiners—in which they asked for a raise that would bring their wages in line with those in the private sector—would have been approved on the very same day if Tingey had not proffered some formal or off-the-record support for their request.

The master mechanics and clerks, all civilians who worked on salary rather than daily wages, were Tingey's assistants in managing the variety of activities under way at the yard, and he needed their cooperation. He routinely took up their cases with the board when he felt that they were deserving of promotion, increased wages, or allowances such as additional apprentices, and in return he had their loyalty and, with the usual exception of Benjamin King, excellent working relations with them all.

Tingey understood the difficult conditions in which the ordinary workmen, who were on daily wages, had to earn their living. With their wages dependent on the ebb and flow of activity at the yard, the vagaries of weather (rain or freezing weather could stop work and hence pay), wintertime reductions in force, and occasional pay cuts mandated by the commissioners, they lived precarious lives and were highly dependent on credit to get by in bad times. It was the wives and children, however, for whom Tingey felt the most sympathy—too many of the men, he was convinced, were prone to spend their money on drink and leave their families in desperate straits. When recommending an individual for employment, promotion, or extra allowances, in fact, his most common justifications were the man's steadiness and sobriety, or the needs of his large and hard-pressed family.

Tingey tried, as much as he could given the seasonal and sporadic nature of the workload, to provide steady employment for as many of the residents of Navy Yard Hill as he could. When work on a project began to taper off, he tried to switch the employees to other tasks or to promote a new project that would employ them. When cost cutting was necessary, his tendency was to recommend across-the-board pay cuts that spread the pain, rather than staff reductions that left some workers in distress. His success rate with the commission in making such arrangements was not particularly high, however: they were interested in efficiency, not welfare. But his arguments at least speak well for his empathy. On occasions when he wanted to find work for his crews, he argued that keeping the work force together was in the long-term benefit of the yard, but also that unemployment was causing "great distress of several industrious families," or that "excellent workmen with families of small children are in a state of Starvation and distress." New work, he argued would "relieve some poor women & children from deep affliction." Sometimes, the commissioners agreed to the changes Tingey wanted, but could not—in writing, at least—bring themselves to endorse his humanitarian arguments. The jobs were approved, but only if they conferred "advantage to the public."[22] The workers and their families knew, though, that their commandant cared for their welfare, which helps explain why to the major part of his civilian work force Tingey was both truly beloved and respectfully feared, the leadership traits that he had, years earlier, advised young midshipmen to strive for.

In spite of the uncertainty, competition for jobs at the yard was constant. It could also become unpleasant, and loaded with racial prejudice. White workers wanted the jobs for themselves, and feared that competition from enslaved and even free blacks dragged down the wage scale. Tingey's correspondence with the board indicates that racially based complaints were, after wage demands, the most frequent issue needing resolution. As in other areas of the yard's administration, the result was mixed: the board (like Secretary Smith before them) taking a nominally authoritative, pro-white stance, with Tingey and his colleagues arguing successfully for exceptions based on convenience or effectiveness. Black workers, both free and enslaved, continued to be hired in a number of the yard's departments throughout Tingey's administration, and beyond. The biggest concentration of black laborers continued to be in the caulking and painting shops, where many were free men, and in the smithies, where most were slaves—a number of whom were owned by salaried yard mechanics and clerks.

The expansion of the blacksmith operation to make all the Navy's anchors brought the problem to a head. To staff up the shop, the yard staff and Tingey preferred to rehire the old black (and mostly slave) sledgehammer men (or strikers), who—as John Davis of Abel, the master mechanic in charge at the time put it—"we found by long experience that Blacks have made the best Strikers in the execution of heavy work & are easily subjected to the Discipline of the Shop—& less able to leave us on any change of wages." The board did not agree, however, and, a few days later, as part of a circular to all navy yards, directed that no slaves or negroes (that is, freemen) were to be hired in any yard, except under exceptional circumstances subject to approval by the board. The circular explained this step with a vague claim that it was justified on account of "abuses having existed in some of the Navy yards by the introduction of improper Characters for improper purposes." Most likely, however, the step was dictated by white pressure for the jobs, as indicated by contemporary instructions to Tingey, John Cassin at Norfolk, and presumably other commandants, that every effort should be made to hire white men to replace the blacks fired by this order.[23]

The white replacements, however, did not work out well. As the shop continued to expand (soon it would also be making iron anchor cables for all new ships), Benjamin King complained that he wanted to rehire some of the old strikers to train the new white workers, who, he told Tingey, were "quite unaccustomed to such kind of work, and thereby endanger burning the iron in a heavy heat and thus to a certainty of spoiling the anchor."[24] The board, however, would not relent. Its policy against hiring blacks was restated in Article 27 of the new regulations for navy yards presented to Congress that April, wages for white strikers were raised, and Tingey and King were told to advertise locally and recruit in other cities for white men. All to little avail. Enough good men could not be found, or would not stay, and before long exceptions began to be granted. By 1821 King had seven black strikers hired under exceptions, but even those caused white workers to complain. Tingey kept the board from accepting all the gripes at face value, however: one complainer he called a drunken wife-beater whom he never wanted to see employed again; others, he claimed, were fired because they had run afoul of the law. In 1823 he fired all the black strikers to satisfy still another complaint to the board, but fairly soon, it seems, rehired them—including several whose pay, he claimed, was the only support of poor widows. The commandant's pragmatic and humane management style, typically, was taking a few of the hard edges off a policy decision by the board.

Expansion of the blacksmith shop was just one of the ways in which the mission of the Washington yard was being transformed by the commission. Taking advantage of the steam engine in place and the known technical skills of the Washington workforce, the commission gradually made Washington the prime supplier to the Navy for a range of products and services: anchors and chains, cambooses (or shipboard stoves), ships' pumps and fire-fighting equipment, blocks, brass work and lanterns, and small arms and ordnance testing. The blacksmith, plumbing (or brass-working), and block-makers' shops, plus a new armory and testing facility, began to rival shipbuilding and repair as the yard's most important set of activities.

Shipbuilding, all the same, continued to expand. A new frigate was begun in 1818, and wood was being stockpiled for yet another. In early 1819, the launching of the 74-gun *Columbus* gave Tingey and the yard's workers the first red-letter chance to celebrate their achievements since the fire. As the *National Intelligencer* gushed, "[T]he noble ship of the line *Columbus* glided from its bed in the navy yard of this city in the most majestic style, in the presence of many thousands of spectators who, in spite of unfavorable weather, had assembled to witness this interesting scene. . . . The vessel was greeted on its descent by a national salute from the artillery, by patriotic airs from the band of the marine corps, and by thousands of Columbians gathered together from every quarter of the Union."[25] The hull—not yet a ship—was then brought up to the wharf, where the joiners, plumbers, painters, and riggers spent another nine months finishing it inside, outside, and topside.

By December the crew for the *Columbus* was beginning to arrive, and was provided with lodging on receiving ships, rations, and suitable duties. But the ship was not yet ready for sea. Tingey and Doughty also faced a major problem, which was getting the ship across the bar at the mouth of the river. Silting had become such a problem over the decades, both in the Potomac and Anacostia Rivers, that, even without ballast, cannons, or supplies on board, the ship's draft would barely allow her to clear the bar.[26] In fact, when the effort was made at high tide in early December, the ship did not clear. She became stuck, requiring several days' strenuous effort to get her into the main stream. She was then guided down the Potomac to an anchorage off St. Mary's in Maryland, where she lay for another six-month period of supply and fitting-out, including some recaulking necessary because of seams that had opened when the ship was dragged over the bar. The inefficiency of this whole process, which involved shipping supplies and men up and down the river by chartered schooners, unfortunately cast a bit of a pall over the successful launch—as well as the future of the yard as a building location for large vessels.[27]

The commissioners were considering a new shipbuilding experiment for the yard. Since assuming office, they had been aware that the new congressional generosity to the Navy might result in more ships being built than were needed for routine peacetime patrols. They were faced with the same

dilemma that Jefferson and Latrobe had faced years before: how to protect out-of-service wooden ships from the elements. Not surprisingly, they
favored the same remedy—dry-docks—although not on such a grandiose
scale as the one Latrobe had designed. Captain Rodgers, in addition, had
proposed a cheaper, intermediate scheme that had been used in Europe. This
idea was a sort of two-way building slip, with wooden rails extending down
into the water that would permit ships to be both launched and dragged up
the ways onto dry land. In 1821 he succeeded in getting approval to make an
experimental "inclined plane" of this type in Washington. The location was
to be close to the one chosen earlier by Latrobe—the stretch of gravel bottom
at the eastern extremity of the yard's waterfront. To protect the ship's upper
works from the weather, a large shed, or ship house, also was approved.

While work on the *Columbus* progressed, first at the wharf and then
downriver, the shipwrights at the yard had a new set of projects. A new
44-gun frigate, the *Potomac*, was begun in August 1819, on the slipway
vacated by the *Columbus*. The next year, two small 12-gun schooners were
also started. The first of those, the *Shark*, was launched in May 1821 and—
much easier to finish and fit out than the ship of the line—was already ready
to sail in July. The second, the *Grampus*, was launched in August, while still
another schooner, the *Peacock*, was brought in for repairs to her hull. All of
these smaller vessels were being prepared for service in the Caribbean, where
the Navy was beginning aggressive patrols against troublesome pirates.

Almost as soon as the schooners were off the ways, the keel of a new
frigate, tentatively called the *Susquehanna*, was laid. Some six months later,
in March 1821, the half-completed *Potomac* was also launched. But by
autumn the latter was back on dry land, as the first ship to put the new
inclined plane to the test. The experiment went well, with the ship on blocks
being pulled up the rails by 140 men on the ropes, while President James
Monroe, members of Congress, diplomats, and other dignitaries witnessed
the new technology in action. It went so well, in fact, that Rodgers was able
to get approval in the 1823 budget for a permanent and improved version of
the inclined plane. The new version was designed to combine a dry-dock at
the tide line with a steam engine to pump it out, and a much sturdier marine
railway to bring vessels up onto the wharf. This was a major undertaking,
involving a great deal of pile-driving and earth-moving, which would suffer
setbacks and take a number of years to complete.

While the dry-dock and railway were being built, of course, the *Potomac*
was stranded up on the wharf, but work continued under the protection of
its boat shed. The second frigate was also rapidly taking shape. In addition,
a stream of small schooners, recently purchased by Captain John Rodgers
in preparation for his new duties as commodore of the Caribbean anti-

pirate squadron, came into the yard for repairs, equipping, or fitting out. Named whimsically the *Jackall*, *Beagle*, *Ferrier*, *Weasel*, and *Decoy*, they were intended for the close inshore work that the Navy's bigger warships could not deal with. While none of those projects imposed major demands on the yard's craftsmen, each had its peculiarities and special demands, and coordination of all the projects and supplies coming in and going out of the yard was a major responsibility for Tingey and his assistants.

The second frigate, renamed the *Brandywine*, was launched in March 1825 and fitted out over the coming months in a politically sensitive rush—which will be described in Chapter 11. Shortly after the launch, Doughty and his carpenters began to lay the keel and sternpost of yet another 44-gun frigate, to be called the *Columbia* in memory of the ship that had been burned in the yard in 1814. The old frigate *Congress*, which as Tingey recalled had last been repaired in the Washington yard some fourteen years previously, had come in once again for extensive repairs. Because of the cold winter and ice in the river, however, the work—which involved the hard and risky job of careening the hull on the shore—had to be put off until spring of 1826.

Ice and a heavy January snowstorm contributed to another delay, caused by the collapse of the coffer dam at the mouth of the new dry-dock. Efforts were made to repair the damage and pump out the dock, but several months later one of the dock walls began to fail as well. The new steam pump and its smokestack had to be quickly dismantled lest they fall into the river. When the second wall also began to fail, the dry-dock project was dropped for the time being. The new inclined railway remained usable, but all the same it took until September to relaunch the *Potomac*. "She went off the ways with probably more ease, but certainly less strain, than any ship of her magnitude ever did before," a relieved Tingey was able to report to Secretary of the Navy Samuel Southard.[28] In its place on the inclined plane, Doughty's men would soon begin to build the frame of the *St. Louis*, one of ten sloops of war that had recently been approved by Congress. The sloop was launched two years later, and was eased over the bar, fully loaded, just before Christmas 1828.

The sheer amount of shipbuilding that took place during those dozen years called for a high degree of coordination between Tingey, as commandant of the yard, and Doughty, in operational charge of the work crews. There were, to be sure, moments of disagreement and even of conflict. They had different opinions, for example, on repairs to the yard's tender. Doughty thought it could be patched together and still do its job, and the economy-minded commissioners sided with him—but Tingey, needing to transport heavy cannon from the Georgetown foundry, then refused to use a boat that he considered unsound. On another occasion, Tingey refused to accept requisitions from Doughty's deputy—trying to make the point, it would seem, that he would

CAPTAIN THOMAS TINGEY, C. 1820

(By John Trumbull; courtesy of Naval Art Center, Naval History and Heritage Command, and reproduced with permission of the owner, Eckford DeKay)

accept the naval constructor's authority over large elements of the work, but would not as commandant take orders from lower-ranking foremen.

On occasion, Doughty tried to ignore Tingey, which did not sit well with the touchy commandant. One such incident caused an uncharacteristic bleat from Tingey to the commissioners. "It is with great unwillingness I find myself compelled to state that I find an extraordinary and most unaccountable reluctance on Mr. Doughty to furnish any information or to comply with any instruction or request emanating from me. If I have no authority to call on Mr. Doughty for information, I shall be glad to have it certified by the Board," he complained. The issue was a minor one about information needed to make cost estimates, but its tone indicates a latent level of frustration and resentment on Tingey's part. The commissioners took his side: "Mr. Doughty is bound, as much as any other civil officer borne on the rolls of the Yard, to comply with your instructions relating to the public service," they answered. But two years later, a similar situation arose when Doughty refused to honor a request that he supply information requested by the board, writing Tingey a letter that the commissioners, when informed of it, called "highly improper. He ought not to have hesitated one moment to execute your order to prepare another draft."[29]

All in all, though, irritations of this sort are infrequent in the written record, and coordination apparently was adequate to both satisfy the commissioners and accomplish a remarkable amount of work. Tingey and Doughty were both professionals, and their disagreements did not hinder a fruitful cooperation.

As 1828 drew to a close, Commodore Tingey could take pride in the success of his yard. Almost fifteen years after it had burned to the ground, and in spite of the initial desire of the commissioners to close it down, it had expanded its importance to the Navy. No longer an important supply and repair yard, it had instead become specialized in the mechanical crafts and was the prime supplier of many essential shipboard items. Five major and two minor warships had been built at the yard, and the yard's labor force was the largest and most versatile labor pool in the national capital. The commandant remained one of the leading citizens of the city, a respected fixture at many ceremonial and civic events. Since the war, he had worked successfully with three secretaries of the Navy and nine naval commissioners, with no indication that, in spite of his advancing age, they questioned in any serious way his capacity to run the yard. He himself showed no inclination to retire, and it almost seemed that he could become a permanent feature of the city that had grown up around him and his navy yard.

CHAPTER ELEVEN

Patriarch

The Board of Naval Commissioners was only one of a number of new institutions that sprang up in Washington after the war. A new sense of national confidence was in the air. Americans had fought the mighty British to a draw, even defeated them roundly on the field of battle at New Orleans, and were poised for a period of consolidation and growth. When local citizens, Thomas Law among them, stepped forward with a promise to build a temporary building for the homeless Congress, that body decisively turned aside the lingering but persistent attempts to relocate the nation's capital away from the Potomac.

Rebuilding began rapidly—not only at the navy yard, but across the town, and expansion soon followed, both private and public. The war's mistakes had taught the administration that it could not defend or govern a growing nation well without more national institutions. Penny-pinching was by no means abandoned, but patriotism and national growth were in the air. The military was once again respected, with the result that a number of the new institutions established in Washington were military ones such as the naval commission, an expanded Army ordnance department, a topographical department, and a general land office.

Captain Tingey was pleased at the prospect of an expanded naval community. Over the years, many of his colleagues had come through Washington on business, a number of them for extended periods as they supervised the fitting-out of their new commands, and he had managed to strike up friendships with most of them. In a service replete with personal rivalries and impetuous, competitive men, Tingey's ability to remain on amicable terms with his colleagues was unusual indeed. Hospitable and gregarious, he welcomed courtesy calls and even opened his house to his colleagues. When he learned that Isaac Hull was joining the new commission, for example, he forwarded an offer to host: "he must quarter with me, and I'll give his good wife the first mess of green peas. I have them already three inches height."[1] He was disappointed in that offer, however, because Mrs. Hull never came to Washington and Hull himself found quarters nearer to the commission offices during the few months he served in the city. John Rodgers' choice to set up house in Georgetown, was another disappointment, in that opportunities for informal contact with his old friend would be limited.

The presence of the commissioners, on the other hand, was a mixed blessing, which over time would serve to diminish Tingey's standing in the community. The commodore was now only one of several senior officers in town, and he was an old shoe—elderly and familiar—whereas the newly arrived captains were younger, war heroes, and rich with honors and prize money. The newcomers rapidly assumed leading places in the town's more elegant society, and took impressive houses in the fashionable quarters: Stephen Decatur near the White House, and David Porter just up Sixteenth Street on what became known as Meridian Hill. Physical and social distance plus the inevitable strains of the work situation, it would seem, eventually made the relationship between Tingey and the commissioners more of a collaborative necessity than a friendly partnership.

The new commissioners, determined to establish their reformist authority at the start, had taken two early actions that could not have been appreciated by Tingey. First was the decision to downgrade the Washington yard to a shipbuilding facility only, and second was their warning to the commandant that they would not approve hiring based on anything other than their definition of the public interest—that is, economy and efficiency. Annoyed, Tingey nonetheless played for time. He applied for a long-delayed leave of absence, and informed the commissioners, just six weeks after they had set up shop, that Secretary Crowninshield had approved his taking a long vacation. He would be stopping at naval yards along the eastern coast as he traveled, he assured them, and would give "prompt attention" to any communications they felt it necessary to send him.

Tingey's intent, beyond perhaps getting away from the commissioners for the moment, was to visit his northern family. The unfortunate death of Ann Dulany Tingey in the spring of 1814 had plunged Tingey once again into a bachelor life, enlivened in a family sense only by the occasional visits to or from his daughter Sarah and her family, which now included two wartime babies, Mary and Daniel French Dulany. The trip to Maine would provide opportunities for visits with both the Cravens and the Wingates. Hannah and Tunis Craven and their children Margaretta, Anna Maria, Thomas, and Alfred had left Washington in 1812 for Tunis' job at the navy yard in Portsmouth. (Another child, Tunis Augustus Macdonough Craven, was born in Portsmouth at the beginning of 1813.) Tingey undoubtedly missed them; they had filled the commandant's house with the company that he always relished. But then, in Maine with the Wingates, he would be able to visit with a daughter he had not seen for years and her two new children, Julia Nesbit and the just-born Sydney Ellen.

Leaving the yard in mid-June 1815, he visited Philadelphia, Boston, Portsmouth, and Bath, Maine, returning to work by the first week of September. The visit, "shorter than I could wish," according to Margaret Gay (who was also a bit troubled by his "unusual silences") must have been a pleasant interlude, with professional concerns pushed to the background during numerous family gatherings. The celebrations did not cover his birthday, however, which fell just after his return to Washington. That occasion was marked by an affectionate "rondomontade" sent by Margaret Gay:

> *How blest the age of sixty-four*
> *When former cares return no more,*
> *When life in retrospect appears*
> *A series of distinguished years,*
> *When nature buds in early youth*
> *Where Virtue, Honor, Wisdom, Truth,*
> *When Justice, most triumphant shone,*
> *And Feeling marked him for her own*
> *With heart most meek and debonair,*
> *Yet courage chose her empire there. . . .*
> *Then blest the age of sixty-four,*
> *When clouds and storms arise no more—*
> *Tranquil the eve of life appears*
> *And Tingey glories in his years.*[2]

Whether in Washington, Philadelphia, New Jersey, or Maine, Tingey was involved with family: he had become patriarch and promoter of a growing family network. Margaret's and his daughters were now firmly established (if not uniformly prosperous), and their new extended families and relatives had also become their father's. A new set of opportunities as well as responsibilities had been created. Even before he left for Maine, for example, Tingey had helped arrange the assignment of Timothy Winn as purser at the Washington yard. Winn was an in-law relation through his marriage to Rebecca Dulany, a sister of Tingey's late wife Ann. In an era when family sponsorship and patronage were accepted parts of the appointment process, Winn's appointment was scarcely controversial—certainly not as much as had been Tingey's earlier effort to land the same job for his son-in-law, Joseph Wingate. Winn was already an established naval purser, and he would hold the Washington yard job without controversy until his death, while also becoming an investor in local businesses.[3] Other, younger Dulany relatives had already entered into Navy careers by the time Tingey married into their family, and his ability to intervene on their behalf would be useful to their careers as well. Among these were Bladen Dulany, Ann's younger brother, and French and Dulany Forrest, both Ann's nephews.

Nor had Tingey forgotten to mentor the relatives of his first wife, Margaret Murdoch. Shortly after his return, he petitioned the Navy secretary to have his great nephew, midshipman John Kelly (grandson of Mary Murdoch Beale) assigned to the USS *Java*. The assignment was made, helping the young man advance in a career that eventually led to the rank of commodore. Still another grandson of Mary Beale, George Beale Jr., also saw Navy service, having been appointed purser back in 1813. As with the Dulany relatives, Tingey's hand in facilitating young Kelly's and Beale's appointments as midshipmen and beyond can be guessed at, but not often documented.

At the yard, work was progressing at the time on two fronts: learning to cope with the increasing paper documentation required by the commissioners, and completing the first round of repairs to the buildings and perimeter wall so as to enable work to proceed over the coming winter in reasonable comfort and security. Tingey's bad experience over the pillage of the yard—particularly his home—at the time of the fire had made him even more than usually concerned over security. He had advertised for a no-questions-asked return of his stolen property, but little had shown up, and the experience appears to have soured his view of his neighbors.

All the same, it was a time in Washington and Navy circles for renewal and celebration. Repairs had begun on the Capitol and White House, the theater and dancing assemblies had reopened, the president had joined in praise for the Navy, money was being appropriated for rebuilding, and the mood was triumphant. Tingey, once again a bachelor but fond as ever of good cheer, hosted lively dinner parties at which, according to Mrs. Crowninshield, the guests "always have high times." The late 1815 visit of the hero of New Orleans, Andrew Jackson, capped a celebratory social year. Tingey was, naturally, on the committee to organize the ball of the season. He informed Margaret Gay of the ladies' intense preparations for the event: "I do not believe there is a mantua maker, a milliner, or a taylor who is not engaged for the occasion and must work night and day," he wrote, even while fretting that the ball might not live up to the expectations of the town's giddily patriotic celebrants.[4]

Tingey's daughters had begun to conspire, at about the same time, on a way to change their father's situation as widower. Sarah, who brought her children to the city from time to time to amuse their grandfather, must have reported to her sisters that their father was lonely. By spring 1816, the conspiracy was hatched, and Tingey apprised of their conclusions: they thought that he should remarry, and had some suggestions. Sarah and Hannah, he reported to Margaret Gay, "appear to feel anxious for me to be once again united to a faithful friend—Alas my darling how is that to be expected at my day? . . . The persons they have severally hinted at are as far as I know them, most excellent and respectable women, yet I think not that either would exactly suit."[5]

But he was not to fend off his daughters—or the idea—so lightly. Some months later, he showed that he was willing to consider their idea, and maybe even their suggestions for a match. At the end of that year he visited Hannah in New Jersey at Willow Hill, the home of Tunis Craven's family. It was a successful family visit, it seems. On his return to Washington, he wrote to Margaret Gay conceding his surrender. Since all three daughters "have fixed their minds on the same object," he acknowledged, he had "written to X at Willow Hill . . . [and] on receipt of her answer you shall know the result."[6]

The lady in question was Tunis Craven's own sister Ann Evelina, unmarried at age thirty. She and her family knew Tingey well; he had been a supportive father-in-law to Tunis during the young man's personal difficulties, and a second family tie could be mutually useful to both families. Ann accepted the commodore's offer, possibly during a short leave he took in April. They were married 19 May 1817, possibly in New Jersey but equally possibly in Washington, where Hannah had given birth just six days earlier to the commodore's latest grandchild, Charles Edmiston Craven.[7] With Sarah and "all her noisy animals" also visiting, the commandant's house at the yard was once again alive with women, children, and commotion, and the genial patriarch would no longer have to maintain a lonely bachelor existence. Moreover, his marriage to Ann Craven, while no romantic match, proved to be a solid and sympathetic union.

Tingey had had to make quick round trips to New Jersey because his deputy, Nathaniel Haraden, was declining both physically and mentally. "The imbecility of poor Haraden has long since thrown the whole of his duty on me," Tingey wrote to Margaret Gay just weeks after his marriage.[8] Haraden soon retired, to be replaced by a welcome face: Master Commandant Stephen Cassin, the son of Tingey's old colleague John Cassin. Theirs was a good collaboration, enabling Tingey to oversee the expansion of the yard's shipbuilding and mechanical activities effectively, deal with the ever-increasing paperwork, and even take leisurely vacations in Philadelphia and New Jersey over the next few years.

Over time, however, Cassin's attention became more and more focused on an ancillary duty as the yard's ordnance expert, leaving Tingey—even while claiming he was not "an advocate for a superabundance of officers"—to feel the need of another senior hand to assist him in managing the yard.[9] His timing was bad, unfortunately: the financial panic of 1819 had caused a serious recession, and Congress was once again determined to cut back expenditures. In the post-war climate, however, the commissioners had support in defending the Navy's interests, and fought back with some success. While agreeing to get rid of some of the ships and equipment left over from the war, they inundated the legislators with figures that justified the work and the staffing of the yards—which in the case of the Washington yard was thirty-four uniformed and 380 civilian employees. All those statistics that Tingey and his colleagues had been gathering so laboriously now helped to justify the Navy's case, and Congress mandated no general reduction of staff. But current appropriations were cut anyway. Pay cuts and periodic layoffs became necessary, and Tingey did not get the second officer he had hoped for. When Cassin left in early 1822 to command the schooner *Peacock* in the West Indies, his successor, Alexander Wadsworth, did not take on the extra ordnance duties, and Tingey consequently felt less strain.

Tingey's request for additional help may have been dictated as well by a simple fact: his normally robust health was beginning to slip. For more than a decade, his only health complaint had been about recurring autumn bouts of what he called influenza, which caused him to "suffer more than people generally [do] by those unpleasant disorders," as he had confided once to Truxtun.[10] In the summer of 1820, he once again made a long summertime visit to his family in the north, and on his return to Washington reported that he was suffering from his usual complaint. He was still able to recover rapidly. That winter saw him as active as ever in his civic enthusiasms: heading up the dancing assembly, presiding at commemorative dinners, or taking his sleigh to make Sunday after-church calls on congressmen. But it was his last year of routinely good health. The following autumn, his usual "indisposition" seems to have turned into a serious illness: Cassin signed all the correspondence for six weeks even though Tingey was still present. Increasingly, too, he was dictating rather than writing his official letters, and at the same time his distinctive signature was becoming less and less emphatic, more and more shaky. In short, he was beginning to show his age.

His management at the yard nonetheless remained solid. His letters to the commissioners—often several a day—continued to show full awareness of all the major activities under way, and clarity of thought in addressing them. Things did occasionally slip, in spite of having more clerks to help keep track of the details, and exchanges with the commissioners did occasionally get testy. But if Tingey had any serious difference with the commissioners—and the record shows none—it would have stemmed more basically from having different underlying priorities. The commandant's desire was to accomplish his assigned work at the yard with maximum efficiency, while the commissioners wanted to create a Navy-wide system that achieved overall cost effectiveness. The two outlooks did not always mesh, but Tingey dutifully toed the line when called to task. And the work got done.

Work there certainly was. *Columbus* was gone, but the two schooners and then the two frigates kept the crews fully employed. Work at the forges and smithies continued to expand. It had become the second major element of the yard's work, employing almost a fifth of the yard's labor force by 1820 in fabricating chain cables and anchors. Major construction projects were also under way on the inclined plane, the armorer's shop, and a new warehouse. Tingey squabbled with the commissioners over the placement of the warehouse, which they wanted to build onto the eastern wall to save money. Tingey insisted that it stand free of the wall, to deter the neighborhood thieves from gaining access. He prevailed. With ever-increasing inventories of valuable supplies on the property, Tingey sought to increase security by raising the perimeter wall, and even extending the eastern wall into the river to block entry across the mudflats. He also strove to clarify his control over the forty-man Marine detachment assigned to the yard, which had been put under his command.

Pilferage had been a concern of Tingey's from the day back in 1800 when he insisted on construction of the first perimeter wall. The speed with which the neighbors had pillaged the yard in 1814 only increased his concerns on this score, and apparently contributed to a healthy cynicism on his part about the moral condition of many of his employees and neighbors. He complained that the yard's laborers, or "the poorer classes (being the majority of the persons employed here) . . . seldom fail to spend the next day after receiving their wages in a constant state of idleness and inebriation, and thus the wives and children are always nearly in a state of beggary and starvation." Such men, he felt, were all too prone to try their hand at pilferage, and the Marine guards entrusted to protect the property were scarcely better. "It is not a very common case, to find a strictly sober sentry on post at evening, or indeed at any time after the middle of the day," he wrote to the commissioners. Moreover, he added, hiring watchmen from "persons residing in this neighborhood" would not resolve the problem, as their "moral characters generally are little, if anything, superior to the marines, and having mostly families to support, have still greater inducements, and more interested accomplices, to facilitate acts of pillage."[11]

What is interesting in his correspondence on this subject is how Tingey's evident distrust of many of his workmen and neighbors is balanced by sympathy for the condition of their families. He evidently knew first-hand the qualities of many of the employees and had distinct opinions about some, not all of them positive. But even though maintaining order was a prime concern in running an establishment like the navy yard, he did not have a free hand in ordering punishment for infractions of the rules. Responsibility for discipline among the civilians was first of all in the hands of the foremen, who had primary authority to fire or punish individuals for cause. Over the uniformed men, Tingey had greater authority, but even there he could apply it only in accordance with the rules of the service. In the Navy, corporal punishment was a normal means to enforce discipline, and Tingey did not flinch from seeing it used against enlisted men or slaves. Blows with a knotted rope, or "starter," were apparently routine incentives to work, or laid on as the cost of misbehavior. More-severe punishment, on the other hand, had to go by the Navy's formal rules and procedures. Tingey could be harsh, but the humane streak he showed in his concern for the workers' families was also evident in his treatment of the uniformed employees. In the case of a Marine who struck a black cook in an attack that Tingey considered outrageous, for example, he opted for leniency when the attacker sobered up and begged for mercy, saying, "I confess myself no friend to the lash, when a delinquent can be made sensible to his error."[12]

Court martials and inquiries were common at a naval establishment such as the yard; because they were matters of public record, they also could be politically and administratively touchy. Sensitive as usual to any derogation of his authority, Tingey complained at one point to the secretary that the report of a court martial held at the yard and under his authority had not been submitted through him. ("I hope I shall not be deemed fastidious on a point of etiquette," he delicately prefaced his demand.)[13] Less than a year later, Tingey would himself preside at two court martials that were much more sensitive, as they touched on the honor, not only of the persons under trial, but also of the service. The trials, which took place in Boston and lasted from March to May 1822, involved charges against Captain John Shaw for demeaning his commodore, Isaac Hull. Tingey had been chosen to preside, as an officer senior to Shaw who had no known prejudice toward the case. His chairmanship was apparently unexceptional, and though Shaw was convicted, it was for a minor offense.

But the most sensitive case on which Tingey served was the 1825 court martial of Commodore David Porter, who had angered the administration when his men invaded the Spanish Puerto Rican town of Fajardo on flimsy pretexts. The case was important for the Navy because Porter, in addition, had taken positions that verged on insubordination toward the Navy's civilian leadership. Navy Secretary Samuel Southard wanted a conviction; the case was closely followed by the national press, much of it sympathetic to Porter. Presiding was Captain James Barron, who held grudges against most of his Navy colleagues, including Tingey for his role in 1805 as the second for John Rodgers in the duel that never took place. Tingey, who was friendly with Porter, thus found himself caught in a political squeeze of the kind he preferred to avoid. He tried to extricate himself from the uncomfortable situation by pointing out that work at the yard was suffering from his prolonged duty on the court (the trial lasted forty days), but he was not excused. Porter was found guilty and was suspended from the Navy for six months, but resigned in anger to become commander of the Mexican navy.

Tingey was indeed needed at the yard that summer, because the establishment was in a frenzy of preparation for another politically significant event. General Lafayette, one of the few remaining revolutionary generals, the friend of Washington and a living symbol of the old French alliance, had been making a triumphal tour of America for the past year. His return to France, President Adams had decided, would be made with much ceremony and symbolism on an American warship, the frigate *Susquehanna*—now renamed the *Brandywine* in honor of Lafayette's first American battle. The only problem was that the decision had been made belatedly and the ship was not at all ready—the hull had been launched (with the president on board) only in late June. It became Tingey's job to see that the deadline was met. That meant borrowing equipment from other vessels (masts, spars, hawsers, and boats from the *Potomac*, sails from the *Congress*, and so on), fitting out the cabin with special furniture, curtains, and fixtures, and generally reordering priorities at the yard to get the president's wish completed satisfactorily and on time. The ship went over the Potomac bar without too much trouble at the end of July, and was fitted out over the summer weeks at St. Mary's. In early September the ship was ready, the honored guest left Washington in a blizzard of speeches and music, received a cannon salute as his launch passed the navy yard, and joined the *Brandywine* for his trip home. Work at the yard could finally return to normal.

Almost a year earlier, at the beginning of the "year of uninterrupted festivity and enjoyment inspired by your presence," as President John Quincy Adams put it his farewell speech to Lafayette, the French guest had visited the navy yard. Not once, but twice. On the more official visit, he had been accompanied by then–President Monroe for a tour of the yard and dinner at Tingey's house. But, on a more interesting personal level, Lafayette had visited the yard ten days earlier, at Tingey's invitation. The key event of that visit had been tea at the Tingey house, to which Ann Tingey had invited a

USS *Brandywine*, launched at Washington, 1825
(Courtesy of Naval Art Center, Naval History and Heritage Command)

number of the "first circle" ladies of the city, to meet the hero of the day in an intimate setting.

The event illuminates the important role the third Mrs. Tingey had come to play in her husband's life. Ann Tingey unfortunately left no personal documents that disclose her character, but her obituary describes her as "one who possessed in an unusual degree the esteem and affection of all who knew her. Her life was marked by deeds of benevolence, and many . . . have had impressive evidence of her deep sympathy for the poor and needy."[14] Glimpses of a hospitable and cultured woman can be seen in the contributions she soon made to the old widower's lifestyle. Improvements were made to the house, the couple subscribed to a project to open an art studio and gallery, they contributed to a fund to open new schools on the Lancastrian model, and Mrs. Tingey herself sat on the board of the recently established girls' orphanage. Apart from the orphanage, these were activities with which Tingey had some familiarity. He had had his portrait painted, and had contributed to the public schools from their inception, even sitting on the board—but those activities had mostly been before the illness and death of Margaret, his first wife, some fifteen years earlier. Ann Tingey, it seems, had brought new energy and purpose, and had reinvigorated life—familial, cultural, and social—at the commandant's house.

That is not to suggest that Tingey had been a social recluse during his widowhood. It was not in his character, and, moreover, his presence and organizing skill were always in demand at the banquets, balls, and celebrations of the capital city. Both his position and his personality led to his having a full social life, but once again he could enjoy it in the company of a wife. One can sense his pleasure at such events from this description of a "most splendid ball and entertainment" given by Colonel Henderson of the Marines, and attended by "nearly all the respectable males and females that now fill our city with youth and beauty, gaiety and gravity. I of course was there, with a part of the household."[15]

The commandant's house had become a lively gathering place for the Tingey family, their friends, and colleagues. Sarah and her children—what Margaret Gay called her "infant tribe"—visited most frequently, and Tingey also rode out to the Dulany farm on his occasional days off. (He called Oak Hill, the Dulany farm, "Poverty Hill"—facetiously it seems, since the Dulanys were the only one of his daughters' families that were doing well financially.) There also appears to have been a considerable amount of visiting back and forth from members of the Craven family in New Jersey, and even occasionally from Hannah and her children who lived in Portsmouth (or later in the Brooklyn navy yard, when Tunis was transferred there). Margaret Gay was able to make the long trip down from Maine less frequently. She did come in the fall of 1822, her father having sent a joking letter to Joseph Wingate authorizing a visit by "the ship Margaret Gay, under the care and conduct of her old proprietor and Commander."[16] When she left just before Christmas that year, her eleven-year-old daughter Virginia stayed behind in Washington so she could attend school. Five years later, the fourteen-year-old Dulany daughter, Mary, similarly began to live in the commandant's house regularly so she could go to school in Washington. Ann Tingey appears to have been a kind and affectionate hostess to all.

Tingey had had a reputation, back on the *Ganges*, of offering good hospitality and now that he could depend on an obliging wife, a large house, and multiple servants, he entertained frequently. "All our Bath and Maine friends, that is those with whom I have any acquaintance, have all dined with me," he wrote to Margaret Gay. He urged her to travel to Washington, because "we want to have the house well filled this winter," and boasted in the fall of 1825 that they were hosting no fewer than twenty-three people.[17] Unfortunately, though, these family reunions were not always entirely joyous. Of the twenty-three in the house that fall, two (Hannah Craven and Daniel Dulany senior) were ill, and Tingey himself was suffering from his usual "influenza." Even sadder two years later was the death of Anna Maria Craven, who had been born in the old Tingey house on G Street almost twenty-two years earlier. She died in late September 1827 while visiting her grandfather, and was buried in the Congressional Cemetery that he had helped establish.

The commandant's house, a substantial, center-hall building on the highest point of the navy yard compound, was an island of domesticity for Tingey yet a place from which he could keep a close watch on work in the yard. He took great interest in the large garden that was attached, and boasted of the vegetables and fruit it produced. The house itself appears to have been simply but amply furnished. In the inventory of his estate, what stands out is the amount of china, glassware, and kitchen equipment kept on hand—surely another sign of the extensive entertaining that took place. A number of outbuildings, including a carriage house and small stable, made that corner of the yard into the commandant's little enclave, yet a place that was thoroughly integrated into the life of the yard.[18]

Living as he did in the big house on the compound, working often from his home but with his office only a short stroll down the main road, and enjoying a twenty-year familiarity with the place and indeed many of the workers, it is scarcely surprising that Tingey was seen by his men as an avuncular figure. In fact, he actually was uncle to two young lieutenants who worked at the yard. Dulany Forrest, a nephew who had distinguished

TINGEY HOUSE, WASHINGTON NAVY YARD, C. 1820
(Courtesy of Naval Art Center, Naval History and Heritage Command)

himself in battle during the 1812 war, was made commander of the navy yard tender in 1822, while his brother, French Forrest, also served at the yard during the same period. Along with Timothy Winn, these relatives presumably had easy access to the commandant's house, but from the absence of any indication to the contrary it can be assumed that Tingey kept his day-to-day dealings with them on a strictly professional level. It may have been easier, in fact, for him to openly assist those of his relatives who lived and worked at a greater distance. His sponsorship of the early Navy careers of his nephew John Kelly, and his grandsons Thomas Tingey Craven and Tunis A. M. Craven, was open and successful; launched on their careers with his assistance, all three eventually reached senior rank.[19]

The Navy had always been considered a gentlemanly and honorable profession, even in its most neglected days, and now Tingey could truly take pride in its resurgence to respectability. His own career, though short on battle heroics, had been entirely honorable, and was an evident model for members of the upcoming generation looking for a respectable career. Margaret Gay wrote that his Craven grandson, Thomas, even called himself "commodore," but that it was his granddaughter Virginia Wingate, who "inherits all your self command . . . and resolution."[20] His had become a naval family. Two other grandchildren, in fact, also had Navy careers of a sort: Henry Wingate, who served as lieutenant for a short time in the 1840s, and Margaretta Craven, who married a short-lived naval officer named Francis Sanderson. Tingey's first family in America, the Murdochs, had been merchant seamen but his later relatives in the Craven, Wingate, and Dulany families had seen him as a naval officer, and were attracted to the career by his example.

His family responsibilities extended, of course, beyond Navy business. He tried to help his sons-in-law make their way, but it was not always easy. The various business projects concocted by Tunis Craven, Joseph Wingate, and occasionally George Beale, never seemed to bring much success, and in 1817 Craven was once again in debt—this time to Wingate, among others. Tingey, "having suffered by that business so unpleasantly and from which embarrassment [I] have but very lately been extricated," as he explained to Wingate, would not step in. That problem eventually was resolved, but Wingate in turn became a source of discomfort. He had obtained the post of collector of customs at Bath, normally a comfortable sinecure. But Wingate was apparently given to political feuding of a nature that aggravated a personality already given to "extreme feeling," as Margaret Gay delicately phrased it. "[T]here were moments," she wrote, "when he would appear to lose all hope." Exactly what the issues were is unclear, but his father-in-law felt it necessary to advise him against getting involved in political maneuvers:

"as an officer in the service of the General Government, mind your own business in preference to all others!" The feuds persisted, however, and when Wingate's customs appointment was up for renewal in Senate in 1824, his enemies opposed it with charges that ships in which he had invested during the 1812 war had engaged in illegal trade. Wingate enlisted his father-in-law's help, and Tingey tried to act as a mediator with "several of my particular friends in the Senate," but he was too late. The vote was being taken even as the commodore appeared at the Capitol, and Wingate's candidacy was crushed on the last day of the session. Tingey would not—indeed could not, given his position—take up Wingate's cause. He limited himself to expressions of concern and solace. "Don't let your chagrin on this business cause you much uneasiness," he wrote the same day, adding on the following day that, though "your enemies become triumphant . . . this triumph I presage will not be of long duration to them."[21] He was, in the end, right: Wingate was elected to Congress in 1827 and served two terms.

With Daniel Dulany, on the other hand, matters were much less complicated. Visits between members of the two households were relatively frequent. "I know nothing delights both Sarah and Mr. D so much as a visit from you—they both mentioned your trip on horse back with great pleasure," wrote Hannah.[22] Focused as he was on developing his farm, Dulany did little or no business with the government or the navy yard, and his major business involvement with Tingey concerned the court cases and land sales connected with settling the estate of Ann Bladen Tingey.

Another close family tie remained that with his first wife's nephew George Beale, who continued to be an occasional contractor to the navy yard and who also was involved in various business schemes with Craven and Wingate. George Beale Jr., the son, had spent a few years as a naval purser, but then settled in Washington, probably in late 1818. His courtship of Emily Truxtun, the daughter of Tingey's old friend Thomas Truxtun, brought the two delighted old captains together again in a sort of collaboration to facilitate the marriage. When the young couple was married in 1819, it cemented that old friendship while expanding family ties; before long Ann Tingey, Emily, and her mother Gertrude Truxtun were exchanging visits in New Jersey and Washington.[23]

In 1823 the senior Beale, who was eight years younger than Tingey, died at his son's house in Georgetown. Old colleagues were passing from the scene. Tingey's navy yard colleague John Cassin, who also was younger, had died a year earlier. Tingey ranked fourth among the Navy's captains, but younger colleagues like John Rodgers and William Bainbridge had long ago passed him, and now he could see an entirely new generation claiming its place. He had helped many, among them Cassin's sons Stephen and

Joseph (the latter a purser whom Tingey had helped get a position on the *Columbus*). Visits by Lieutenant John Dale, a fellow whom he "used to dandle on my knee" brought home to Tingey the point of his advancing age. He wrote nostalgically to the father, his old friend Richard Dale, about his sixty years of sea duty, the deaths of their colleagues, and "reminiscences of our former social days [that] occupy my earnest and most pleasing thoughts."[24]

By 1825, indeed, Tingey's good health was beginning to desert him. His absences from the office due to "indipositions" were more frequent and longer, and while he was often able to work from home, excuses were increasingly offered for delays, forgetfulness, or even inability to attend to matters. The situation was not chronic, however: most of the periods of illness fell during the cold weather when work at the yard was slow. The first ten days of September 1826 were a case in point. The commandant's clerk, Mordecai Booth, reported to the commissioners that Tingey was confined to his room because of "extream indisposition," and Tingey reported that he had been obliged to watch the launching of the *Potomac* from his bedroom window.[25] Yet by the end of the period, his detailed reporting picked up where it had left off, and was as crisp and business-like as ever (although most of it by this time was dictated, and his signature more shaky and spidery than ever).

That Secretary Southard and his colleagues continued to respect Tingey's work was made clear in the spring of 1827, when vacancies on the board of commissioners led to his name being considered as a potential member. Tingey was not interested. He had work to do—Congress had recently passed an authorization for more ships, a sloop of war and a frigate were on the ways at the yard, and long-awaited landfill, wharf repair, and building projects had been approved. He had no desire to change jobs or move, and let it be known. President Adams delayed making a final decision, having learned from the Marine commandant about "the reluctance with which Commodore Tingey quits the station for the office of Commissioner of the Navy, and of the regrets of the inhabitants at the yard upon his leaving them." Hoping perhaps that the appointment would not go through, Tingey took a six-week trip north, visiting the Brooklyn navy yard for sure and possibly reaching as far north as Maine. On his return to Washington in late August, he wrote to Margaret Gay optimistically that the secretary "left no instructions relative to new duties for me. I consider myself still attached to my old station and do hope I shall not be urged to change it." But he was wrong. The board needed a senior captain, Tingey was available and was not capable of sea duty, and the president and secretary could delay no longer. Tingey was made a commissioner, and began sitting with his colleagues in mid-September. But it turned out to be only an interlude: by the end of October he had been released back to his old job.[26]

Somehow, Tingey had persuaded the secretary and the president to reverse their decision. President Adams gave several reasons when he wrote up the affair in his journal: "Commodore Rodgers, since his return from the command of the squadron in the Mediterranean, has been re-commissioned to the Board. But Tingey is extremely desirous of withdrawing from the Board and going back to his command at the navy yard here, particularly as there is an unsettled question of rank between him and Rodgers, which may slumber unless they are brought together as members of the same Commission." The first reason—Tingey's preference for the job (and the house) at the yard—is undoubtedly true. But whether Tingey, outwardly one of the less status-proud captains in the Navy, would really have balked at working for his old friend Rodgers is less clear, as is his pretension to actually be the senior officer. Perhaps that was simply a pretext. It if was, it served its purpose; Tingey was back at the yard.[27]

He arrived back at the yard just in time to make plans for implementation of a commission order he had probably helped draft while serving on the board: that the Washington yard would henceforth be the Navy's prime supplier of a whole range of metal, mechanical, and technical supplies. He queried his branch chiefs as to what they needed to put the plan into operation, received the predictable answers (more men, more machines), and began gradual implementation. The steam machine was to be made stronger, trip hammers and bellows added, the block-maker machinery increased, the armory expanded, and many other changes started that would make the yard into a true industrial site. Even so, shipbuilding continued side by side with the new industrial emphasis, the lumber storage areas and lumber docks were improved, and in late summer of the next year the sloop *St. Louis* was finally launched.

The launching tuned into a sort of comedy, though it was not intended as such. With the president, the commissioners, and other dignitaries present amidst the usual decoration and ceremony, at the designated moment the ship refused to move down the ways—hung up on a misdriven ribbing nail. John Rodgers, ever a Type A leader, solved the problem by having every available worker and sailor climb up onto the ship with him, and jump up and down on the quarterdeck to his cries of, "Shake yourselves, my brave fellows, and dance her down, for she must go down."[28] Finally, the vessel came free and slid into the river, presumably to the merriment of all. All, perhaps, but Tingey, who must have been a bit embarrassed by the circumstance. And he did not yet know that the ship would be a further embarrassment to him and the yard.

Fitted out and fully loaded with ballast and cannon, the *St. Louis* passed over the bar in late December and proceeded to Norfolk for sea trials and final

WASHINGTON NAVY YARD, 1840, SHOWING BOAT SHEDS
(Courtesy of Naval Art Center, Naval History and Heritage Command)

preparations. But, according to her captain John Sloat, she had been badly caulked above the water line. The squadron commodore, James Barron, took up Sloat's complaint with some vehemence, sending along some samples of faulty oakum to the commission and demanding an explanation. Nor were the commissioners gentle in demanding answers from Tingey. "This fact is calculated to bring the reputation of the yard seriously into question," they charged, adding that they would welcome explanations but "it is impossible to resist the interpretation that this has been great neglect, should Capt. Sloat's opinion prove to be correct."[29]

Tingey, as was typical when a matter was raised that might reflect on his honor, fought back. He admitted that the state of his health had not allowed him to oversee the work directly, "not that I pretend to arrogate to myself infallibility in having the duties performed." But the oakum used, he claimed (with written affidavits of support from Doughty and the chief carpenter), was fully up to standard and approved by the board. He also noted that Sloat had been present during the entire process, and had even been told that the ship might need recaulking. As to Sloat's complaints, he dismissed them scornfully by commenting, "I have in a long life seen much more of the state and condition of new ships than that officer, & scarcely ever knew one, that went perfect tight to sea, the first time."[30]

It was Tingey's last tussle with the commissioners, and it was one he would neither win nor lose. His health had deteriorated further; he could no longer stay outdoors to make surveys or supervise the work, and his bad health had kept him out of the office for more than a month in the fall. (His physical disabilities and consequent lack of first-hand attention also may have contributed to a deterioration in the yard's order and appearance, which was criticized by his successor.) Tingey continued all the same to correspond actively with the commissioners and the secretary's office, on matters large and small. One request he made was one he perhaps should have made years previously, as no other navy yard commanders carried responsibilities similar to his: he asked to be relieved of the extra duty of serving as naval agent. He concluded his appeal with a summation of his condition, saying that in "justice to myself in my present infirm state, and approximating the close of my seventy-eighth year, I am incapable of the lively energy of a youthful seaman and require some relaxation, at least from the multiplicity of cares these double duties require. I am therefore constrained to solicit your further endeavors to have me released from the duties of the agency altogether."[31] The request was promptly granted, but Tingey never found the relaxation he had hoped for. Two weeks later, he affixed his spidery signature on the last letter he would send to the commissioners. Number 3133, it dealt with the mundane task of sending some shipbuilding patterns to the navy yard at Norfolk.

A week later, on 23 February 1829, a day with snow on the ground, clear skies, and gale-like winds, Commodore Thomas Tingey died in his bed, at 10:00 o'clock in the morning.

"A fine officer he was and a gentleman," one of the yard's painters wrote in his diary for that day.[32] That memorial was written by a slave, a menial employee who worked for paltry daily wages at the mercy of the budget cycle and the weather, and whose owner took most of his earnings for himself. Yet in its simplicity and honesty, it probably captures what most of the men who had built the yard and the ships thought of their long-time boss. Tingey had been hard but fair; he had sought both fear and affection from his men, and had won their respect. He had at the same time succeeded in building a strong and lasting institution, and his early decisions would set patterns for the management of navy yards for generations afterward.

On the afternoon of the day he died, the muster bell did not ring at the yard, and the men were given a half day off. (Tingey would have been pleased if they had raised a glass in his memory, but unhappy had they gone on to drink to excess.) The next day was a normal workday at the yard, marked only by the lowering of the flag to half-mast, and a salute of thirteen guns—a ceremony also conducted at the other naval yards, stations, and vessels. Officers of the Navy and Marine Corps also wore black crepe armbands for thirty days to mark their colleague's departure. The *National Intelligencer*, whose editors had sat on many a dais with the commandant and whose presses had on occasion been repaired at the yard, wrote of the man who needed little introduction to its readers,

To his exalted worth every one who has ever known him will bear testimony. His irreproachable character must be to his bereaved widow and affectionate children an invaluable legacy. His commission in the Navy was nearly coeval with its existence. For almost 50 years he has sustained the character of an officer of the Navy with unsullied reputation. As the head of a family he was a venerable and true patriarch. As a man he was humane, kind and generous. As a citizen, faithful and loyal. His death, though it happened to him in the fullness of years, will be mourned by all who knew him.[33]

Among those who had known him during his Washington years, the memories were more personal. Margaret Smith wrote that Tingey had been "our first kind friend and acquaintance" in the city, while Anna Maria Thornton noted his passing in her diary with a simple tribute: "a worthy man."[34]

The funeral was held two days later, under clouds and rain. The procession started from the commandant's house at 1:00 p.m., taking the still-unpaved streets of the bustling community that had grown up around the yard, to the Congressional Cemetery that Tingey and his church had established a generation earlier. There, he was laid to rest next to his first wives, Margaret and Ann, and the two granddaughters who had died in the Washington seat of the family. It was an entirely suitable location: a short walk from the navy yard that he had spent more than a quarter of a century developing, in sacred ground of the church in which he had played such a vital part, and in the bosom of a family that had provided him with constant moral purpose and support.

The young sailor who had come to America more than half a century earlier, a man with little family and uncertain prospects, had established himself soundly and left a lasting legacy. His contribution to the growth of the Navy, while not heroic like that of some colleagues, was vital. But perhaps an equal achievement had been the creation of a large and loving family. He and Margaret had seen their children well raised and well married, their progeny were connected to some of the better families of the seaboard, and his subsequent marriages had expanded the family network still further. He had left a reputation his widow and children could honor, and an estate that would ensure her comfort, while the Navy would continue to benefit from the tradition of service that was passed down in the Tingey blood through succeeding generations.[35]

Notes

CHAPTER ONE A New American

1. Admiral John Byron to Thomas Tingey, 31 July 1771, Tingey Papers, Lewis D. Cook Collection, Historical Society of Washington. Thomas Tingey is hereafter referred to as "Tingey" in the endnotes.

2. Tingey's ancestors recently have been traced by Eben W. Graves, whose study "The English Ancestry of Captain Thomas Tingey, U.S.N. (1750–1829)" is as yet unpublished.

3. Charles Creighton, *A History of Epidemics in Britain*, Vol. 2 (London: Cambridge University Press, 1894).

4. Years later, Tingey wrote to an old friend that 12 May would mark the sixtieth anniversary of his entering on "sea duty." Tingey to Richard Dale, 29 April 1825, Richard Dale Papers, Library of Congress Manuscript Division.

5. Tingey's life story, as relayed to and subsequently by his family, has some elements of invention. Family tradition has it that he claimed to be the son of a Church of England minister, yet no evidence has been presented or found to support that claim—and now Mr. Grave's genealogical work, cited above, has shown that claim to be untrue. Similarly, family lore has it that Tingey served in the continental or a state navy during the revolutionary struggle, yet again there is no evidence to support the claim. But Tingey's 1800 claim to his superiors in the newly formed United States Navy that he had experience in British navy shipyards does ring true, and is supported by his satisfactory performance in the navy yard job that he held for more than a quarter of a century.

6. Admiral Hugh Palliser to Samuel Davys, 2 August 1767, Labrador Boundary Commission, The Record Book, St. John's Newfoundland, Vol. 4, 19. Last accessed at Newfoundland and Labrador Heritage, http://www.heritage.nf.ca/law/lab3/labvol3_1006.html, on 27 September 2010.

7. The activities of the *Nautilus* and the *Otter* have been traced through the logs of their captains and sailing masters at the British National Archives: ADM 51/629 and 52/1380, respectively, for the *Nautilus*, ADM 51/663 and 52/1387, respectively, for the *Otter*. The logs, while very informative on the activities of the ships and their crew, unfortunately are not so forthcoming on incidental matters such as passengers or supernumeraries such as the fort garrison.

8. Muster books of the HMS *Panther*, British Archives, ADM 36/7660. Tingey was carried on the *Panther*'s payroll and muster roll from May to December, regardless of any detached duty or his actual physical location.

9. Admiral Molyneux Shuldham to Lord Hillsborough, 6 July 1772, British Archives CO 194/32, 93.

10. The family history given here is predominantly drawn from Lewis D. Cook, "William Murdoch (1705–1761) and his Descendants," in *Genealogies of Pennsylvania Families* (Baltimore: Genealogical Publishing, 1982), Vol. 16 (October 1948), 350–385.

11. Ibid., 353.

12. Tingey to J. Collins, 7 January 1793, Thomas Tingey Letterbook 1788–1793, Historical Society of Pennsylvania, Tingey-Craven Family Papers (hereafter "Letterbook," 49.

CHAPTER TWO **Merchant Captain**

1. Tingey to John Wilcocks, 5 August 1790, Letterbook, 17.

2. Memorandum, 24 March 1789, Letterbook, 81–86.

3. Tingey to John Wilcocks, 5 August 1790, Letterbook, 17.

4. Ibid.

5. Sirajul Islam, "Americans in Calcutta Bazaars," Asiatic Society of Bangladesh, Dhaka. Last accessed at http://www.asiaticsociety.org.bd/journals/Golden_jubilee_vol/articles/H_474%20(SI%20Sir).htm, on 28 September 2010. To give Tingey credit, he did have a book on Bengal in his family library at the time of his death.

6. The life-saving incident may have been a slight exaggeration by the banyan, who was seeking a favor some years later. Mohampersand Takoor to Tingey, 21 December 1810, Tingey letters held by Eben W. Graves.

7. Tingey to Edward Gardner, 18 November 1792, Letterbook, 43. Emphasis in original.

8. Tingey to Tyson and Vaux, 17 December 1789, Letterbook, 8.

9. Tingey to T. W. Francis, December (undated) 1789, Letterbook, 9.

10. Tingey to Willing, Morris & Swanwick, 21 January 1791, Letterbook, 23.

11. Tingey to Willing, Morris & Swanwick, 17 November 1791, Letterbook, 80.

12. Tingey to Robert Smith, 10 December 1791, Letterbook, 33.

13. Tingey to Brown & Francis, 18 September 1792, Letterbook, 39.

14. Tingey to John Brown, 12 November 1792, Letterbook, 42.

15. Tingey to Brown & Francis, 29 March and 13 April 1793, Letterbook, 59–60.

16. Certificate of ownership, Naval Historical Center. Last accessed at http://www.history.Navy.mil/library/manuscript/tingey1795.htm, on 28 September 2010.

17. Unless otherwise noted, details of the voyage are from the Tingey Papers, *Ganges* journal, Library of Congress Manuscript Division.

18. Tingey to Willing & Francis, 19 June 1795, Gratz Collection, Historical Society of Pennsylvania, Box 35.

CHAPTER THREE A New Naval Uniform

1. Margaret Tingey to Tingey, 9 and 25 March 1800, Commodore Thomas Tingey Research Collection, Historical Society of Washington, DC (hereafter "Family Letters").

2. The key source for documents regarding the Quasi-War is the Office of Naval Records, *Naval Documents Related to the Quasi-War between the United States and France* (Washington, DC: U.S. Printing Office 1935–1938) (hereafter *Naval Documents*). The quote is from Stoddert to John Adams, 1 September 1798, *Naval Documents*, Vol. 1, 367.

3. Bill of sale for the *Ganges*, 3 May 1798, *Naval Documents*, Vol. 1, 63.

4. Tingey to Margaret Gay Tingey, 6 February 1797, Family Letters.

5. Tingey to Benjamin Stoddert, 27 January 1799, *Naval Documents*, Vol. 2, 285.

6. Ibid.

7. Tingey to Benjamin Stoddert, 18 February 1799, *Naval Documents*, Vol. 2, 368.

8. First quote is from Tingey to Benjamin Stoddert, 18 February 1799, *Naval Documents*, Vol. 2, 368; second quote is from the *Connecticut Current* of March 18, 1799, quoted in *Naval Documents*, Vol. 2, 382.

9. Tingey to Margaret Gay and Hannah Tingey, 25 March 1799, Family Letters.

10. Benjamin Stoddert to Tingey, 19 March 1799, *Naval Documents*, Vol. 2, 479.

11. Tingey to Benjamin Stoddert, 21 April 1799, *Naval Documents*, Vol. 3, 81. The capture of the *Eliza* led to a legal battle that wound up in the U.S. Supreme Court. In *Bass v Tingey*, decided 15 August 1800, the justices ruled in a controversial decision that the United States and France were indeed in a state of war, that the French had held the ship for the requisite amount of time, and that Tingey and his crew were consequently entitled to half of the sale proceeds of the recaptured ship.

12. Benjamin Stoddert to Thomas Truxtun, 6 May 1799, *Naval Documents*, Vol. 3, 142; Benjamin Stoddert to Thomas Truxtun, 24 May 1799, *Naval Documents*, Vol. 3, 245. The quotation is from Benjamin Stoddert to Tingey, 28 May 1799, *Naval Documents*, Vol. 3, 268.

13. *Naval Documents*, Vol. 3, 257.

14. Tingey to Benjamin Stoddert, 11 June 1799, *Naval Documents*, Vol. 3, 326–328.

15. Tingey to Willing & Francis, 29 June 1799, *Naval Documents*, Vol. 3, 430.

16. Tingey to Benjamin Stoddert, 26 June 1799, *Naval Documents*, Vol. 3, 346, 348.

17. Benjamin Stoddert to Tingey, 13 July 1799, *Naval Documents*, Vol. 3, 496; Benjamin Stoddert to Tingey, June 22 1799, *Naval Documents*, Vol. 3, 384.

18. First quote is from Benjamin Stoddert to John Adams, 15 July 1799, *Naval Documents*, Vol. 3, 500; second quote is from Benjamin Stoddert to Tingey, 22 June 1799, *Naval Documents*, Vol. 3, 384.

19. Tingey to Benjamin Stoddert, 26 July 1799, *Naval Documents*, Vol. 3, 544.

20. Tingey to Benjamin Stoddert, 29 August 1799, *Naval Documents*, Vol. 4, 132.

21. Tingey to Benjamin Stoddert, 19 August 1799, *Naval Documents*, Vol. 4, 95.

22. Benjamin Stoddert to Tingey, 9 September 1799, *Naval Documents*, Vol. 4, 169.

23. Tingey to Moses Brown, 18 September 1799, *Naval Documents*, Vol. 4, 202.

24. Tingey to Robert Thomson, Commander in Chief British Forces, 2 October 1799, *Naval Documents*, Vol. 4, 248.

CHAPTER FOUR   **A Shaky Start to a New Command**

1. President John Adams to Secretary of State McHenry, 6 August 1799, *Naval Documents*, Vol. 4, 34.

2. Benjamin Stoddert to Washington, 16 September 1798, *Naval Documents*, Vol. 1, 410.

3. George Washington to Benjamin Stoddert, 26 September 1798, *Naval Documents*, Vol. 1, 455.

4. Benjamin Stoddert to William Marbury, 23 May 1799, *Naval Documents*, Vol. 3, 242.

5. Benjamin Stoddert to William Marbury, 22 January 1800, *Naval Documents*, Vol. 5, 114.

6. Benjamin Stoddert to Tingey, 22 January 1800, *Naval Documents*, Vol. 5, 113.

7. Tingey to Benjamin Stoddert, 7 February 1800, *Naval Documents*, Vol. 5, 212.

8. Margaret Tingey to Tingey, 25 January and 25 March 1800, Family Letters.

9. Tingey to his daughters, 15 February 1800, Family Letters.

10. Tingey to Robert Brent, 11 March 1800, *Naval Documents*, Vol. 5, 291.

11. Tingey to his daughters, 16 and 25 May 1800, Family Letters. The quote is from the 25 May letter.

12. Benjamin Stoddert to Lieutenant Colonel William Burrows, USMC, 23 June 1800, *Naval Documents*, Vol. 6, 74.

13. First quote is from Thomas Jefferson to James Monroe, 11 August 1786; second quote is from Thomas Jefferson to Edmund Pendleton, 22 April 1799. Both quotes are from Thomas Jefferson Papers, Library of Congress, Series I, # 117 and 954 (hereafter "Jefferson Papers"). Last accessed at http://memory .loc.gov/ammem/collections/jefferson_papers, on 2 October 2010.

14. Margaret Tingey to Tingey, 9 March 1800, Family Letters.

15. Thomas Jefferson to Benjamin Henry Latrobe, 2 November 1802, in Edward C. Carter, *The Papers of Benjamin Henry Latrobe* (New Haven, CT: Maryland Historical Society 1984–1988) (hereafter "*Latrobe Papers*"), Vol. 1, 221.

16. Thomas Jefferson to Samuel Smith, 9 March 1800, Jefferson Papers, Series I, # 162.

17. *Annals of Congress*, 7th Congress, House 2nd session, 408.

18. First quote is from Tingey to Robert Smith, 12 March 1803, Jefferson Papers, Series I, # 1212; second quote is from Thomas Jefferson to Robert Smith, 19 March 1803, Jefferson Papers, Series I, # 5.

19. Tingey to Robert Smith, 16 January 1805, National Archives, Record Group (hereafter "RG") 45/M125.

20. Christopher McKee, *A Gentlemanly and Honorable Profession* (Annapolis, MD: Naval Institute Press, 1991), 544n. McKee's evidence identifying Tingey as the probable drafter (in 1802) appears convincing.

21. Robert Smith to John Rodgers, 21 December 1803, National Archives, RG45/M149.

22. Gershom Craven to Tingey, 6 May 1805. Quoted in Kenneth Craven, "The Craven Family of New Jersey," History Society of Hunterdon County, NJ, 1978, 8. Dr. Craven, the father of Tingey's son-in-law Tunis Craven, was responding to a letter from Tingey and, I assume, recycling Tingey's language.

CHAPTER FIVE Building the Yard

1. Secretary Robert Smith's brother, Congressman Samuel Smith, was the main speaker against the proposed 1801 legislation. *Annals of Congress*, 6th Congress, House 2nd session, 1076 ff.

2. Henry Latrobe to Nathaniel Ingraham, 9 September 1813, in *Latrobe Papers*, Vol. 3, 4.

3. Robert Smith to Tingey, 22 May 1805, National Archives, RG45/M149.

4. Henry Latrobe to Tingey, 10 May 1805, National Archives, RG45/M149.

5. The house, one of the few large brick-built houses in the area at that time, was at 423 Sixth Street SE.

6. First quote is from Henry Latrobe to Philip Mazzei, 19 December 1806, *Latrobe Papers*, Vol. 2, 328; second quote is from William Thornton in the *National Intelligencer*, 20 April 1808.

7. The magazine was constructed, for safety reasons, on a second plot of government land up the Anacostia River, near the eastern end of the present Congressional Cemetery where G Street would reach the river.

8. Henry Latrobe to Paul Hamilton, 29 June 181, *Latrobe Papers*, Vol. 3, 105.

9. Isaac Hull, Memorial to Congress, 3 January 1833, Register of Debates, 22nd Congress, 2nd session, document 18.

10. Henry Latrobe to Tingey, 16 July 1810, *Latrobe Papers*, Vol. 2, 877. This concerned raising funds for the Washington Canal Company, which both men supported.

11. First quote is from Robert Smith to Tingey, 26 May 1808, National Archives, RG45/M441; second quote is from Robert Smith to Tingey, 12 May 1808, National Archives RG45/M441. Smith was actually arguing in the first citation for more systematic purchases of supplies such as tar, pitch, and turpentine, but the same sentiment applied to lumber procurement.

12. First quote is from Thomas Jefferson to Robert Smith, 5 November 1808, Jefferson Papers, Series I, # 906; second quote is from Robert Smith to Thomas Jefferson, 3 November 1808, Jefferson Papers, Series I, # 898.

13. Paul Hamilton to Samuel Hanson, 22 March 1810, National Archives, RG45/M441.

14. Paul Hamilton to Tingey, 2 August 1809, National Archives, RG45/M441.

15. First quote is from Tingey to Paul Hamilton, 3 August 1809, National Archives, RG45/M125; second quote is from Tingey to Charles Goldsborough, 15 August 1809, National Archives, RG45/M125.

16. Paul Hamilton to Tingey, 16 December 1809, National Archives, RG45/M441.

17. First quote is from *Spirit of Seventy-Six*, 3 July 1810; second quote is from *Spirit of Seventy-Six*, 17 July 1810; third quote is from *National Intelligencer*, 22 October 1810.

18. Tingey to Paul Hamilton, 17 December 1810, National Archives, RG45/M125.

19. Henry Latrobe to Mary Elizabeth Latrobe, 15 April 1815, *Latrobe Papers*, Vol. 3, 645.

20. William Jones to Tingey, 15 April 1814, National Archives, RG45/M441.

21. William Jones to Tingey, 20 September 1814, National Archives, RG45/M441.

CHAPTER SIX **Managing the Work**

1. Tingey to Midshipman Beekman Van Hoffman, 14 November 1810, National Archives, RG45/M125.

2. Tingey to Robert Smith, 10 December 1807, National Archives, RG45/M125.

3. First quote is from Tingey to Robert Smith, 6 March 1807, National Archives, RG45/M125; second quote is from Tingey to Robert Smith, 12 March 1807, National Archives, RG45/M125; third quote is from Robert Smith to Commander Edward Preble, Portland, Maine, 13 March 1807, National Archives, RG45/M441.

4. Tingey to Paul Hamilton, 1 August 1809, National Archives, RG45/M125.

5. First quote is from Paul Hamilton to Tingey, 12 August 1809, National Archives, RG45/M441; second quote is from Paul Hamilton to Cassin, 1 July 1809, National Archives, RG45/M441.

6. First and second quotes are from Tingey to Paul Hamilton, 6 November 1809, National Archives, RG45/M125; third quote is from Paul Hamilton to Tingey, 29 November 1809, National Archives, RG45/M441.

7. Tingey to L. Archibald McElroy, 5 November 1798, *Naval Documents*, Vol. 2, 7.

8. Blacksmith petition to Secretary Paul Hamilton, 12 October 1812, National Archives, RG45/M124.

9. Robert Smith to Tingey, 12 April 1808, National Archives, RG45/M441.

10. First quote is from Robert Smith to Tingey, 25 May 1808, National Archives, RG45/M441; second quote is from Tingey to Robert Smith, 26 May 1808, National Archives, RG45/M125 (emphasis in original). Smith's comparison with the perquisites of other American military services may have been correct, but Tingey also was correct in that the practice, following Royal Navy tradition, had become accepted in the American Navy even though there were no regulations actually permitting it (McKee, *A Gentlemanly and Honorable Profession*, 333).

11. A little more than a year later, Tingey freed a slave Abraham, who was almost surely the same Lynson. Whether or not Abraham had been able to buy his manumission with a share of his wages is not known (District of Columbia Archives, Liber no. 22, of 21 July 1809, 146–147).

12. Tingey to Robert Smith, 12 July 1809, National Archives, RG45/M125.

13. Fox to Congressman Benjamin Talmadge, 15 April 1810, quoted in Merle Westlake, *Josiah Fox, 1763–1847* (Philadelphia: Xlibris, 2003), 76.

14. Josiah Fox to Robert Smith, 7 May 1806, Westlake, *Josiah Fox*, 69.

15. Tingey to Robert Smith, 3 June 1806, National Archives, RG45/M125.

16. Tingey to Robert Smith, 12 June 1807, National Archives, RG45/M125.

17. Paul Hamilton to Tingey, 1 August 1810, National Archives, RG45/M441.

18. Tingey to Paul Hamilton, 7 October 1812, National Archives, RG45/M125.

19. First quote is from *Latrobe Journal*, 11 August 1806, in Edward P. Carter, ed. *The Journals of Benjamin Henry Latrobe, 1799–1829*, Maryland Historical Society, 1980, 68; second quote is from Paul Hamilton to Tingey, 25 January 1811, National Archives, RG45/M441.

20. Tingey to Paul Hamilton, 16 May 1809, National Archives, RG45/M125.

21. *Centinel* [sic] *of Liberty*, open letter from William Marbury, 30 September 1800.

22. William Jones to Tingey, 17 May 1813, National Archives, RG45/M441.

CHAPTER SEVEN **At Home, In Town**

1. Tingey to Margaret Gay and Hannah Tingey, 16 May 1800, Family Letters.

2. The prize money estimates are from McKee, *A Gentlemanly and Honorable Profession*, 336.

3. Tingey to Willing & Francis, 23 September 1800, Gratz Collection, Historical Society of Pennsylvania, Box 35. Emphasis in the original.

4. First quote is from Margaret Tingey to Tingey, 25 January 1800, Family Letters; second quote is from Tingey to Willing & Francis, 23 September 1800, Gratz Collection, Historical Society of Pennsylvania, Box 35.

5. Both would marry Americans and remain in their adopted country. Susanna married a Dr. John Barry, who was reportedly a U.S. Navy surgeon (although no record of his service exists), while Robert became a merchant sailor and married Elizabeth Eldridge of Philadelphia.

6. Sukey's quote from Margaret Tingey to Tingey, 25 January 1800, Family Letters; Tingey's advertisement in the *National Intelligencer*, 8 August 1821.

7. First quote is from Margaret Tingey to Tingey, 9 March 1800, Family Letters; second quote is from Tingey to Margaret Gay Tingey, undated (summer 1808), Family Letters.

8. Quotations are from Margaret Smith to Mrs. Kirkpatrick, 16 November 1800; Gaillard Hunt, ed., *The First Forty Years of Washington Society* (New York: Ungar, 1965), 1.

9. Margaret Gay Tingey Wingate to Tingey, 23 July 1809, Family Letters.

10. *National Intelligencer*, 6 July 1801.

11. The monument, made in Italy of white Carrara marble, was damaged in the 1814 fire and is now on the grounds of the Naval Academy in Annapolis.

12. John Edward Semmes, *John H. B. Latrobe and His Times* (Baltimore: Norman Remington, 1917), 36.

13. Tingey to Willing & Francis, 11 September 1801, Gratz Collection, Historical Society of Pennsylvania, Box 35.

14. Robert Smith to Joshua Wingate, 24 June 1804, National Archives, RG45/ entry 11, "Letters sent concerning supplies for the Dey of Algiers, 1803–1808."

15. Tingey to James Greenleaf, 12 December 1805, Family Letters.

16. First three quotes are from (in order) from Tingey's letters to John Rodgers, of 18 October 1806, 4 February 1807, and 20 March 1807, Rodgers Papers, Library of Congress Manuscript Division, III, 1; obituary is from *National Intelligencer*, 1 May 1807.

17. John Rodgers to Tingey, 27 April 1807, Family Letters.

18. First quote is from Tingey to Margaret Gay Tingey, undated 1808; second quote is from Tingey to Margaret Gay Tingey, 12 July 1808, Family Letters.

19. Henry Latrobe to Isaac Hazelhurst, 16 November 1808, *Latrobe Papers*, Vol. 2, 669.

20. First quote is from Elizabeth Latrobe to Julianna Mille, 17 February 1812, Semmes, *John H. B. Latrobe and His Times*, 17; second quote is from Tingey to Margaret Gay Wingate, 18 May 1810, Family Letters.

21. Margaret Gay and Joseph Wingate's first child, Tingeyanna Margaretta, had been born in August 1809 in Massachusetts, but had survived only twelve months. She died in Washington during a visit from Margaret Gay and Joseph Wingate to her mother's family home.

22. Tunis Craven to Joseph Wingate, 20 February 1810, Family Letters.

23. John Rodgers commented to his wife just a few months after the wedding, "Margaret Tingey looks, I think, as if matrimony did not agree with her, for altho she appears to be in good spirits I consider she looks several years older

than she did when we last saw her" (John Rodgers to Minerva Rodgers, 22 December 1808, Rodgers Papers, Library of Congress Manuscript Division, Series I:13). A few years later, Margaret Smith found Wingate's sudden and unexplained departure from Washington to be a "new misfortune" for Margaret Gay—implying other problems at his hands (Margaret Smith to Mrs. Kirkpatrick, 6 May 1810, Hunt, ed., *The First Forty Years*, 85).

24. Tingey to Willing & Francis, 5 October 1813; Tingey to George Simpson, 12 January 1814; both are from the Gratz Collection, Historical Society of Pennsylvania, Box 35.

25. The house had been built in 1803–1804 when John Cassin was commandant of the yard, and was occupied by Cassin and his family until his assignment to head the navy yard at Gosport, Virginia (National Register of Historic Places application for Tingey House, 3). See also Michael W. Fazio and Patrick A. Snadon, *The Domestic Architecture of Benjamin Henry Latrobe* (Baltimore: Johns Hopkins Press, 2006), 633.

26. Initial quotes are from William to Eleanor Jones, 10 February 1813, quoted in McKee, *A Gentlemanly and Honorable Profession*, 86; second quote is from Henry Latrobe to Nathaniel Ingraham, 9 September 1813, *Latrobe Papers*, Vol. 3, 480.

CHAPTER EIGHT **Ships or Boats**

1. Thomas Jefferson to Robert Smith, 4 July 1804, Jefferson Papers, Series I, # 1111.

2. Robert Smith to Thomas Jefferson, 3 July 1804, Jefferson Papers, Series I, # 1004.

3. Ibid.

4. Thomas Jefferson to Wilson Cary Nicholas, 6 December 1804, Jefferson Papers, Series I, # 895.

5. Rodger's letter is worth quoting, because it illustrates the kind of reaction King's behavior occasioned.

> "Sir," he begins, "Your conduct has been so Derogatory to the principles of truth & so particularly neglectful to the Work you had to do for the Congress, that I am determined to make a report of the same to the Gover[n]m[ent]. A Man in your situation ought at least to be a Man of principle & truth; as by your want of Boath, I shall be forced to go to Sea, without many Articles which are of the Utmost Importance. . . . It is your Interest to pray that my Head may be Knock'd off before I return, for be assured if you are not punished before that period I will revenge the Injury you have done me, with my own hands." (*Naval Documents Related to Wars with the Barbary Powers*, [Washington, DC: U.S. Office of Naval Records and Library, 1939–1944], Vol. 4, 193–194)

6. That is not to say that some of his fellow officers did not criticize the yard's management, covet his job, or hope that Tingey would retire or move on. Thomas Truxtun in 1804 and Edward Preble in 1806 both indicated their readiness to replace Tingey (Robert Smith to Thomas Jefferson, 19 July 1804,

Jefferson Papers, Series I, # 1121; Edward Preble to Charles Goldsborough, 25 May 1806, as discussed in Christopher McKee, *Edward Preble: A Naval Biography, 1761–1807* (Annapolis, MD: Naval Institute Press, 1972), 344.

7. First quote is from Tingey to John Rodgers, 13 September 1806; second quote is from Tingey to John Stricker, 4 February 1807; third quote is from Tingey to John Rodgers, 4 February 1807; all in Rodgers Papers, Library of Congress Manuscript Division, III, 1.

8. Tingey to Robert Smith, 27 March 1807, National Archives, RG45/M125.

9. Tingey, unaddressed, 9 February 1807, *American State Papers, Naval Affairs*, Vol. 1, 164.

10. Margaret Gay Wingate to Tingey, 23 July 1809, Family Letters.

11. First quote is from Thomas Truxtun to Tingey, 27 July 1807 (emphasis in original), Truxtun Papers, Library of Congress Manuscript Division, Naval Historical Collection; second quote is from Tingey to Margaret Gay Wingate, 7 August 1807, Family Letters.

12. Quote from Tingey to John Rodgers, 17 March 1807, Rodgers Papers, Library of Congress Manuscript Division, III, 1.

13. First quote from George Clinton, 22 January 1807, *Annals of Congress*, 9th Congress, House 2nd session, 385; second quote from John Smilie, 5 February 1807, *Annals of Congress*, 9th Congress, House 2nd session, 469.

14. *Annals of Congress*, 10th Congress, 1st session, 34.

15. Attachment to Tingey to Robert Smith, 7 January 1809, National Archives, RG45/M125.

16. Robert Smith to Tingey, 6 February 1808, National Archives, RG45/M441.

17. First quote is from Thomas Jefferson to Robert Smith, 12 August 1808, Jefferson Papers, Series I, # 16; discussion of Tingey's reaction is from Henry Latrobe to Fulton, 6 June 1813, in *Latrobe Papers*, Vol. 3, 468.

18. In the 1810 test Fulton's rowboat with her harpoon gun and torpedoes were pitted against the *Argus* and John Rodgers' careful advance planning. Rodgers had surrounded the vessel with so many defensive measures—nets, booms, swinging pikes, and so on—that the attackers could not affix their weapon to the hull. Rodgers and his Navy colleagues gloated at thwarting the infernal weapon, and Fulton essentially abandoned the project to concentrate on his steamboat. But the proponents of mines had the last word—a torpedo floated with the current hit and sank a British ship of four hundred tons at Norfolk in November 1813.

19. Thomas Jefferson to Benjamin Stoddert, 18 February 1809, Jefferson Papers, Series I, # 713.

20. The *Essex*'s armament was changed while she was repaired in Washington. In view of the fact that she was forced to strike her colors in early 1814 because she was outgunned by two British ships armed with long guns, while she had only short-range carronades, the question arises as to when her armament was converted to carronades, and what role, if any, Tingey played in the decision. While the documentary record is incomplete as to exactly who made the

decisions and when, all changes in armament were by rule to be approved by the secretary of the Navy. Early in the rebuild, Tingey requested instructions from Secretary Paul Hamilton as to the armament of the ship, saying he presumed the present arrangement, "was such as will need no alteration" (Tingey to Paul Hamilton, 10 January 1808, National Archives, RG45/M125). There is no record of an answer, yet a decision must have been made to alter the armament, because by June of the following year carronade carriages were being fitted for the ship. According to Portia Takajian's *Anatomy of the Ship* (London: Conway Maritime Press, 1990, 15), the *Essex* left the yard in 1809 armed with twenty-eight long 12-pounders and eighteen 32-pound carronades. According to the same source, she was not converted to a predominately carronade-armed ship (forty 32-pound carronades and six long 12-pounders) until 1810, at Norfolk, per the request of Captain John Smith and with the approval of Secretary Paul Hamilton.

21. Act of 21 April 1806, *Statutes at Large*, 9th Congress, 1st session, 390.

22. Tingey to John Rodgers, 21 November 1809, Rodgers Papers, Library of Congress Manuscript Division, III, 1.

23. John Randolph, 25 April 1809, *Annals of Congress*, 11th Congress, House 2nd session, 1970.

24. First quote is from James Barron to Edward Preble, 7 May 1806, in McKee, *Edward Preble*, 344; second quote is from Tingey to Charles Goldsborough, 9 August 1809, National Archives, RG45/M125.

25. First quote is from Paul Hamilton to Tingey, 1 December 1809, National Archives, RG45/M141; second quote is from Tingey to Margaret Gay Wingate, 9 August 1809, Family Letters.

26. Tingey to Paul Hamilton, 13 December 1809, National Archives, RG45/M125.

CHAPTER NINE **War and Disaster**

1. *Annals of Congress*, 12th Congress, Senate 1st session, 14.

2. Paul Hamilton to John Rodgers, 9 June 1810, quoted in Charles O. Paullin, *Commodore John Rodgers* (New York: Arno Press, 1980), 212.

3. Tingey to Margaret Gay Tingey, 8 September 1807, Family Letters.

4. Samuel Mitchill to Catherine Mitchill, 10 December 1812, quoted in *Harper's New Monthly Magazine 58*, no. 347 (April 1879).

5. Thomas Jefferson to John Adams, 27 May 1813, Jefferson Papers, Series I, # 810.

6. *Statutes at Large*, 12th Congress, 2nd session, 821.

7. Henry Latrobe to Nathaniel Ingraham, 9 September 1813, *Latrobe Papers*, Vol. 3, 480.

8. First quote is from William Jones to Eleanor Jones, 23 January 1813, in William S. Dudley et al., eds., *The Naval War of 1812: A Documentary History* (Washington, DC: Naval Historical Center, 1985), Vol. 2, 35 (hereafter "*The Naval War of 1812*"); second quote is from William Jones to Isaac Hull, 9 April 1813, National Archives, RG45/M441.

9. The fort had been built in 1809 in the flurry of war preparation caused by the Chesapeake affair. Tingey and Secretary of War Dearborn had visited the site in August 1807, with Tingey optimistically calling the situation "a little Gibraltar on the Potomac" (Tingey to Jonathan Williams, 12 August 1807, Records of the U.S. Military Philosophical Society #85, New York Historical Society Manuscript Division).

10. William Jones to Tingey, 18 July 1813, National Archives, RG45/M441.

11. *Annals of Congress*, 13th Congress, House 2nd session, 1870.

12. Miss Jones, c. 22 August 1814, quoted in Anne Hollingsworth Wharton, *Social Life in the Early Republic* (Philadelphia: J. B. Lippincott, 1903), 163.

13. William Jones to Congress, 3 October 1814, *Annals of Congress*, Appendix to 13th Congress, 3rd session, 1674. The secretary, who had received some criticism for his actions, was here providing a strong justification, for the record.

14. Ibid, 1672.

15. Mordecai Booth to Tingey, 22 August 1814, Dudley, ed., *The Naval War of 1812*, Vol. 3, 202.

16. Mordecai Booth to Tingey, 23 August 1814, Dudley, ed., *The Naval War of 1812*, Vol. 3, 205.

17. William Jones to Congress, 3 October 1814, *Annals of Congress*, Appendix to 13th Congress, 3rd session, 1672.

18. The quote is from William Jones to Congress, 3 October 1814, *Annals of Congress*, Appendix to 13th Congress, 3rd session, 1674. In that report, Jones puts his appearance at the yard at 2:00 in the afternoon, but an earlier memo of his, dated 27 August 1814, cited in Dudley, ed., *The Naval War of 1812*, Vol. 2, 214, mentions the later hour, and appears more accurate.

19. Mordecai Booth to Tingey, 10 September 1814, in Dudley, ed., *The Naval War of 1812*, Vol. 3, 209 ff, as are all subsequent quotes from Booth's report.

20. Tingey to William Jones, 27 August 1814, attachment to William Jones to Congress, 3 October 1814, *Annals of Congress*, Appendix to 13th Congress, 3rd session, 1679.

21. William Jones to Congress, 3 October 1814, *Annals of Congress*, Appendix to 13th Congress, 3rd session, 1675.

CHAPTER TEN Rebuilding

1. *Annals of Congress*, 13th Congress, House 3rd session, 1047.

2. Ibid., 1060.

3. Tingey to Captain Charles Morris, 18 March 1815, quoted in Linda M. Maloney, *The Captain from Connecticut: The Life and Naval Times of Isaac Hull* (Boston: North Eastern University Press, 1986), 266.

4. First quote is from Benjamin Crowninshield to John Rodgers, 23 May 1815, James Madison Papers at the Library of Congress, Series 1, # 445; second quote is from Benjamin Crowninshield to James Madison, 23 May 1815, James

Madison Papers at the Library of Congress, Series 1, # 442. Last accessed at http://lcweb2.loc.gov/ammem/collections/madison_papers, on 5 October 2010.

5. Board Journal, 1 May 1815, National Archives, RG45/E303, Vol. 1.

6. The senior, salaried mechanics had been laid off shortly after the fire by order of Secretary William Jones. A number of them complained, and some even sued the government for the loss of their personal property. Those claims were not settled for years, even decades, and in some cases only posthumously.

7. John Rodgers to Tingey, 11 May 1815, National Archives, RG45/E307, Vol. 1.

8. Quote is from Tingey to John Rodgers, 15 May 1815, National Archives, RG45/E314, Vol. 71. Punctuation has been changed for better comprehension.

9. Tingey to Margaret Gay Wingate, 6 May 1815, Family Letters.

10. Tingey to Margaret Gay Wingate, 5 December 1815, Family Letters.

11. Tingey to John Rodgers, 17 July 1816, National Archives, RG45/E314, Vol. 71.

12. John Rodgers to Tingey, 17 July 1816, National Archives, RG45/E307, Vol. 1.

13. First quote is from Tingey to Rodgers, 12 April 1819, National Archives, RG45/E314, Vol.71; second quote is from John Rodgers to Tingey, 13 January 1824, National Archives, RG45/E307, Vol. 4.

14. First quote is from Tingey to Margaret Gay Wingate, 10 October 1820, Family Letters; second quote is from Tingey to Margaret Gay Wingate, 21 January 1821, Family Letters.

15. Captain Samuel Evans had been found guilty of "misconduct" in the 1823 case, in which he was accused of misusing government property; he was subjected only to a reprimand and an exhortation (from Secretary of the Navy Smith Thompson) that he be "more cautious about blending his public and private concerns" (Niles Register, Vol. 24, 30 July 1823).

16. Tingey to John Rodgers, 12 September 1817, National Archives, RG45/E314, Vol. 71.

17. John Rodgers to Tingey, 15 September 1817, National Archives, RG45/E307, Vol. 1.

18. John Rodgers to Tingey, 13 August 1816, National Archives, RG45/E307, Vol. 1.

19. First quote is from Tingey to Benjamin Crowninshield, 27 January 1816; second quote is from Tingey to Benjamin Crowninshield, 16 January 1816; both quotes are from National Archives, RG45/M125.

20. Tingey to Benjamin Crowninshield, 5 February 1816, National Archives, RG45/M125.

21. Board Journal, 26 February 1817, National Archives, RG45/E303, Vol. 1.

22. First quote is from Tingey to John Rodgers, 30 August 1821, National Archives, RG45/E314, Vol. 74; second quote is from Tingey to John Rodgers, 16 January 1822, National Archives, RG45/E314, Vol. 76; third quote is from John Rodgers to Tingey, 21 January 1822, National Archives, RG45/E307, Vol. 3.

23. First quote is from John Davis of Abel to Tingey, 15 March 1817, National Archives, RG45/E314, Vol. 71; second quote is from Board Circular of 17 March 1817, National Archives, RG45/E307, Vol. 1.

24. Tingey to John Rodgers, 17 February 1818, National Archives, RG45/E314, Vol. 72.

25. *National Intelligencer*, 2 March 1809.

26. A few years later, in 1826, a two-horse powered scoop dredge, or mud machine, was built to keep the wharf clear of sediment, and the spoil also used for landfill. The dredge was also loaned periodically to the city government to remove obstacles in the river.

27. The *Columbus* turned out to be the largest vessel ever built in Washington. She and her sister ships turned out to be fairly poor sailers, and though she had a long record of service, she never distinguished herself. She was sunk at the beginning of the Civil War to prevent capture by Confederate forces.

28. Tingey to Samuel Southard, 7 September 1826, National Archives, RG45/M125.

29. First quote is from Tingey to Captain William Bainbridge, 29 March 1824, National Archives, RG45/E314, Vol. 78 (Bainbridge was Rodger's replacement as chairman of the board); second quote is from William Bainbridge to Tingey, 31 March 1824, National Archives, RG45/E307, Vol. 4; third quote is from William Bainbridge to Tingey, 7 February 1826, National Archives, RG45/E307, Vol. 5.

CHAPTER ELEVEN **Patriarch**

1. Tingey to Charles Morris, 18 March 1815, quoted in Maloney, *The Captain from Connecticut*, 266.

2. Margaret Gay Wingate to Tingey, 11 September 1815, Family Letters.

3. Winn was a partner in the Navy Yard Bridge Company, which built a toll bridge in 1819 over the Anacostia River, just upstream of the yard at Eleventh Street. William Marbury was another partner; Tingey owned eleven income-producing shares in the enterprise.

4. First quote is from Mary Crowinshield to her mother, 24 December 1815, Francis Crowinshield, ed., *The Letters of Mary Boardman Crowninshield 1815–6* (Cambridge, MA: Riverside Press, 1935), 32; second quote is from Tingey to Margaret Gay Wingate, 5 December 1815, Family Letters. A mantua is a full-skirted gown that was fashionable at that time.

5. Tingey to Margaret Gay Wingate, 25 April 1816, Family Letters.

6. Tingey to Margaret Gay Wingate, 15 February 1817, Family Letters.

7. Another grandchild, Henry Wingate, had been born in Maine in March of the same year.

8. Tingey to Margaret Gay Wingate, 31 May 1817, Family Letters.

9. Tingey to Navy Secretary Smith Thompson, 24 September 1820, National Archives, RG45/M125.

10. Tingey to Thomas Truxtun, 28 October 1808, Truxtun Papers, Historical Society of Pennsylvania.

11. First quote is from Tingey to John Rodgers, 12 April 1819, National Archives, RG45/E314, Vol. 73; second and third quotes are from Tingey to John Rodgers, 26 July 1821, Rodgers Papers, Historical Society of Pennsylvania, Series I, Box 1, Folder 5.

12. Michael Shiner, a slave at the time, wrote in his diary that he and a slave of Tingey's were both threatened with a "starting" after drinking, fighting, and "cutting some shines." *The Diary of Michael Shiner*, 4 July 1828, Navy Department Library, 27. Last accessed at http://www.history.Navy.mil/library/online/shinerdiary.html#diary, on 8 October 2010. Quote is from Tingey to Secretary Smith Thompson, 12 September 1821, National Archives, RG45/M125.

13. Tingey to Secretary Smith Thompson, 13 July 1821, National Archives, RG45/M125.

14. Lewis D. Cook, "William Murdoch of Philadelphia and his Descendents," *Pennsylvania Genealogical Magazine* 16 (October 1948): 382.

15. Tingey to Joseph Wingate, 21 February 1823, Family Letters.

16. Tingey to Joseph Wingate, 16 April 1822, Family Letters.

17. Tingey to Margaret Gay Wingate, 20 September 1822, Family Letters.

18. The house, called Tingey House, still stands, and is currently the official residence of the Chief of Naval Operations.

19. Tingey did not live to see the full scope of their successes, though he did know of one death: Dulany Forrest died in 1825, in command of the schooner *Decoy* in the Caribbean. French Forrest reached the rank of captain in 1844, served as commandant of the Washington navy yard for short time in 1855, and joined the Confederate Navy during the Civil War. John Kelly retired in 1862 with the rank of commodore. Thomas Tingey Craven rose to the rank of rear admiral before his retirement in 1869. His first wife was Virginia Ann Wingate, Margaret Gay's daughter—whom he presumably met at the Tingey house in Washington. Tunis Augustus Macdonough Craven, a commander at the time, died in the battle of Mobile Bay in 1864 in command of the USS *Tecumseh*.

20. Margaret Gay Wingate to Tingey, 4 October 1819, Family Letters.

21. Quotes, in order of appearance in paragraph, are Tingey to Joseph Wingate, 30 January 1817; Margaret Gay Wingate to Tingey, 25 March 1820; Tingey to Joseph Wingate, 27 February 1822; Tingey to Joseph Wingate, 11 May 1822; Tingey to Joseph Wingate, 26 May 1822; and Tingey to Joseph Wingate, 27 May 1822. All quotes are from Family Letters.

22. Hannah Tingey Craven to Tingey, undated, 1817, Family Letters

23. Those ties were doubled some years later, in 1840, when Thomas' grandson, Thomas Tingey Craven, married Truxtun's granddaughter, Emily Truxtun Henderson.

24. Tingey to Richard Dale, 24 April 1825, Richard Dale Papers, Library of Congress Manuscript Division.

25. Mordecai Booth to Charles Morris, 2 September 1826, National Archives, RG45/E314, Vol. 80.

26. First quote is from John Q. Adams, *Memoirs*, Charles F. Adams, ed. (Freeport, NY: Books for Libraries Press, 1969), Vol. 7, 296; second quote is from Tingey to Margaret Gay Wingate, 30 August 1827, Family Letters.

27. Quote is from Adams, *Memoirs*, Vol. 7, 343. Tingey may have believed that he had a claim to seniority: when he and Rodgers both entered the service for the first time in 1798, he entered as a captain and Rodgers only as a lieutenant. Rodgers had served continuously, however, whereas Tingey's current commission dated only from 1804.

28. From the colorful description of the event in *The Diary of Michael Shiner*, 16 August 1828, 28.

29. John Rodgers to Tingey, 6 January 1829, National Archives, RG45/E307, Vol. 6.

30. Tingey to John Rodgers, 10 January 1829, National Archives, RG45/E314, Vol. 83.

31. Tingey to Secretary Samuel Southard, 2 February 1829, National Archives, RG45/M125.

32. *The Diary of Michael Shiner*, 23 February 1829, 1829, 38.

33. *National Intelligencer*, 24 February 1829.

34. First quote is from Margaret Smith to Mrs. Boyd, undated 1929, Hunt, ed., *The First Forty Years*, 290; second quote is from Anna Maria Thornton diary, 13 January 1829, Thornton Papers, Library of Congress Manuscript Division.

35. The estate was valued at just under $12,000, and included almost $3,000 from the auction of household furnishings, the proceeds from selling three slaves, and other property, including some thirty lots in Washington. The commodore died intestate, but the estate was apparently divided amicably among the family, with the daughters—their husbands having waived their potential claims—receiving the real estate (which was finally divided in 1837). Ann Evelina left Washington to live in Lambertville, New Jersey, where she died in 1861—leaving a portion of her estate in turn to two unmarried granddaughters of Thomas Tingey, Julia Wingate and Margaret Dulany.

Selected Bibliography

The major sources for this work are Tingey's correspondence with his superiors in the Navy, his business and naval colleagues, and his family. Many other sources have informed the discussion, either as background to the period and its politics or because they provided insights into the character of Tingey and his contemporaries. I have listed only those works that were consulted frequently or on principal points and that would prove to be valuable references to others interested in this life or this period. Where a source served as an authority for only a point or two, it will be cited in the endnotes but not necessarily in this bibliography.

Principal Works Consulted

American State Papers, Naval Affairs, Vols. I–III, and *Military Affairs* Vol. I. Library of Congress, Washington, DC. Accessible at http://lcweb2.loc.gov/ammem/amlaw/lawhome.html.

Annals of Congress. Library of Congress, Washington, DC. Accessible at http://lcweb2.loc.gov/ammem/amlaw/lawhome.html.

Carter, Edward C. *The Papers of Benjamin Henry Latrobe.* 3 vols. New Haven, CT: Maryland Historical Society, 1984–1988.

Cook, Lewis D. "William Murdoch (1705–1761) and his Descendants." Vol. 16 in *Genealogies of Pennsylvania Families.* Baltimore: Genealogical Publishing, 1982 (October 1948), 39–74.

Creighton, Charles. *A History of Epidemics in Britain,* Vol. 2. London: Cambridge University Press, 1894.

Dudley, William S., et al., eds. *The Naval War of 1812: A Documentary History.* Vols. I–III. Washington, DC: Naval Historical Center, 1985.

Ferguson, Eugene. *Truxtun of the Constellation: The Life of Commodore Thomas Truxtun, U.S. Navy, 1755–1822.* Baltimore: Johns Hopkins Press, 1956.

Furber, Holden. "The Beginnings of American Trade with India, 1784–1812." *The New England Quarterly,* 11, no. 2 (1938, June).

Graves, Eben W. "The English Ancestry of Captain Thomas Tingey, U.S.N. (1750–1829)." Unpublished study.

Hibben, Henry B. *Navy Yard, Washington: History from Organization, 1799 to Present Date.* Washington, DC: Government Printing Office, 1896.

Hunt, Gaillard, ed. *The First Forty Years of Washington Society* (edited compendium of Margaret B. Smith's letters). New York: Ungar, 1965.

Jefferson, Thomas. The Thomas Jefferson Papers. Library of Congress, Washington, DC. Accessible at http://memory.loc.gov/ammem/collections/jefferson_papers.

Madison, James. The James Madison Papers. Library of Congress, Washington, DC. Accessible at http://lcweb2.loc.gov/ammem/collections/madison_papers.

Maloney, Linda M. The Captain from Connecticut: The Life and Naval Times of Isaac Hull. Boston: North Eastern University Press, 1986.

Marolda, Edward J. The Washington Navy Yard: An Illustrated History. Washington, DC: Naval Historical Center, 1999.

McKee, Christopher. A Gentlemanly and Honorable Profession: The Creation of the U.S. Naval Officer Corps, 1794–1815. Annapolis, MD: Naval Institute Press, 1991.

Office of Naval Records. Naval Documents Related to the Quasi-War between the United States and France, 7 vols. Washington, DC: Government Printing Office, 1935–1938.

Paullin, Charles O. Commodore John Rodgers. New York: Arno Press, 1980.

Peck, Taylor. Round-Shot to Rockets: A History of the Washington Navy Yard and U.S. Naval Gun Factory. Annapolis, MD: Naval Institute Press, 1949.

Pitch, Anthony, The Burning of Washington: The British Invasion of 1814. Annapolis, MD: Naval Institute Press, 1998.

Porter, David D. Memoir of Commodore David Porter. Albany, NY: Munsell, 1875.

Reed, Parker M. A History of Bath and Environs. Portland, ME: Lakeside Press, 1894.

Semmes, John E. John H. B. Latrobe and His Times. Baltimore: Norman Remington, 1917.

Sharp, John G. History of the Washington Navy Yard Civilian Workforce. Stockton, CA: Vindolandia Press, 2005.

Symonds, Craig L. Navalists and Antinavalists : The Naval Policy Debate in the United States, 1785–1827. Newark: University of Delaware Press, 1980.

U.S. Senate. "History of the Congressional Cemetery." 59th Congress 2nd Session, Document #72, December 1906.

Van Horne, John C., and Lee W. Formwalt, eds. The Correspondence and Miscellaneous Papers of Benjamin Henry Latrobe. New Haven: Yale University Press, 1984–1988.

Votaw, Henry C. "The Sloop-of-War Ganges." United States Naval Institute Proceedings 98, 7 (July 1972), 82–84.

Westlake, Merle. Josiah Fox, 1763–1847. Philadelphia: Xlibris, 2003.

Archival Sources

The National Archives, Washington, DC, Naval Records, Record Group 45.
  • Microfilm correspondence of secretaries
    —Letters Received by Secretary (M124):
    —Letters Sent by Secretary (M209)
    —Letters to Naval Officers (M149)

—Letters from Captains (M125)

—Letters to Commandants (M441)

—Letters Sent Concerning Supplies for the Dey of Algiers, 1803–1808 (Entry 11).

- Records of the Board of Naval Commissioners (subgroup of RG45; original documents in copybooks, not microfilm)

—Letters Sent (E304)

—Letters to Commandants (E307)

—Letters from Commandants (E314)

—Commission Journal (E303)

—Report on the Removal of Powder from the Washington Navy Yard, 1814 (E491)

—Washington Navy Yard Logbook (E492)

The National Archives, London (Kew)

- Admiralty files ADM 52/1380/6 and ADM 51/629/3: Logs of HMS *Nautilus*
- ADM 51/663 and 52/1387: Logs of HMS *Otter*
- Colonial Office Files CO 194/27, 194/28, 194/30 and 194/32

Lodge Records, Naval Masonic Lodge, Washington, DC (one record book for the period.)

Parish Records. Christ Church SE, Washington, DC (chronological record of meetings of the parish vestry).

Richard Dale Papers. Manuscript Division, Library of Congress, Washington, DC.

Rodgers Family Papers. Historical Society of Pennsylvania, Philadelphia.

John Rodgers Family Papers. Manuscript Division, Library of Congress, Washington, DC, Naval Historical Collection.

Thomas Tingey Papers. Lewis D. Cook Collection, Historical Society of Washington, DC.

Thomas Tingey Letterbook 1788–1793. Historical Society of Pennsylvania, Philadelphia.

Tingey-Craven Family Papers, Historical Society of Pennsylvania, Philadelphia.

Thomas Tingey file, Navy Department Library, Washington Navy Yard; call number "ZB 220 file."

Thomas Tingey folders, Pennsylvania Historical Society, Philadelphia, Gratz Collection, Box 35.

Thomas Tingey file, Manuscript Division, Library of Congress, Washington, DC, Naval Historical Collection.

Thomas Truxtun Papers, Manuscript Division, Library of Congress, Washington, DC, Naval Historical Collection.

Thomas Truxtun Papers. Historical Society of Pennsylvania, Philadelphia.

Thomas Truxtun Papers. Manuscript Division, Library of Congress, Washington, DC (two sets).

Index

About the Author

AN AUTHOR AND RETIRED DIPLOMAT, Ambassador Gordon Brown's books include *Incidental Architect* (about early Washington, D.C.), *Toussaint's Clause: The Founding Fathers and The Haitian Revolution,* and *The Norman Invasion of Southern Italy and Sicily.* During a thirty-five-year career in the U.S. Foreign Service he was ambassador to Mauritania 1991–94, political adviser to General Schwarzkopf during the first Gulf War, and director of Arab Gulf affairs in the State Department.